W9-BDZ-381

Kansas School of Religion
At the University of Kansas
Smith Hall, Rm. 109, Library
Lawrence, Kansas 66045-2164

PELICAN BOOKS

THE QUEST FOR ETERNITY

John Gaskin is an Anglo-Scot who has worked for most
of his adult life in Dublin. He is a graduate of
Oxford University where he also took a postgraduate
degree after working for a time in one of the great
Scottish financial institutions. He has been a Fellow
of Trinity College Dublin since 1978. He is a
countryman, gardener and writer of ghost stories
by disposition, but an academic and city dweller by
profession. He is married and has two children.
Professor Gaskin's widely praised *Hume's Philosophy
of Religion* was published in 1978.

gift James Woelfel
11-84

BL51
.634
1984

J. C. A. GASKIN

THE QUEST FOR ETERNITY

AN OUTLINE OF THE PHILOSOPHY OF RELIGION

PENGUIN BOOKS

KANSAS SCHOOL OF RELIGION
UNIVERSITY OF KANSAS
1300 OREAD AVENUE
LAWRENCE, KANSAS 66044

Penguin Books Ltd, Harmondsworth, Middlesex, England
Penguin Books, 40 West 23rd Street, New York, New York 10010, U.S.A.
Penguin Books Australia Ltd, Ringwood, Victoria, Australia
Penguin Books Canada Ltd, 2801 John Street, Markham, Ontario, Canada L3R 1B4
Penguin Books (N.Z.) Ltd, 182–190 Wairau Road, Auckland 10, New Zealand

First published 1984

Copyright © J. C. A. Gaskin, 1984
All rights reserved

Made and printed in Great Britain by
Richard Clay (The Chaucer Press) Ltd, Bungay, Suffolk
Filmset in 9 on 12 pt Photina

Except in the United States of America, this book is sold subject
to the condition that it shall not, by way of trade or otherwise, be lent,
re-sold, hired out, or otherwise circulated without the
publisher's prior consent in any form of binding or cover other than
that in which it is published and without a similar condition
including this condition being imposed on the subsequent purchaser

1) Religion - Philosophy
2) God · Proof

FORETHOUGHT

Either there must be an inevitable necessity, ... or a gracious Providence, or chaos without order or meaning. If necessity, wherefore resistance? If a Providence that is ready to be gracious, then make yourself worthy of such divine grace. But if a chaos, then be pleased that in such a trackless sea, you have within you a guiding reason.

Marcus Aurelius
Emperor of Rome
Meditations, XII:14

CONTENTS

PREFACE

This book is written for anyone who thinks critically about the real existence of God, for the student of theology who may want an account of some of the main philosophical questions which undermine or support his religious beliefs, and for the student of philosophy who is taking an outline course in the philosophy of religion. It is also written because I believe that whether *there is a God* or *there is no God* is a matter of very great consequence. It makes a tremendous difference to our entire attitude to life which of those two brief propositions we consider to be true, and the actual truth of one rather than the other makes a tremendous difference to the total reality of the world. If I am right in saying this, then it is surely desirable that thought, rather than blind faith or dogmatic atheism, should take us as far as possible. We cannot prove the existence of God. But there are indicators which can be assessed, and I wish to try to assess them.

Intentions

The eight chapters – apart from forming what I hope is a logical and coherent map of some of the main areas in the philosophy of religion – are united by two basic persuasions which are currently unfashionable in certain theological and philosophical quarters. The first is that there is a root concept of deity (the theistic concept) which is of great historical persistence, and is still common to, and ordinarily assumed by, the Jewish, Christian and Islamic religions in their normal language and operation. The second basic persuasion is that it is when they have this root concept (or something like it) in mind that people ask, and legitimately ask, whether God exists; and, having asked this question, expect, and legitimately expect, reasons or evidence to be produced in support of whatever answer is given.

In chapter one I argue the case for these basic persuasions. Chapter two deals with some of the confusions and road blocks which result from disregarding them. In chapters three and four I look at the main lines of evidence in support of belief in God – first at the ancient but still lively evidence drawn from 'the starry heavens above'; then at the more intimate evidence which seems to come to us in our own experience of the world. Chapters five and six deal with objections to theistic belief – first with the external objection that the theistic concept of God is not only incredible but meaningless or incoherent; secondly with such internal dilemmas for theism as the problem of evil. In chapter seven I look at some of the problems unleashed by the presumption of atheism. My conclusions, such as they are, follow in chapter eight.

It has been my objective to avoid philosophical jargon as far as possible and to present the issues without presuming more than a willingness to think hard about these subjects. But not all of what follows is easy and some of it presents both a difficult road and an uncertain destination. If this were not so, the philosophy of religion would have been at an end long ago and all reasonable men and women would agree in matters concerning the existence of God, and perhaps also concerning the origin of the universe and the destiny of man. My only claim is that I have not made these matters superfluously difficult.

The professional philosopher may object that the arguments of some important writers (such as Alvin Plantinga or P. T. Geach) have been ignored. This is deliberate policy. It results partly from limitations of space, partly from my judgement of what is most relevant to the questions at issue, and partly from a decision to omit certain material which has a place in publications aimed at other professional philosophers but which most people would find unrewardingly difficult.

Avoiding jargon does not mean avoiding all words and phrases which are special to the subject under discussion. A short glossary of such terms in the philosophy of religion is given at the end of the book. It includes familiar words such as 'agnostic' and 'atheist' which are given a somewhat more carefully defined sense than is sometimes the case, conventional labels such as 'ontological argument', and certain critically important (but sometimes vaguely understood) terms of which 'theism' and 'deism' are examples.

Conventions

All quotations from the Bible are given in the text of the Revised Standard Version. This combines modern accuracy with some of the glories of the original translations into English. Quotations from the Koran are from the Penguin edition translated by N. J. Dawood (London, 1956).

There are two species of notes: footnotes which are marked with an asterisk and placed at the bottom of the page of text to which they relate; and end notes which are numbered consecutively in the text of each chapter and grouped together at the back of the book. The footnotes (there are few) contribute comments or explanations which would disrupt the flow of ideas in the main text but which I hope will be read. The end notes contain sources, references, afterthoughts and apologies.

On first mention I give the dates of important historical figures. The very few technical terms not included in the Glossary (e.g. *a priori* and *a posteriori*) are explained in footnotes if they are not discussed in the main text. There is just one exception to this and it needs to be explained now.

Philosophers freely (and rather thoughtlessly as far as non-philosophers are concerned) employ the group of terms 'impossible', 'logically impossible' and 'incoherent' in unexplained contrast to 'possible', 'logically possible' and 'coherent'. I shall use these notions at various stages in the text, but at present let the distinction between the first group and the second group be informally understood as follows. Saying that something is 'logically impossible' etc. means that the thing cannot make sense, or is not a possible thing, in any world. It is, for example, logically impossible to come across a round square. But it is logically possible etc. (however factually improbable) to suppose that a man could jump twenty-five feet or fly to any height at will. The thing may never happen, but it makes sense to suppose that it could. It was logically possible (indeed unsurprising) for Alice to see the *head* of the cat after the rest of its body had faded away. It was logically impossible for her to see its *grin* in the absence of the face whose grin it was.

Appreciations

My thanks are due to many friends and relatives who have assisted this enterprise in various ways but in particular I wish to thank John Bartlett who read through and corrected the final typescript at short notice and under great pressure of other work. David Berman, Michael Slote and

Timothy Williamson among my colleagues in Trinity College Dublin were also of great assistance. Their critical reading of various chapters saved me from many pitfalls. Those which remain I stray into on my own responsibility. I am also deeply indebted to Olive Murtagh whose patient and accurate typing and retyping of the manuscript has made possible this book.

Some of the ideas concerning the design argument in chapter three are abbreviated from my *Hume's Philosophy of Religion* (London and New York, 1978). A few paragraphs in chapters six and seven are drawn from articles in *Ratio* 1975 and *Hermathena* 1978 respectively. I am indebted to the editors of those journals for permission to reproduce the material here. An early draft of part of chapter four was read at the 1983 meeting of the Irish Philosophical Club at Ballymascanlon.

In the eight chapters which follow, a few readers may discern occasional traces of the lectures given by me in Trinity College during the past decade. The subject has always interested me, and the interest those lectures evoked indeed gave me the stimulus to develop my ideas. But what has resulted, for what it is worth, is a new work: not old notes in new covers.

A final word of thanks is due to my father, H. J. Gaskin, who, as a very senior citizen, developed the powers of a proof-reader – a task for which my own mediatric impatience renders me singularly ill adapted.

J. C. A. Gaskin
Trinity College Dublin

1 THE WAY FORWARD

The question which lies ahead concerns the existence of God: not the activity of Pan or Thor or some other localized spirit of the earth, not the importance of whatever we put as our highest values, but the real existence of the one God who is the personal and intelligent origin and destiny of all things and to whom we are all supposed to be of special concern.

Belief in God in something like this sense – theism – is, as I shall argue later in this chapter, the root belief shared by Jew, Christian and Muslim. It is important not only because of its intrinsic intellectual and personal claims, but also because if it is false or incoherent then the great monotheistic religions of the world, despite any particular historical revelation they may be supposed to contain, lose their characteristic claims to be fundamental truths about a reality which lies beyond the personality of the believer. The claim of theism is that certain things of enormous personal and cosmic significance are so, and will remain so, whether you accept or reject them. The question is, are they so, or, at the very least, is it reasonable or unreasonable to accept that they are so?

But the case for and against theism as a reasonable belief has been argued before, and recently. Antony Flew produced a flamboyant and stimulating attack upon it in *God and Philosophy* (London, 1966). Richard Swinburne has developed a massive defence in three recent volumes.[1] A judiciously argued atheistic assessment, *The Miracle of Theism* (Oxford, 1982), was delivered posthumously by J. L. Mackie; and there are dozens of other books: some biased, some nicely balanced, some so fastidiously indecisive as to be almost self-extinguishing. So why write again? I have three objectives.

(i) *The Objects of the Quest*

In the first place, as a man certain of his existence for only a brief space of time, I want to try to understand whether the universe is somehow explainable, or makes sense, in terms of the activity of a cosmic intelligence. I am interested in whether the things which may be said about that intelligence relate in any way to the historical revelation claimed by Abraham or Jesus or Mahomet. I am interested in whether certain (common?) human experiences direct one to, or are of, some living thing which lies beyond all ordinary things. I want to explore, to think through, these and other matters while I can, and perhaps to take others with me even if, as I write these words, I do not know exactly to what conclusions I am leading in the last chapter.

My second objective in writing about theistic belief is to resist the influence of those philosophers and theologians who retain the linguistic appearances of religion, particularly the Christian religion, but so redirect the meaning of the language that the religion turns out to be something quite different from what its critics, and for that matter most of its adherents, always thought it was. (See 'personalism', p. 190.)

Among philosophers the attitude is epitomized by D. Z. Phillips. Thus in a review of Mackie's 1982 book he remarks 'what informs such labours is Mackie's assumption that religious belief *is* belief in theism. He equates religious belief with this particular philosophical account of it.'[2] One is inclined to retort that what informs Phillips's labours[3] is his assumption that religious belief is *not* theistic. He equates religious belief with his own particular philosophical account of it. But the point is that one highly respectable philosopher can readily question whether another highly respectable philosopher is well employed in taking seriously the claims of theistic religion. I think Mackie and others like him are well employed, and I wish to defend this view before similarly employing myself.

Among theologians, the enterprise of finding an understanding of Christianity which will replace its familiar theistic assumptions has many distinguished names associated with it: Tillich, Bultmann, John Robinson and, more recently and more extravagantly, Don Cupitt, to list but a few. Their enterprise seems to be motivated by the desire to find an interpretation of Christianity which will allow it to exist *along with* secular atheism or even, in Cupitt's case, in company with the now largely abandoned anti-religious philosophy of the logical positivists. As long ago as 1963

Alasdair MacIntyre put this enterprise on the point of a needle when he wrote:

> Turning aside from this arid in-group theology, the most perceptive theologians wish to translate what they have to say to an atheistic world. But they are doomed to one of two failures. Either they succeed in their translation: in which case what they find themselves saying has been transformed into the atheism of their hearers. Or they fail in their translation: in which case no one hears what they have to say but themselves.[4]

My purpose is to show that such translations are neither legitimate nor necessary. They are not legitimate because they twist religious belief into something remote from its own traditions and different from what most of its own adherents still believe. They are not necessary because the main theistic tradition can still be taken seriously as a possible belief about the ultimate reality of things.

My third and final objective is to resist irrational rejection or acceptance of religion. The person who refuses to consider the reasons or evidence which the religious believer may put forward in defence of his claims is just as culpably irrational as the believer who refuses to attend to the reasonable objections of the sceptic. The atheism of a closed mind is no improvement upon the faith of a thoughtless religion. If theism is important – and it is – then it has to be sustained by its coherence and at least made to some degree probable by the evidence it can produce. And the same, I am inclined to think, applies to atheism.

Given these three objectives – my desire to understand, to show that theism is arguably the main line of religion, and to apply cool reason to its claims – the general questions at issue can be stated as follows. First, whether there is in fact an agreed concept of God which is taken for granted in the ordinary working of theistic religions. Secondly, whether there is evidence which confirms beyond reasonable doubt, or makes probable, the existence of anything corresponding to such a concept. Thirdly, whether the theistic concept of God is covertly incoherent. Finally, whether the evidence makes any alternative account of deity (e.g. dualist, pantheist or deist) more probable than the theistic account, or suggests agnosticism, scepticism or atheism as the wise man's conclusion.

The first task, however, is to resolve, for present purposes, a cluster of questions about the meaning of the central religious term 'God'. Is there, as I maintain, a concept of Deity which is, in an acceptable sense, common to the beliefs of the great theistic religions of the world and which is the legitimate object of philosophical inquiry? What might that concept be? Is it of any interest to the faithful in any actual world religion? Without some measure of agreement concerning these matters all discussion will be confusion and futility.

(ii) *Theism and Personalism*

'If you want to browse around looking for a religion to your taste, then you should read books on comparative religion. If you want to ask which of the claims of a religion are true or coherent, then the correct study, if you are within the Anglo-Saxon tradition, is the philosophy of religion.' But already in those elementary and simplistic opening sentences of my lecture the words 'true' and 'coherent' grated upon some of the audience. Some of them demurred at the black-or-white, take-it-or-leave-it sound of the alternatives true/false, coherent/incoherent. These sharp disjunctions failed to echo the state of unclear belief or hesitant doubt which they experienced, and the question 'Is it true that God exists?' had, to them, an insensitive ring to it, quite apart from problems about what might be meant by the word 'God'. Perhaps, they suggested, religion and belief in God should be regarded as a way of life rather than as assent to some sort of existential proposition about a named entity 'God'.

On the one hand I would certainly agree that religion is not *merely* assent to a proposition about God, or even assent to a whole creed, despite the evident appearance that most religious language and practice presumes such assent. On the other hand, I hold that responses of the sort I have just described suggest, not so much the inappropriateness of the question 'Does God exist?', as a modern loss of nerve about what theists – Christians in particular – believe: how they should state their beliefs and whether their religion makes any straightforward truth claims at all. Religion, I hear from various sources, is an essential phenomenon of man's nature. It is a way of life. It is a recipe against ultimate existential despair. It is a way of reconciling our mortality and our ultimate aspirations. It is a way of expressing one's involvement in the world through performative language. It is a myth with moral connotations. It is an affirmation of spiritual values. I shall call these accounts of religion (and the new understandings of God upon which they depend) 'personalist' accounts. The word is intended to emphasize that they are the in-group ideas of those who seek to present the essentials of a religion in ways which are radically different from the general theistic tradition upon which the religion is founded and with which it is historically associated.

These personalist accounts filter down to the doubting layman, living in a sceptical and science-centred society, from two main sources. One is from philosophers who have sought interpretations of religion which avoid the charge of other, somewhat dated, philosophers that religious language is factually meaningless. The second, and far more important influence, is the various personalist re-thinks of Christian theology evolved in the middle decades of this century and given such remarkable publicity in John Robinson's popular *Honest to God* (S.C.M. Press, 1963). I do not mean that every sincere Christian has felt obliged to turn to one of these re-thinks in order to salvage his faith. Clearly a remarkable number, Pope John Paul II evidently included, manage to rely on a basically theistic belief come what may. I mean that Christians who are a prey to contemporary doubts and hesitations about their beliefs often look to a personalist theology as a resting place before they either return to a more conventional statement of their faith (as John Robinson appears to have done) or become atheists (as appears to be the recent decision of Michael Goulder of Birmingham University). From the point of view of the thoughtful layman who *wants* to retain an allegiance to Christianity but who *feels* the incongruities of full-blooded traditional belief, one of the outcomes of the proliferation of personalist theologies is vagueness about what should be understood by the word 'God'. Another is uncertainty about the legitimacy of asking about God's existence. Does this vagueness and uncertainty matter? I think it does, both because it confuses the issues and because it is untrue to a main historical presumption of theism. What is this presumption?

With the exception of the word 'Father', the first sentence of the ancient Christian formulation known as the Apostles' Creed expresses a belief which, as far as it goes, could have received the assent of Jew or Muslim: 'I believe in God the Father Almighty, Maker of heaven and earth.' The word 'maker', since it has several different senses (see below, p. 51), will need exploration before the formula can be clearly understood, but, with that exception, the affirmation has a bold and decisive look which is followed in many other basic statements of Christian belief, for example in the Nicene Creed: 'I believe in God, the Father Almighty, Maker of heaven and earth and of all things visible and invisible.' At this stage it may be objected that these formulations do not actually assert the *existence* of God (an obscure notion since what God is said to be makes him so unlike all other existent entities); but it is difficult to imagine what could be meant by belief in a named entity if the belief did not carry the implication that the named entity existed in some way. The point is made explicit in the first sentence of Article One of the Anglican Articles of Religion (1571) which again, as far as I take the quotation (i.e. leaving out the second sentence in the Article which becomes specifically Christian in its reference to the Holy Trinity), could probably receive the assent of most other Christian denominations and of Jews and Muslims: 'There is but one living and true God, everlasting, without body, parts, or passions; of infinite power, wisdom, and goodness; the Maker and Preserver of all things both visible and invisible.'

Now the point about all these formulations is that they are attempts to state what was already built into and presumed by the normal activity and common language of Christianity. Because in each case I have stopped at the point at which the specifically Christian affirmations begin, they can also function as statements of what is taken for granted in the Judaic and Islamic religions. When the Jew reads 'In the beginning God *created* the heavens and the earth' (Genesis 1:1) or 'Then the Lord *answered* Job out of the whirlwind . . .' (Job 38:1); when the Christian reads 'the Father who *sent* me has himself *given me commandment* what to say' (John 14:49) or recites the Lord's Prayer; when the Muslim says 'In the Name of Allah, the Compassionate, the Merciful: Praise the Name of your Lord, the Most High, who has *created* all things and *well proportioned* them; who has *ordained* their destinies and *guided* them . . .' (Koran, 'The Most High'), the believer is in each case assuming that he can talk to and about a God who, whatever else he may be, is *at least a single, active agent who creates, commands, answers, guides, and ordains all things.* It is this common assumption which unites theistic religions as such. It justifies a critical discussion without detailed cultural, social or historical exegesis of the more particular concepts of deity which identify God as the *Christian* God, or the Christian God as understood in fourteenth-century Padua, or Allah as understood by al-Kindi rather than by Averroes, etc.* What is more, it is this basic assumption of theism which comes near enough to pre-Christian, non-Jewish monotheism for some of the Pagan philo-

---

* al-Kindi was a ninth-century, Averroes or ibn-Rushd a twelfth-century, Muslim philosopher. They differed, among other things, in that al-Kindi did *not* believe in the eternity of the universe and of matter, Averroes did believe in it.

sophical arguments (conspicuously what we now call the design argument and the cosmological argument) to have appealed to Christian *and* Muslim theologians from the earliest times, and it is this basic assumption of theism of which it is historically and philosophically legitimate to ask such questions as 'Does this God exist?'

(iii) *God and gods*

The contrast between this historically sanctioned theistic concept of God and both the hesitations of modern laymen and the radical inventiveness of modern theologians could scarcely be more striking. Let us take the lay hesitation first. In 1979 I asked a class of third-year honours students, *before* I discussed the subject with them, to write down briefly what they meant by the word 'God'. The class was about 50 per cent Roman Catholic; the other 50 per cent included other Christian denominations, atheists, Jews and two Muslims. Here are some of their replies:

1. 'God is the father of Mankind and his existence leads one to believe that life has some hidden meaning.'
2. 'God is a being who demands love and obedience, who can interfere with the workings of the world (because he is the author of the world).'
3. ' "God" is the name of a non-existent being.'
4. ' "God" is the name for a benevolent, all-powerful, intelligent, supernatural creator.'
5. 'God is eternity.'
6. ' "God" is the answer to questions which have no satisfactory answer, such as "Why anything?".'
7. 'Being asked what I understand by "God" leaves me in a predicament, because I know I have been listening to people talking about God all my life and never had any difficulty understanding that the conversation was sensible. Yet I can't say what I understand by "God".'
8. ' "God": the power which designed, created and now maintains the Universe.'
9. 'When using the term "God" I mean it in the sense in which it is understood in Roman Catholic theology.'

Apart from the suggestions of a creator and of an active agent contained in 2, 4, 8 and, by coy implication, also in 9, it is hard to discern much common ground between these answers and the basic statements of theism quoted above from Christian sources. Answers 1, 3 and 5 are hopelessly vague, while 6 and 7, although perceptive and perhaps important, tell us very little at this stage of the investigation. These student replies are, however, conservative by the standards set by some allegedly Christian theologians.

Consider, for example, the radical inventiveness of Paul Tillich's much quoted account of God:

> The name of this infinite and inexhaustible depth and ground of all being is God. That depth is what the word God means. And if that word has not much meaning for you, translate it, and speak of the depths of your life, of the source of your being, of your ultimate concern, of what you take seriously without any reservation.[5]

The startling thing about Tillich's concept of God is not that it is new, but that it simply will not allow *any* traditional theistic religious formulations to be expressed. 'The ground of all being' is an existentialist abstraction, not an *agent* which can be said to love, create, command, etc., and the idea that God is somehow an agent, an initiator of action in some ways analogous to what is understood by agency in a human person, is so integral to theism in general and to Christianity in particular that without it historical theism would be at an end. It would not merely exclude the Greek philosophical component in theism; it would also *silence* the Judaic direct speech to and about God. One can only repeat Alasdair MacIntyre's trenchant comment: 'Clearly, however, the conversion of the unbeliever is only so easy for Tillich because belief in God has been evacuated of all its traditional content.'[6]

The view that I am advocating – that there is a basic and enduring theistic concept of God, on the one hand drawn from Greek philosophy and on the other hand originally assumed in the ordinary expression of the Judaic religion – is categorically opposed to such unselective pluralism as that expressed in Don Cupitt's *The Leap of Reason* (London, 1976). Cupitt seems to argue that because we welcome, or have to tolerate, a pluralistic society (one 'in which it is publicly acknowledged that there are entrenched and apparently unsettlable differences of approach to and belief about fundamental questions of morality, religion, politics, and some other topics'), therefore a 'trans-religious' definition of God, 'some common metaphysical claim made by all the various theistic religions', must give way to a belief in God 'which bears a specific meaning and is justified in relation to a particular religious community and its universe of discourse – but only in that relation' (pp. 106f.).

The defect in this view of how we should understand belief in God is
that it makes the concept 'God' so narrowly sectarian, so emphatically
culture-related, and potentially so idiosyncratic, that not only is any
general theistic concept destroyed, but any claim to continuity or unity
in Christian (or Jewish or Islamic) history is likely to be also lost. Are we
to understand, for example, that the prayers of a tenth-century Pope are
directed at the same or at a different God from the prayers of a twentieth-
century Pope? If to the same, then there must be some discernible continuity in what is understood by the word 'God', and I have endeavoured
to discern part of this continuity in certain sentences from the Creeds. If
to different Gods, then the history of Christianity is radically discontinu-
ous and the God of Moses or Jesus or Mahomet is of no more than
historical interest to us, being merely their culturally isolated concepts.

In a more recent publication (*Taking Leave of God*, London, 1980)
Cupitt carries his personalist remaking of Christian theism to an excess
which even he describes as 'Christian Buddhism'. We are no longer
allowed even a pluralist deity. Traditional theistic belief has now become
a sign of mere childishness: 'it is spiritual vulgarity and immaturity to
demand an extra-religious reality of God' (p. 10). 'God's reality is not a
matter of facts and evidence, but of the unconditional authority of religious categories in a person's life' (p. 56). The real external existence of
God 'is of no religious interest' (p. 96). 'God is the religious concern,
reified' (p. 9). Why not? Others have explained at length why not,[7] but
there are two obvious reasons. One is that Cupitt's personalist religion is
totally and explicitly at variance with almost every aspect of any recognizable Christian tradition. (It is as if he had told you what Marxism
was in descriptions appropriate to medieval Christianity.) The other is
that his internalized religion entirely lacks reasons to support it. He can
do nothing with the person who says 'I don't feel the authority of any
religious categories – unconditional or otherwise.' The theistic tradition
of Christianity, on the other hand, is not only *the* historical main line of
development from first to last; it is also a tradition which makes claims to
present a coherent and true account of the way reality is: claims which it
has almost always been able to support with some sort of reasoned
evidence (whether good or bad we shall see later).

So I say again: it is possible to discern a minimum concept of deity
which is the common starting point of Jewish, Christian and Islamic
belief in God. (Some evidence that this is so is provided by the Masonic
Lodge in which men of all three faiths can and do unite in assenting to

belief in a God who is fundamentally the theistic God without the embellishments of particular religions.) This starting point is taken for granted in the prayer and worship of each religion but it is *not* the object of worship of either Jew, Christian or Muslim. In each religion God is additionally credited with the characteristics, no doubt culture-bound to a degree, of the particular historical religion, or sect within the religion. But the starting point is *assumed* by the distinctive developments of each religion and has, since the earliest developments of Christian and Muslim theology, been associated in its expression with the arguments and concepts of Greek philosophy (particularly those drawn from Plato, Aristotle and the Stoics). In the case of Jewish theology, the same association dates at least from Philo of Alexandria (c. 20 B.C.–c. A.D. 50). Concerning *this* concept of God it does make sense to ask if the concept is coherent, and it also makes sense to ask if there is any evidence which would hint at, make probable, or prove the existence of anything corresponding to the concept.

It will be noted that I am not committing myself to the ecumenical fallacy that 'really we all worship the same God'. I take it to be only too evident that we do not. In detail there are many concepts of God, and to that extent Cupitt's theological pluralism is no doubt right enough. My point is that there is, and has always been, a root concept of God, common to the three great theistic religions of the world, which is so fundamental to them that without it they lose their characteristic and historical claims to rest upon a profound and all-pervading truth about the nature of things. Can this root concept of God which is the theistic concept be delineated more precisely than by the brief credal formulas quoted earlier?

In his useful book *Concepts of Deity* (London, 1971) H. P. Owen begins: 'Theism may be defined as belief in one God, the Creator, who is infinite, self-existent, incorporeal, eternal, immutable, impassible, simple, perfect, omniscient and omnipotent.' But this will not do. In the first place no mention is made of any moral characteristic which would make such a God either concerned with or even the concern of mankind. Hence no distinction is made between a God thus defined and a deistic god. Secondly, no reference is made to an essential feature of theism, namely, that God is always spoken about in ways which imply that he is an active *agent* (something like a 'person' in the modern acceptation of that term).

A much more detailed and very astutely argued account of the theistic concept of God is set out by Richard Swinburne thus:

I take the proposition 'God exists' (and the equivalent proposition
'There is a God') to be logically equivalent to 'there exists a person
without a body (i.e. a spirit) who is eternal, is perfectly free, omnipotent,
omniscient, perfectly good, and the creator of all things'. I use 'God' as
the name of the person picked out by this description. I understand by
God's being eternal that he always has existed and always will exist
. . . By God's being perfectly free I understand that no object or event
or state (including past states of himself) in any way causally influences
him to do the actions which he does – his own choice at the moment of
action alone determines what he does. By God's being omnipotent I
understand that he is able to do whatever it is logically possible (i.e.
coherent to suppose) that he can do. By God's being omniscient I
understand that he knows whatever it is logically possible that he
know. By God's being perfectly good I understand that he does no
morally bad action. By his being the creator of all things I understand
that everything which exists at each moment of time (apart from
himself) exists because, at that moment of time, he makes it exist, or
permits it to exist.[8]

This evidently goes a great deal further than either of the sentences I
quoted earlier from the Apostles' or the Nicene Creed although it is quite
close, in its opening statement, to the first sentence in Article One of the
Thirty-Nine Articles. I take mild exception to it at three points. The first is
that although it is, I think, implied by the definition of 'omnipotence' that
there could only be one such God, this is not brought out explicitly in the
words quoted. Secondly, I would have preferred to leave out the expression 'perfectly good'. It invites almost limitless controversy with the critical philosopher (and from the sharply different moral standpoints of the
three theistic religions) about what it is to be good. I would prefer to say
that God is morally concerned with mankind and leave it at that for the
moment. (What is more, Swinburne's explication of 'perfectly good' suggests that goodness is a mere absence of doing bad. Many would regard
this as too negative an account: goodness is *doing* good, not simply
avoiding evil.) Thirdly, I am not entirely at ease with Swinburne's use of
the word 'person'. He explains the word in *The Coherence of Theism*
(Oxford, 1977, pp. 99–102) and it is clear from what he says there that
to be a person something must satisfy complex and even elusive criteria.
I do not want to say that the theistic God is not a person, but I would
prefer to say that he has the characteristics of being an agent. By 'an

agent' I understand something which can act, will, compel, create, and display certain other of the dispositional or intentional characteristics *normally* associated with being an intelligent person. (See chapter five for further discussion.) Being a person will certainly entail being an agent, but I am not convinced that every agent will be a person, and it looks as if the activity of an agent rather than the somewhat more extensive character of being a person is the essential attribute of a theistic God.

Having regard to the various ancient and modern expressions of theism I have quoted, the following would, I think, be an expression of the root belief which would receive the assent of Jew, Christian and Muslim without either invoking the particular beliefs of one of these religions or shrinking the concept of God to the point at which it would be unacceptable to any of them:

> There exists one God who is creator and sustainer of all things; who is omnipotent, omniscient and eternal; who is an agent able to act everywhere without a body, and who is morally concerned with mankind.*

When I refer to God in this sense I shall, for the remainder of the book, speak of 'the theistic God' or simply of *God*. When God is given any of the specific characteristics which associate him with a particular theistic religion, e.g. 'the Father of our Lord Jesus Christ', I shall always use a qualifying phrase or a special name, thus: 'the Christian God', or 'the Muslim God' (or 'Allah'). When a god is referred to who is neither specifically the theistic God nor the God of a particular theistic religion, I shall refer to 'god' without the capital letter. I am aware that this will on rare occasions lead to my making covert philosophical or theological judgements, as when I might refer to 'Tillich's concept of god'. I hope, however, that the usefulness of the conventions I adopt will, in the present context, excuse my occasionally employing them to present unargued conclusions. I can now repeat my original questions: is God's existence coherent or incoherent, is there evidence which makes his existence certain, or probable, or possible? I shall begin to look for answers to these questions in chapter three; but before doing so two moves to rule out of court all attempts to treat belief in God as a serious rational commitment require examination.

* I shall on occasions give a less formal characterization of God than this. For example at the end of chapter four I speak of God as 'an invisible, all-permeating, intelligent force operating as an agent throughout the universe and to whom man matters as a tiny, pale reflection of himself'. My intention is that these characterizations should be consistent with the main statement above (except, of course, where they relate to a god with a small 'g').

2 INITIAL OBSTRUCTIONS

One of the ways in which the devout believer may seek to insulate his religion from criticism is by adopting a fideistic attitude: 'The certainty of my faith comes by the grace of God alone, not from dubious evidence and uncertain chains of reasoning.' One of the ways in which the atheist may do most harm to religion is by agreeing with him. But fideism has a venerable lineage, particularly in protestant Christian theology. It is, for example, strongly suggested in the 1571 Articles 11 and 17. The claim is that what is believed is in a special category where faith is autonomous and all objections can be disregarded. The other side of this coin invites the critic to dismiss the claims of religion in the terms in which they are made: if reason and evidence are not relevant, then the psychologist or sociologist can be invited to explain the phenomenon of belief as best he may in terms of its causes.

In this chapter I shall argue (a) that a correct understanding of the differences between reasons and causes of a belief makes fideism a disastrous option for a religion which expects to be taken seriously as a claim about things which exist apart from the personality of the believer; (b) that such an option is contrary to the main historical traditions of theism; and (c) that even the most insidiously plausible accounts of the causes of belief in God do not, of themselves, obviate the need to examine the reasons and evidence for the belief if any can be produced.

(i) *Reasons and Causes*

The eighteenth-century Scottish philosopher David Hume (1711–76) – one of the dominant influences in modern philosophy – very clearly understood and made use of the two categories of explanation of belief which arise from a distinction between reasons and causes. Indeed he devoted separate books to the two areas: the *Natural History of Religion* (1757) being an account of the causes of religious belief, and the *Dialogues concerning Natural Religion* (published in 1779 and perhaps the most important book on the philosophy of religion in the English language) being a discussion of the reasons for belief in a god or God. In the 'Introduction' to the *Natural History* he wrote:

> As every enquiry, which regards religion, is of the utmost importance, there are two questions in particular, which challenge our attention, to wit, that concerning its foundation in reason, and that concerning its origin in human nature.

It is this distinction and its consequences which I must now open up.

Suppose I am staying at an old and isolated country house. Nearby there are several high walled enclosures, one of which had been a rose garden but is now wild and ruinous. The boy who comes to dig vegetables tells me that the rose garden is haunted by the ghost of an evil old man who in life had tended the garden. I ask him why he thinks it is haunted. His answer may well take the form of *reasons* or *evidence* for his belief: 'Because I hear a voice talking to itself there sometimes; twigs snap on still evenings, and I sometimes see an old rose bush beautifully pruned and tended when I come here in the mornings.' Suppose I now account for the voice and the cut roses. It is my host (he often talks to himself) who goes to the old garden alone in the evening and sometimes makes an attempt to tidy a bush. What I now expect from the boy is something like 'Ah, of course! That's the explanation!' or possibly more evidence or counter-objections to my explanation. But what I might get is a stubborn refusal to budge in the face of evidence: 'I don't care. I know there's a ghost there.' I now lose interest. The boy's belief can tell me nothing which would, for example, justify my staying in the garden all night on the off-chance of encountering the supernatural. Later my host explains that the boy's father was a schizophrenic, and that the boy himself had been brought up by aged grandparents who filled his head with all manner of superstitious stories which the boy took for real. I am now at ease again. I have some sort of *causal* explanation of his curious belief about the rose garden. The belief is a product of his upbringing and possibly also of his mental inheritance. It is not a conviction about a possible state of affairs in the public world we both inhabit, although it seems this way to him. In short, in Hume's words, the belief has no foundation in reason. Its origin is to be found in causes operating within the boy's (peculiar) nature.

This story can be generalized. It is possible to ask of any statement of belief 'Why do you believe it?', and such a question normally expects reasons to be produced. But a number of different responses are possible according to which the belief will be classified as reasonable or unreasonable. Before looking at these responses note that the classification 'reasonable or unreasonable' is not the same as the classification 'true or false'. The former classification is made by reference to the presence or absence of grounds for holding the belief and to the way in which the belief is entertained (whether it is responsive to further evidence or not). The latter classification is made by finding out whether what is believed is or is not the case (something by no means always possible). Thus an unreasonable belief *could* turn out to be true (e.g. he had no grounds for what he believed, and his belief was not responsive to evidence, but it just happened he was right); and a reasonable belief *could* turn out to be false (e.g. he had grounds for his belief but he did not realize they were mistaken). With this in mind, let us now see what responses there could be to the question 'Why do you believe it?'

1. *Good* reasons are produced. If the reasons are good enough, in our judgement, we may even adopt the belief ourselves (i.e. accept it as true). But even if they are not good enough to persuade us to accept it as true (because, for example, we attach more importance to a certain imponderable factor than the other man does) we may still acknowledge the reasonableness of the belief. Thus what the boy told me about the garden and what I found out for myself could have been sufficient to persuade me that the boy's belief was held on reasonable grounds, although I am not yet convinced that the garden is in fact haunted. The same could happen with belief in God: I examine the reasons which are produced for the belief and, although they may not entirely convince me, I acknowledge that the belief has reasonable grounds.

2. *Bad* reasons are produced; but when this is pointed out the belief is modified or abandoned. Again, the belief, though now abandoned, was entertained in a reasonable way: it was responsive to evidence. Thus the boy could have accepted my explanation of the phenomena in the rose garden and ceased to believe in the ghost. The believer could abandon his belief in God if he recognized that the reasons for his belief were inadequate. The atheist could be shifted from his atheism by the appearance of new evidence or by reassessment of old. Such shifts of belief about

fundamental issues may well occur slowly, but the possibility of their occurring as a response to evidence is the indication that the belief is reasonable.

3. *Bad* reasons are produced or no reasons at all ('it's a matter of faith'); but when this is pointed out to the believer he keeps his belief intact: it is not responsive to evidence. We are then inclined to say (as with the boy in my story) that his belief is unreasonable or, more strongly, irrational. As I have already indicated, it is evident that belief in God is sometimes entertained in this irrational way, and some Christians rejoice in the irrationality ('belief cannot argue with unbelief: it can only preach to it!'). It is equally evident that many religious people, and Christians throughout most of their history, have been willing to justify at least some of their beliefs by appeal to reasons and evidence. In the former case the uncommitted man is driven to explain the phenomenon of religion by appeal to causes: social and psychological factors which could give rise to the belief. In the latter case, since there is a claim that the belief is reasonable, the uncommitted man must first consider whether what is believed could be true on the basis of the evidence produced.

4. I have so far spoken as if the notions of 'good' and 'bad' evidence presented no difficulties, but this is not always so. It may happen that the believer and his critic genuinely and legitimately disagree about what constitutes good and bad evidence in the case in question. Thus, for example, part of the believer's evidence may be that in a moment of despair he felt the presence of God. But the non-believer refuses to accept this sort of thing as evidence: it is too private, ambiguous or vague. Again, the believer may cite as evidence something which the critic is inclined to regard as among the causes of the belief. For example, the boy explains to me that he is specially sensitive to ghosts because of his upbringing; or the religious man tells me that he is more alive to the presence of God than I am because of his habits of prayer and fasting. What then should count as good evidence for a religious belief, particularly belief in God? There is unfortunately no general answer to this question. Some of the evidence, in particular the ancient and profound arguments which are dealt with in the next chapter, does not depend upon the special personal circumstances of the person considering the evidence. But other evidence does. Religious experience *is* of a personal character and presents special problems. I will therefore examine it separately in chapter four.

Now there are two consequences of all this which need particular emphasis. One is this: sometimes it is assumed that you need not bother with a person's *reasons* for his belief once you have succeeded in showing that there are *causes* why he holds the particular belief. Such an assumption is wholly unjustifiable. A person may be causally disposed to believe something for which he can produce perfectly respectable reasons. It may, for example, be possible to show that I am causally disposed to regard smoking as a dirty and unhealthy habit. I suffered from bronchitis as a child and smoking tortured me, etc. But this in no way devalues my excellent reasons for the belief that smoking is dirty and unhealthy. Look at the statistics for lung cancer and heart disease. Look at the fingers of the heavy smoker. Look at the ash on the carpet. Notice the fetid smell of their clothes, and so on. So I say again: to show that there are causes of a belief – psychological or environmental factors which predispose the person to hold the belief – is not *in itself* sufficient to show that the belief is irrational. It has also to be shown, either that the believer has no reasons for his belief, or that he is going to stick to his belief quite apart from what he alleges to be his reasons for holding it.

The second consequence is to show why fideism is such a disastrous option for the believer. If the central theistic belief in God is entirely a matter of ungrounded faith* and at no point made probable, or even perhaps coherent, by rational analyses or attention to evidence, then belief in God will have the same status from the point of view of the non-believer as the boy's refusal to be disabused of his fears about the ghost in the garden. Belief in God will not be something anchored by evidence in a reality beyond the believer's mind. It will be the result of a highly personal anti-rational gulp of the sort described so well in William Sargent's *Battle for the Mind* (London, 1957); or it will be the product of general psychological, sociological or environmental factors which explain the belief in terms of general causes.

* Faith and belief (and for that matter knowledge) are related terms which require analysis and discussion at a length which cannot be attempted here. In briefest outline the position I would wish to defend is this. Belief *in* x (where x is a named entity such as God or the Communist Party) is always reducible to some one or more beliefs *that* p (where p is one or more propositions at least one of which is x exists). Belief that God exists means assent to the existence of God upon grounds which, even if reasonably entertained, fall short of allowing one to legitimately claim knowledge that God exists. Faith in God is simply belief that God exists *plus* a decision to make that belief the point of trust and the focus of one's life. Belief, in a religious context, is an acceptance that something we cannot know to be so, is so. Faith is the acceptance actively and truly lived. For a thorough discussion, and a position somewhat different from my own, see Richard Swinburne, *Faith and Reason* (Oxford, 1981), particularly chapters 1 and 4. A useful collection of more general essays is edited by A. Phillips Griffiths, *Knowledge and Belief* (Oxford, 1967).

However, as I indicated at the outset of this chapter, theism, to those who ask about its beliefs, is not offered for consumption in a large anti-rational gulp. It has been *argued* by Christian theologians since St Paul, and by Islamic theologians at least as early as al-Kindi. Theism is a long-standing, historically founded, attempt to communicate something which the believer claims to be true and important about the world. The process of communication may well involve non-rational techniques of conversion and persuasion. The process of passing on the religion from one generation to another may well harness to its purpose general psychological traits of mankind. The faith, once communicated, may well involve, and indeed as faith *must* involve, trust and hope and belief which goes beyond the evidence. But when challenged, what is communicated, particularly concerning the existence of God, has not in the past, and cannot now without altering its whole status, insulate itself entirely from what the rest of the world would recognize as reasons and evidence. What is more, this tradition of argument is not some alien element of Hellenic philosophy somehow grafted onto the pure root-stock of Semitic fideism. It is, as I urged in the first chapter, a natural outcome of the concept of God which is implied by what is said in worship by Jew, Christian and Muslim. This concept relates God, not merely to the internal world of the believer's private consciousness, or to his own private language club, but to the external world we all inhabit. God is the creator and sustainer of *that* world as well as the object of devotion of the mystic.

No clearer or firmer expression of the public and rational claims of theism can be found than in the canonized mentor of the Roman Church, Aquinas (*c.* 1225–74). In *Summa Theologicae* (I, Quest. II, Art. 2) he writes:

> On the contrary, the Apostle says, 'Ever since the creation of the world his invisible nature, namely, his eternal power and deity, has been clearly perceived in the things that have been made' (Romans 1:20). But this would not be unless the existence of God could be demonstrated through the things that are made; for the first thing we must know of anything is whether it exists ... The existence of God, and other truths about God, which can be known by natural reason, are not articles of faith, but are preliminaries to the articles: for faith presupposes natural knowledge ...

In the pages which follow Aquinas sets out the 'Five Ways', the seminal arguments for the existence of God, to some of which we shall return in chapter three. My point here is simply that the central belief of theism – the existence of God – not only *needs* to be related to evidence because of its claims to be about the world we all in some measure know, and in order to avoid being treated as a 'merely' social or psychological phenomenon; it has also been *offered* as a rational belief, not by an ephemeral sect, but by a main stream of Christianity from St Paul through Origen, Aquinas and many others to the present day, as well as by the Kalam Islamic philosophers and Jews in the tradition originally of Philo and later of Maimonides (1135–1204). (Kalam was the natural theology of Islam, about A.D. 800–1300.)

A weakness of theism in grounding its basic belief upon evidence and reason is that it may be shown to be incoherent or false, and it is probably this fear more than anything else which has motivated the more eccentric and unhistorical theologies of the twentieth century. But a strength is undoubtedly its ability to reply to those who seek and provide *causes* for belief in God. There almost certainly are many causes for belief in God, but that fact alone does not 'explain away' a belief for which reasons are also offered. It is only when the fideist abandons reason and evidence that theism is wholly given over to the anatomizing of the psycho-analyst, the sociologist or the anthropologist. Among these anatomists none has subjected belief in God to a more insidiously destructive causal analysis than Sigmund Freud (1856–1939). As a way of devaluing evidence and reasons without examining them, what Freud says is in a class of its own. I propose to look at what he has to say as a final preliminary to examining the evidence itself. Some of the lessons of the look are relevant to other causal explanations or 'natural histories' of religion.

(ii) *A Psycho-analysis of Belief*

It would be unfair and untrue to say that the great psychologists and psycho-analysts have all attempted to explain (in the sense of 'explain away') religion by reference to its origins in human nature, its causes. Nevertheless many of them have said some things and some of them have said many things which are capable of being read in this way. In particular Freud has often been taken to say that belief in God is nothing more than an unconscious projection onto the cosmos at large of the human need for a father figure who will be more reliable and enduring than the earthly father which nature provides. As a commentator remarks: 'The whole status of theological beliefs, as based upon an apparently delusional process of "projection", has been brought into prominence by Freud's book bearing the challenging title, *The Future of an Illusion*, which appeared in 1927.'[1]

What Freud actually has to say is, however, much more complex and guarded than a quick paraphrase might suggest, but the following remark from his memoir of *Leonardo da Vinci* is fairly characteristic of his thinking:

> Psycho-analysis has made us familiar with the intimate connection between the father-complex and belief in God; it has shown us that a personal God is, psychologically, nothing other than an exalted father, and it brings us evidence every day of how young people lose their religious beliefs as soon as their father's authority breaks down. Thus we recognize that the roots of the need for religion are in the parental complex; the almighty and just God, and kindly Nature, appear to us as grand sublimations of father and mother . . .[2]

The word 'psychologically' might seem to imply a qualification: that Freud allows for the possibility that the personal God may be *rationally* or *experientially* something other than an exalted father. But in his major works on the psychology of religion – *Totem and Taboo* and, more especially, *The Future of an Illusion* – it is made perfectly clear how little Freud himself thinks of the possibility. His frequently repeated contentions are that 'the psychical origin of religious ideas . . . are illusions, fulfilments of the oldest, strongest and most urgent wishes of mankind'; that 'religion would thus be the universal obsessional neurosis of mankind'; and that 'the primal father was the original image of God'. The cumulative emphasis of what Freud says seems to indicate that at least *he* thinks that nothing much else can be or need be said in order to answer the question why men believe in God; once the *causes* of this particular religious belief are laid bare, the reasons become of little consequence. The reasons, if any can be found, are just pseudo-reasons for what we want to believe:

> To assess the truth-value of religious doctrines does not lie within the scope of the present enquiry. It is enough for us that we have recognized them as being, in their psychological nature, illusions. But we do not have to conceal the fact that this discovery also strongly influences our attitude to the question which must appear to many to be the most important of all. We know approximately at what periods and by what kind of men religious doctrines were created. If in addition we discover

the motives which led to this, our attitude to the problem of religion will undergo a marked displacement. We shall tell ourselves that it would be very nice if there were a God who created the world and was a benevolent Providence, and if there were a moral order in the universe and an after-life; but it is a very striking fact that all of this is exactly as we are bound to wish it to be.[3]

Now what Freud has to say about religion can be taken to do either or both of two distinct things. It can explain the origins in human nature of the central theistic belief in God. It can also be a way of giving the word 'God' a new meaning.

The first possibility is not particularly damaging to the claims of religion providing the distinction between reasons and causes is kept in mind, and providing it is remembered that a belief may have both an origin in human nature and a foundation in reason. Taken in this way Freud's account of the origin of belief in God is apparently no more damaging to religion than, for example, Hume's account in the *Natural History of Religion* where he traces the origin to fear of the unknown (and apparently capricious) aspects of nature which influence human happiness and misery. Even if Freud is correct (and most of his theories have been subject to heavy destructive criticism), all he shows, it may be said, is that men are psychologically disposed to believe in something for which there may also be perfectly respectable evidence. But of course what he has to say (and what Hume and others have had to say about the natural origin of religious belief) does become damaging if it is found or suspected that belief in God does *not* have any good evidence to substantiate it. In such a case the psychologists provide a well worked out, ready-made answer to the question 'How is it that so many people believe in God or some god if there are no good reasons for such a belief?' Such a question often enough implied in the past that there may be reasons which you (the doubter) have failed to recognize. The Freudian answer is that most people believe because they are similar to each other in the make-up of the psyche. Hume's answer is that most people believe because they are (or were) subject to similar environmental influences. On this showing the old argument from general consent loses virtually all its force: the consent is an explainable psychological datum, not an indication that good evidence is available for those who bother to look for it.

I have thought it worth while devoting some pages to Freud's views on religion because, although other psychologists by no means all agree with his particular account of its origins, his ill-concealed implication that an understanding of origins invalidates a quest for reasons (an implication not shared, for example, by William James in his classic work *The Varieties of Religious Experience*, 1902) has become an assumption which underlies much twentieth-century work on the psychology and sociology of religion. As I have tried to show, such an assumption is not warranted. We cannot *rule out* the possibility of truth in the boy's story about a ghost in the garden even if we know his grandparents were superstitious; causes do not *preclude* reasons. Nevertheless the sort of thing Freud has to say *is* very damaging to the truth claims of religion. If we concede for a moment that his account is correct, then not only does he explain the origins of religious belief in primitive human society (which Hume does); he also shows that the explanation still holds good for educated man in civilized society (which Hume does not). The normal human being *needs and wishes* to believe in a God. Thus Freud is able to make the statement (prophetic in view of the subsequent rise of dogmatic political cults): 'If you want to expel religion from our European civilization, you can only do it by means of another system of doctrines; and such a system would from the outset take over all the psychological characteristics of religion – the same sanctity, rigidity and intolerance, the same prohibition of thought – for its own defence.'[4]

It is clearly a very powerful way of shedding doubt upon the rational integrity of a belief if I can both explain the causes of the belief and show that these involve wanting or needing to believe what is in fact believed. The case against the reasonableness of the belief is not proved, but the demand for evidence becomes very insistent and cannot be turned aside by a retreat into fideism.

The second and potentially more damaging possibility in Freud's account of religion is that it can be used to provide a new meaning for the word 'god'; 'god' *means* 'father figure in the sky' (or something of this sort).

Attempts to make 'god' mean something less than is normally understood in theistic religions are by no means new. There is one, for example, in Hobbes's *Leviathan* (1651), chapter 12, where he says that men desire to know the causes of natural events and postulate 'one First Mover ... which is that which men mean by the name God'. Another suggestion, from which Freud drew some of his ideas, is urged with powerful and repetitive eloquence by the German atheistical philosopher Ludwig Feuerbach. In *The Essence of Christianity* (1841), his major thesis is that god is identical with man's own image, magnified and projected upon the universe at large:

> Consciousness of God is self-consciousness, knowledge of God is self-knowledge . . . Religion, at least the Christian, is the relation of man to himself, or more correctly to his own nature; but a relation to it, viewed as a nature apart from his own. The divine being is nothing else than the human being, or, rather the human nature purified, freed from the limits of the individual man, made objective – i.e., contemplated and revered as another, a distinct being.[5]

What is being said is that despite what religious people *say* they understand by the word 'God' or 'god', what they are really entitled to understand is only 'projected father figure' (Freud), 'incomprehensible first cause' (Hobbes) or 'objectified human nature' (Feuerbach). Moreover the restriction upon what should be understood by the word 'god' is not put forward as an arbitrary stipulation of a new meaning which the believer can dismiss by saying 'Oh, but that's not what *I* mean, and what *I* mean is the normal and accepted meaning.' The new meaning is put forward in each case on the grounds that it is the one which is alone justified by a proper understanding of the phenomena which give rise to the use of the word 'god'.

It is, I think, obvious that as they stand none of these new definitions of 'god' are going to be acceptable to the theist. None of them describe God as he is spoken of in the normal religious language of the Jew, Christian or Muslim. So how is the religious man to defend *his* usage and understanding of the word 'God'?

One objection to any attempt to stipulate a new meaning for a commonly used word like 'God' is that the stipulation is likely to produce an absurd *Through the Looking Glass* situation: '"When *I* use a word," Humpty Dumpty said in rather a scornful tone, "it means just what I choose it to mean – neither more nor less." "The question is", said Alice, "whether you *can* make words mean different things." "The question is," said Humpty Dumpty, "which is to be master – that's all."' But if I am master over words in Humpty Dumpty's sense, the result is confusion and misunderstanding. 'Glory' does *not* mean 'a knock-down argument' for those who normally use the word. 'God' does *not* mean 'incomprehensible first cause' for the multitude who speak of him and to him in language which implies that he has the theistic features outlined in chapter one. In other words the believer *can* object that a new, stipulated meaning of the word 'god' is not his, the normal, meaning and he *can* demand that his meaning of the word be considered.

But even if this linguistic objection is disallowed, the theist can still defend his understanding of the word 'God' on exactly the sort of grounds upon which the new meaning is itself urged. If the phenomena which give rise to use of the word 'god' indicate that 'god' should mean 'projected father figure', other phenomena – or evidence – may indicate that it should mean something closer to the normal. Thus it might be urged that the orderly structure of the world suggests an intelligent, powerful and independent agent as its creator and that *this* is part of what all men mean by 'God'. It may well be that *part* of the meaning of 'God' should be 'projected father figure'. Another part may be 'first cause'. Yet another may be 'preserver of all things both visible and invisible'. But the father figure component cannot be magnified into a definition which excludes all the rest. The reasons and evidence which would make probable the existence of God in a sense of the word 'God' *other* than Freud or Feuerbach (or for that matter Marx) suggest have still to be examined on their own merits (if they have any). Such evidence cannot be legislated out of court because the word 'god' is declared to mean something which palpably it does not mean, even as a minimum definition, to most of those who regularly use it.

Thus I conclude that while a 'natural history' of religion may prove to be highly successful in accounting for the origins in human nature of belief in God, such an account would not rule out evidence and reasons if any can be produced. Nor can restrictive accounts of what 'god' means (derived from psychology or political theory or any other source) be used to rule out meanings of the term which might be suggested by other evidence. But in both cases the legitimate challenge to the believer is the same: produce reasons or evidence which will show that belief in God is reasonably grounded and is thus something *more* than it seems to be from the accounts of its origin. If you do not, then it will be presumed that religion in general and belief in God in particular are 'merely psychological': more like the boy's belief in the ghost in the garden than like a conviction about the world we all experience.

3 THE EVIDENCE FOR BELIEF IN GOD: PUBLIC ARGUMENTS

The totality of evidence which has been offered for the existence of God since the first coming together of Jewish monotheism and Greek philosophy about two thousand years ago is immense. Some of it – the argument from general consent for example – is of very little intrinsic significance. Some of it depends upon philosophies which are now unfamiliar and unlikely to be adopted. (I am thinking, for example, of George Berkeley's theory of immaterialism in the early eighteenth century and the argument for God's existence to which it gives rise.) Some of it – for example what *we* would regard as an excessive credulity towards reports of divine interventions in human affairs – is the product of particular historical and cultural circumstances. But there is also evidence which is very ancient, very persistent, and which still influences belief.

One part of this evidence consists in the powerful and commanding experiences which a surprising number of people describe in terms of a direct encounter with, or perception of, the divine. Such evidence is private in the sense that it can have very little influence with those who do not have such experiences. But it is important because of its prevalence and immediacy. I shall consider the special problems and ambiguities associated with it in the next chapter.

Another part, and a very important part, of the evidence for theistic belief is made up of two objectively ascertainable arguments. They are concerned with the origin of the world we know. They constitute the theistic reasons for rejecting an atheistic cosmology. The bulk of the present chapter is concerned with them.

But there is a further argument, less ancient (only about a thousand years old!) and much less likely to occur spontaneously to a thinking or imaginative person. It is of great philosophical complexity, but of importance inasmuch as it forces us to focus upon what is meant by the existence of such a spectacularly unusual entity as God. I examine it first.

(i) Real, Necessary, and Eternal Existence

An argument which is the single-minded invention of one man is rare in the history of thought but, if one excludes the enigmatic hint in what Jehovah said of himself to Moses: 'I am who I am' (Exodus 3: 14–15), then Anselm (1033–1109, Archbishop of Canterbury 1093–1109) in the *Proslogium* seems to have achieved a pure philosophical original. What he has to say is brief, ingenious, perceptive and puzzling to the point of irritation for an opponent. Nevertheless in its original presentation it was not offered as an argument to convince atheists or doubters, but as a devout prayer which seeks to understand how God is what we already believe him to be. Thus before embarking upon his statement of the single, clear, uncluttered argument which he wanted, Anselm wrote, 'I do not seek to understand so that I may believe; but I believe so that I may understand.' The *belief*, the commitment to God, is first; the *argument* is opened to us by the belief. Despite this avowal, what Anselm wrote has frequently been treated as a serious attempt to prove the existence of God, and it is largely in that light that we must now take it. The argument is in the second of the very brief chapters of the *Proslogium*. The concluding sentences are drawn from chapter 3:

> Therefore, O Lord, thou who givest understanding to faith, grant that I may understand (as far as thou knowest it to be expedient) that thou art as we believe, and that thou art what we believe. Our belief is that thou art a being than which no greater can be conceived [*id quo nihil maius cogitari potest*]. But it might be thought that no such being exists, for 'The fool hath said in his heart, *There is no God*' [Vulgate, Psalms 13 : 1; Authorized Version, Psalms 14 : 1]. Yet this same fool, on hearing of 'that than which no greater can be conceived', understands what he hears, and what he hears is in his understanding [*esse in intellectu*] even if he does not understand that such a being exists. For there is a distinction between having a thing in the understanding and understanding that it is in existence. For instance, when a painter prepares in his mind what he is about to make, he has the conception of it in his understanding, but he understands that what he has not yet made is not yet in existence. Thus even the fool is convinced that something

'than which no greater can be conceived' is in his understanding, for when he hears this phrase he understands it, and what is understood is in the understanding. Now certainly that than which no greater can be conceived cannot *merely* be in the understanding because if it were *only* in the understanding, then it could further be conceived to exist in reality as well; but then it would be a greater thing. *Therefore*: if that than which no greater can be conceived were only in the understanding, there would be something still greater than it. But this is impossible. *Therefore* something undoubtedly exists than which no greater can be conceived, and it exists both in the understanding and in reality . . . Thou art this, O Lord our God . . . And indeed all that exists, saving thee alone, can be conceived to be non-existent. Thou, therefore, alone most truly of all beings hath existence. For all else that exists, exists less truly and has less of existence than thou.

This argument produced an almost immediate critical response (from one Gaunilo, a monk living near Tours) to which Anselm offered a reply which has survived in a somewhat disordered form. The argument was well known to Aquinas (1225–74) but rejected by him. It was revived by Descartes (1596–1650) in *Meditations* V, and totally rejected by Kant (1724–1804) in the *Critique of Pure Reason* (Transcendental Dialectic, Book II, chapter iii, section 3, where it is called 'the ontological or Cartesian argument'. It is now almost always known by the former of these two names). In the second half of the twentieth century it has attracted an almost incredible amount of philosophical analysis[1] as well as being given several theological rehabilitations, notably in the process theology of Charles Hartshorne.[2] It is entirely impossible, and would be most unwelcome within the limitations of this book, to follow these often intricate discussions in the detail which they deserve. All I can realistically attempt is an indication of the character of the argument and a brief look at the main objections. This scanty treatment matters less as part of an examination of the reasons and evidence for theistic belief than might be expected. As I have already hinted, the importance of the ontological argument is not as a proof to the unconvinced, but as an insight into what theistic belief would be when properly understood, and this aspect of the argument's importance does not depend upon following out in full the philosophical criticisms.

The character of Anselm's argument is highly unusual. It is an attempt to reach a conclusion about the real existence of something (and the inconceivability of the non-existence of that thing), not by observation or inference from what is anywhere existent in the universe, but from the concept of the thing itself. Quite apart from any more full-blooded definition which could be given to the concept of God, there can be little doubt that an essential part of the theistic definition would have to be 'that than which no greater can be conceived'. Even the fool (the atheist) can accept this definition and can understand it. But if the fool conceives of God, thus defined, as existent only in his understanding, then a greater being could exist. Namely, the God who exists also in reality. Thus the being than which no greater can be conceived must exist both in the understanding *and* in reality. What is more, the non-existence of a being thus defined is inconceivable. Therefore God thus defined could not not-exist. It will thus be observed that the argument has *two* conclusions: (1) that God, as defined, actually exists in reality, and (2) that God, as defined, could not not-exist, i.e. necessarily exists.

From the point of view of those who do not believe in God (those to whom Anselm did not appear to be addressing himself but who have always felt addressed by him) the movement of the argument *from* the definition of a concept *to* the real and necessary existence of an object which corresponds to the concept, is exasperating. It is exasperating because there is an instinctive and strong feeling that definition of a concept, however strange, cannot guarantee the existence of anything corresponding to the definition; yet this instinctive feeling cannot easily find any *decisive* point at which to fault the argument, despite the consensus of philosophers, even of most believing philosophers, that it is invalid. The best that can be produced are objections which lead to an intricate philosophical labyrinth. Let us look briefly at four of these objections.

1. Gaunilo's reply to Anselm, *On Behalf of the Fool*, contains a number of astute criticisms, at least one of which is seminal. In it Gaunilo maintains that an argument of exactly the same form as Anselm's could prove the real existence of the most excellent island you could conceive. Thus: think of the most excellent island. Now if the island you are thinking of exists only in your understanding, then it is not the most excellent island because the island you are thinking of would be more excellent if it existed in reality as well as in your understanding. Therefore the most excellent island exists in reality *and* in your understanding, and so on for the most excellent wife, cake, etc.

Anselm's reply is that he would certainly recommend anyone to go and look for the most excellent island *if* it could be shown that the logic of the definition 'that being than which no greater can be conceived' could be applied to anything other than God. Bonaventure (1221–74) sharpened Anselm's good-humoured reply. He pointed out that 'island' refers to an intrinsically defective entity. God is *alone* the non-limited perfect being to which the definition can be applied. This difficult claim, that the argument works because it applies uniquely to God, and shows up his uniqueness, will emerge again in connection with other objections to the ontological argument. But let us leave it for the moment.

2. Many critics of Anselm's argument have objected that the comparative 'greater' in the key expression 'than which no greater can be conceived' is vague. The instinctive question to ask is 'Greater by comparison with what other things and with reference to which qualities?' But the straight answer: 'by comparison with all other things and with respect to all qualities' will not do for the theistic God since *all* qualities will include 'destructiveness', 'malevolence', etc., which few people would want to attach to God. From the text of the *Proslogium* Anselm could reply that something is 'greater' than something else, in the sense of his argument, if it exists in the understanding *and* in reality, rather than merely in the understanding. In his important essay 'Anselm's Ontological Arguments' (*The Philosophical Review*, 1960) Norman Malcolm suggests (critically) that Anselm is able to say this only because he tacitly shares the view which Descartes was to make explicit in the *Meditations*, namely that existence is a perfection. In this way a being would be 'greater' – would have a larger accumulation of perfections – if it had the perfection of existing in reality as well as merely the perfection of existing in the understanding. But apart from sounding very strange (very 'medieval'!) in our ears, such an account of 'existence' would involve treating it as an *attribute* of things and, as we shall shortly see, it is very questionable whether this can be or should be done.

The great German theologian Karl Barth, in his study of Anselm,[3] construes 'greater' in a superficially less worrying way:

> Here 'great' suggests, as is shown by the variant *melius* and by the whole application of the formula, quite generally the large mass of all qualities of the object described and therefore as much its 'greatness' in

relation to time and space as the 'greatness' of its spiritual attributes or of its power, or of its inner and outward value or ultimately the type of its particular existence. The 'greater' which cannot be conceived beyond the thing described is therefore quite generally: anything *superior* to it.

As an account of the 'greatness' of God in general this is admirable; but the problem remains that the 'greatness' in the argument appears to relate in particular to two existences: *in the understanding* and *in reality*. The question is: is existence an attribute at all, let alone an attribute which admits of degrees?

3. The layman's sense that definitions cannot create realities has a long history of philosophical supporters from Hume and Kant onwards. Their argument is as follows. In forming an idea of X (whatever X may be) various descriptions are attached to X so that X is progressively more and more precisely defined. Thus if I start with the idea of a tomato I can give it the descriptions: fruit, edible, green when first formed, red (or occasionally yellow) inside and out when ripe, thin skinned, containing small soft pips divided by fleshy sections, etc. Each description adds to the idea of a tomato for one who does not know what a tomato is (i.e. for one who does not know the meaning of the *word* 'tomato' irrespective of whether he has ever encountered such an object in his experience). But suppose I am describing a tomato to someone who has in fact never encountered one in his experience, and does not know whether I am describing a real thing or an imaginary fruit of paradise. I tell him towards the end of my description that tomatoes exist. Now the question is this: in telling him that tomatoes exist, have I added a further description to the idea of a tomato, *or* have I said that what is already (fully or partly) described bears a relationship to the real world which, for example, hobbits do not bear, namely, that of having a real instance. Hume, followed later by Kant, has a strong argument in favour of the latter alternative. It is this. If I build up an idea of something by means of descriptions and then add 'it exists' as a final *description*, then the idea of the existent thing will be a different idea from the idea of the thing before it was asserted to exist. Thus:

> The idea of existence . . . is the very same with the idea of what we conceive to be existent. To reflect on any thing simply, and to reflect on it as existent, are nothing different from each other. That idea,

when conjoin'd with the idea of any object, makes no addition to it.[4]

And again:

'Tis also evident, that the idea of existence is nothing different from the idea of any object, and that when after the simple conception of any thing we wou'd conceive it as existent, we in reality make no addition to or alteration to our first idea ... When I think of God, when I think of him as existent, and when I believe him to be existent, my idea of him neither encreases nor deminishes.[5]

So the point is: 'existence' is not part of the description of what is said to exist, but is an assertion that what has already been described is a real thing. But the ontological argument, in Descartes's variety (*Meditations* V) and also in Anselm's root stock, depends upon treating existence as a part of the description of God. The argument turns upon the crucial definition 'than which no greater can be conceived' and this, in virtue of its own wording, must involve an existent thing, God. God's existence is thus treated as one of his descriptions along with being single, creator and sustainer of all things, an agent, etc. But treating 'existence' in this way (even in connection with such a singular entity as God) does not show, according to the critics of the argument, that God exists. It simply begs the question.

Philosophical analysis of the logic of 'exists' is probably not yet at an end, but even if it were, and it were agreed that 'exists' is not a description which functions equally with other descriptions, the users of the ontological argument have a defence. It is that in the case of God, and God alone, existence *is* one of his descriptions: not accidentally like the colour of a tomato, but essentially and necessarily like the description of a point in Euclidean geometry as 'that which has location without dimension'. But it will be remembered that the ontological argument has two conclusions: that God, as defined, actually exists in reality (let us follow Hume in calling this *real existence*) and that God, as defined, could not not-exist (let us follow others in calling this *necessary existence*). Now the contention that existence is not a description applies to real existence, and it is the real existence of God, when woven into Anselm's definition, which begs the question whether or not God (really) exists. On the other hand, *necessary* existence may well be a rather peculiar description which could be part of the idea of God, and if this were so, then one of the conclusions of the ontological argument would stand, and the question

would be: what is meant by necessary existence,* and: how does necessary existence relate to real existence?

4. In 1948, in one of the most celebrated and illuminating discussions
ever broadcast by the B.B.C., Bertrand Russell and Professor F. C. Copleston,
S.J., debated the existence of God.[6] Quite early in the discussion they came
into irreconcilable disagreement over the phrase 'necessary being': Russell
holding that 'necessary' could only be used meaningfully with reference to
a certain type of proposition, Copleston holding that 'necessary' applied
meaningfully to at least one existent entity, namely God:

> RUSSELL: . . . The word 'necessary', it seems to me, is a useless word,
> except as applied to analytic propositions, not to things . . .
> COPLESTON: . . . Well, we seem to have arrived at an impasse. To say
> that a necessary being is a being that must exist and cannot not-exist
> has for me a definite meaning. For you it has no meaning.

The disagreement arose out of discussion of an aspect of the cosmological
argument to which I shall return in section iii of this chapter but, as
Russell was quick to point out, Copleston's defence of the notion of
necessary existence was also a defence of the ontological argument.

The point between them was this. In the well established tradition of
logic and epistemology which runs through Leibniz (with qualifications),
Hume, Kant, Mill, and many in this century (of whom Russell is one of
the foremost), 'necessary' is a characteristic of those propositions which
are – and here the wording and degree of sophistication can vary con-
siderably – true in virtue of the meanings of the signs or words employed.
Examples are: 'irrational animals are irrational' and 'a triangle has three
internal angles'. These are *necessarily true* propositions inasmuch as the
predicate repeats, or brings out, an essential part of the meaning of the
subject. They say nothing about the existence of anything. They merely
hypothetically imply that *if* there really were irrational animals they
would necessarily be irrational; *if* there really were a triangle it would
necessarily have three internal angles. But if this analysis of 'necessary'
is applied to the phrase 'necessarily existent being', then either the phrase
must be meaningless – propositions, not things, can be said to be necessary – or, just possibly, God's necessary existence will be expressed by the
proposition 'necessarily God exists' which will assert the unhelpful taut-

---

* To speak of God's necessary existence is ambiguous. It could mean either (a) necessarily
God exists, or (b) if God really exists then necessarily God exists. Of these (a) begs the question
of God's real existence, (b) does not. But (a) is what Anselm's argument seems to require.

ology 'the necessarily existent God necessarily exists'. This leaves open the vital question whether such a necessarily existent God *really* exists, although it implies, perhaps valuably, that if God really exists, then he must necessarily exist. At which point one reverts to the questions I have already posed: what could be meant by necessary existence and how will necessary existence relate to real existence?

One, unpromising, attempt to show that the expressions 'necessary existence' or 'necessarily existent being' can have meanings, despite the Hume/Kant/Russell epistemology, consists in showing that there are true existential propositions in mathematics which assert the necessary existence of an entity. For example: 'There necessarily exists a number which is greater by one than any number you can name.' If those exceptions are admitted, why not an exception to admit a proposition asserting the necessary existence of God? But whatever sort of existence a mathematical entity might be supposed to have, the existence of God can hardly be similar. The one has either the peculiar ontological status given by the Platonic tradition or the conventionalist necessity of an entity in a logical system; the other is (presumably) the most gigantic matter of *real* existence which we could begin to apprehend.

A superficially more promising way in which the necessary existence of God could be understood is as the existence of a being which always has existed and never will go out of existence. In Psalm 90 this attribute of God is explicitly affirmed of Jehovah: 'Before the mountains were brought forth or ever thou hadst formed the earth and the world, from everlasting to everlasting thou art God.' Similarly the atoms spoken of by the Greek Epicureans are 'necessary':[7] if they exist as described then they have always existed and always will exist. But this understanding of the phrase 'necessarily exist', apart from being more naturally expressed by saying that something is *eternal*, is misleading. To say that something necessarily exists will simply affirm that, *if* the thing really exists, then the thing is eternal, i.e. as a matter of fact it never came into existence and as a matter of fact it will never go out of existence. Now *if* God really exists, there can be no doubt that we would want to say (at least in the theistic tradition) that he must be eternal; but asserting this hypothetical proposition commits us to no conclusion about whether this allegedly eternal thing really exists, and sheds no useful light upon the tantalizing phrase 'cannot not-exist' as that phrase is required by Anselm's argument.

The most authentic attempt (in the sense that it is enshrined in the Aristotelian and Thomistic traditions of Roman theology) to give meaning to talk about a necessarily existent being, is by contrast with the idea of contingently existing beings. All contingent beings (as opposed to beings which have always existed) might not exist in the sense that there was a time when each of them did not exist. Now if all beings were contingent in this sense – or so the argument goes – there must once have been a time when nothing existed. (The reader will note the massive apparent fallacy here.) Therefore, since nothing comes from nothing, nothing can exist now, which contradicts observation. Therefore some being or beings must have always existed: which is to say they could not not-exist. Furthermore no contingently existent beings can provide the sufficient reason for their own existence: their existence always has to be explained by reference to something else present or previous, and this will apply *ad infinitum* to contingent beings *and* to things that could not not-exist. Therefore, to avoid this infinite regress, we must reach a being which could not not-exist *and* which contains within itself the sufficient reason for its own existence. This necessarily existent being is God.

I do not wish to press the logic of this argument here. It is very close to the third [8] of the famous Five Ways towards belief in God which Aquinas sets out near the beginning of *Summa Theologiae*. A version will be considered in section iii of this chapter. My point in introducing it here is to indicate how a meaning might be given to the idea of a necessarily existent being by argument to, and contrast with, the idea of contingent beings. For the sake of reference, let us call this idea of necessary existence 'Aquinas's concept'. Now the question is, why should Aquinas's concept not function in Anselm's argument as the explication of the being which 'cannot not-exist'?

The answer is given by Aquinas himself when he rejects Anselm's argument. Aquinas points out that the 'opposite of the proposition "God exists" can be thought', and that Anselm's argument will not persuade the doubter because

> even if the meaning of the word 'God' were generally recognized to be 'that than which nothing greater can be thought', nothing thus defined would thereby be granted existence in the world of fact, but merely as thought about. Unless one is given that something in fact exists than which nothing greater can be thought – and this nobody denying the existence of God would grant – the conclusion that God in fact exists does not follow. (*Summa Theologiae*, 1a. 2, 2)

But this amounts to little more than an admirably succinct and lucid reiteration of the commonsense view that verbal manipulations which start off with a statement about something *thought* of as existing cannot go on to guarantee the *real* existence of the thing thought of. Nevertheless Aquinas's rejection of Anselm's argument should alert us to the reason why Aquinas's conception of a necessary being will not function in Anselm's argument: it is not the same conception. Aquinas's words which contrast 'contingent' with 'necessary' are close to a contrast between what is impermanent and what is eternal, and, as we have already seen, necessary = eternal will not do in Anselm's argument.

So how does real existence relate to necessary existence? So far as Anselm is concerned it does not relate. Outside the structure of his un-accepted argument (we are not as yet entitled to say his *invalid* argument) he has given the concept of necessary existence no meaning. But the account of necessary existence arrived at by Aquinas does relate to real existence. If God has the nature which we ascribe to him in theistic religions, and if he really exists, then he must indeed be the eternal being which contains within itself the sufficient reason for its own existence: *if* God really exists, *then* God necessarily exists. But, of course, from this it is still an open question whether God really exists, whether there really is any eternal being which contains within itself the sufficient reason for its own existence. Aquinas tries to close the question by showing that such a being must really exist if we are to explain the existence of anything. But his argument may be inconclusive – as we shall see later.

What then should we finally make of Anselm's argument? We have seen from Gaunilo's objection that, if it is valid at all, it is valid only for one being, God, since God alone satisfies the crucial negative comparison upon which the whole argument depends. Furthermore, if we agree that it is a mistake to regard real existence as a description or 'perfection' of anything, then the argument is simply defective. From the point of view of Aquinas and common sense, it is defective anyway, since no one who doubts the real existence of God is going to have his doubts resolved by a definition which evolves from the thought existence of God. But all this still does not add up to a rejection of Anselm's argument which is as clear, unequivocal and apparently decisive as the argument itself. I am inclined to think that such a decisive rejection may never be found despite the consensus of philosophers and of common sense that the argument gives no good reason to believe in the real existence of God.

But Anselm originally presented his argument as an insight into belief in God rather than as a proof to the sceptical or agnostic. As such it has value. If I already believe in God, then I could not believe anything to be greater, and I would also believe that my God could not not-exist. If he really exists, then he *must* necessarily exist. But does he really exist? That is the substantial question to which we must now turn.

(ii) *Cosmic Questions*

Part of the common theistic root of the Judaic, Christian and Islamic religions involves belief in the real existence of one (and only one) God who in the beginning created heaven and earth. It is this very ancient Jewish belief which found support in two strands of Greek thought which were developed by Christian and Islamic philosophers into what more recent philosophy has usually called the 'cosmological argument' and the 'design argument' for the existence of God. These arguments, and the theistic account of creation with which they are historically associated, are products of a general questioning (common to most cultures) about the ultimate origin of things: a questioning which in Israel resulted in a religion and a creation story, and in Greece resulted in philosophical and scientific speculation and argument. But what does this questioning amount to when it is articulated rather than merely left as a vague wonder and awe evoked by the mysterious universe which everywhere surrounds us? I suggest that the questions themselves, which I shall call *cosmic questions*, are typically:

1. Where does the stuff which the universe contains come from? or, What is the reason for the existence of the universe as a whole? or, Why is there something rather than nothing?
2. Why does the stuff move or change?
3. Why does it change according to orderly and intelligible processes and settle into relatively stable entities?
4. What purpose, if any, does man have in the cosmic scheme of things?

We know, as soon as they are stated, that these questions are probably unanswerable; that they may even be beyond our understanding or incoherent – a product of language cut adrift from its proper points of reference – but most of us still feel moved by them. We are enthralled by the ultimate enigma of things and must take *some* stance with respect to that enigma. We must offer ourselves *some* answers, even if our final answer is that there are no answers. It is therefore still of profound interest to note that in western cultures, at least since the fourth century B.C., these questions have evoked two irreconcilably contrary responses: the religious, dominant for about two thousand years, the archetype of which is Jewish theism; and the atheistic, now more evident than ever before, the archetype of which is Hellenistic atomism. The fundamental characteristic of the theistic response is that it looks *beyond* the world to an eternal and infinite being who somehow explains or gives purpose to all things. The fundamental characteristic of the atheistic response is that its explanation stops with man and the world itself. Now since Hellenistic atomism is both the first coherent atheistic system in the history of the western world, and one which has most in common with the rather vague scientific atheism (or 'positivistic naturalism') of the present day, I propose to give an account of it and then to use it as a paradigm of typically atheistic answers to the cosmic questions.

In the atomist system,* the universe consists of material bodies and void. Material bodies are known, and known to exist, by sensation; void is that in which material bodies exist, move and have place. This void is not the logically absurd non-being of Parmenides, but is, in a sense, existent. It is the 'out there'. The material bodies which are out there are, or are agglomerates of, uncuttable particles (atoms). The universe of void and of material bodies is infinite and eternal, i.e. it has no centre, no spatial boundaries, and no beginning or ending in time; it just *is*. A cosmos is a relatively stable and ordered grouping of material bodies which forms, endures for a while, and then decays, until eventually its constituent atoms fall away again into the primeval rain of the universe. The number of these atoms is, like the universe itself, infinite, and each one is eternal, subject neither to creation nor destruction. This means that the atomist system very emphatically adopts the dogma (which it

---

* The first statements of the atomist philosophy were provided by Leucippus and his younger contemporary Democritus (*c.* 460–370 B.C.). Only fragments and short paraphrases survive. Their ideas were reworked, perhaps in the light of Platonic and Aristotelian criticism, by Epicurus (341–270 B.C.). Three letters and forty short paragraphs of 'Principal Doctrines' are preserved by Diogenes Laertius (a second-century A.D. collector of philosophical anecdotes, paraphrases and bibliographies). There is also a short collection of paragraphs, some evidently spurious, known as the 'Vatican Sayings' discovered in 1880. But the atomist system was given the fullest statement which has survived to us from classical antiquity in *De Rerum Natura*, the great didactic poem by Lucretius dating from about 55 B.C. In speaking of these sources I shall simply refer to 'the atomist system', since for present purposes it is not important to try to distinguish the thought of Democritus (inasmuch as it survives) from that of Epicurus, or that of Epicurus from his apparently faithful exponent Lucretius. (References to Lucretius are by book and line.)

shares with the Stoics and many other systems of philosophy and science) that things cannot come into existence out of nothing. The refrain 'nullam rem e nilo' (less archaically 'nihil ex nihilo') – no thing from nothing – occurs repeatedly in Lucretius, and carries with it the consequence which he makes boldly clear: 'Nothing is ever created by divine power out of nothing' (I, 150). Notice that in the atomist system, a god *neither* creates the stuff, the atoms, from which bodies are formed (they are eternal), *nor* does a god form this or any other cosmos or ordered part of the universe. Nevertheless, weak as it may seem in its ancient version, and much as it invites the theistic challenge of the design argument, there *is* a mechanism for cosmos formation.

It starts from the atomist account of the origin of motion: the second cosmic question. Motion and matter are co-eternal. No unmoved mover or other origin of motion exists. Atoms and their uniform motion 'downwards' (in some absolute sense which is difficult and mechanically superfluous to specify) are from everlasting to everlasting, and there is no 'outside' power which begins or which can turn aside their motion (Lucretius, II, 307). But what does happen, and this is again part of the given nature of things, is that at random times and places individual atoms swerve a little in the cosmic rain, setting up collisions and groupings which can, over enormous periods of time, become a cosmos of material bodies.

The regular structures and ordered processes which are apparent in the cosmos familiar to us do not have their origin in design, but come, like the cosmos itself, from multiple random collisions and combinations of atoms (Lucretius, V, 416–71) which eventually yield results which are relatively stable or have a tendency to repeat themselves. The earth itself is just such a fortuitous concourse of atoms.

For the atomist, the fourth cosmic question, concerning the destiny of man, is quickly and bleakly answered. Man and all living creatures grew out of the earth. This process has now ceased. Many species have already perished due to their unstable forms, and the earth is already past its prime. Man's existence is purely accidental, of no significance to anyone but himself, and of no concern to those blessed intelligences called gods if any there should happen to be.* 'The universe was certainly not created

---

* It is a somewhat moot point whether the Epicureans genuinely wished to acknowledge the existence of some gods; but if they did, it is certain that these gods were mere examples of blessedness who did nothing, created nothing, promised nothing to mankind, and demanded nothing from us.

for us by divine power' (Lucretius, II, 160). Man has no future, either individually in an after life, or corporately as a species. All we can say for ourselves is that: 'Some species increase, others diminish, and in a short space the generations of living things are changed, and like runners pass on the torch of life' (II, 77–9).

This brief account of the atomist response to the four cosmic questions is given in the terms evolved by a school of Greek philosophers several centuries before the birth of Christ. But I trust it will be immediately apparent to the reader that a materialist or atheistic reading of modern accounts of evolution, of atomic physics, and of astronomy, could be woven into the atomist account with very little philosophical alteration: the details, not the structure, of this fundamentally atheistic system would change. The points at which it was in conflict with theistic cosmogony (or indeed with almost any recognizably religious view of things) would remain. I shall henceforth refer to this archetypal system as *classical atheism*.

The theistic account of the origin of the universe is, by contrast, a creation story, but it is one which has an ambiguity at its source. The first two verses of the Book of Genesis are usually read 'In the beginning God created the heavens and the earth. The earth was without form and void, and darkness was upon the face of the deep.' Despite the peculiarity of the Hebrew verb *bārā'* – a notion of creation which is only used in the Old Testament with God as its subject – these verses may mean *either*[9] (a) 'In the beginning God created [out of nothing] the heavens and the earth, and [when he had done this] the earth was without form and void . . .' *or* (b) 'In the beginning the earth was without form and void and [from that pre-existing condition] God created the heavens and the earth . . .'. The first time that meaning (a) appears unequivocally in the Hebrew canon is in 2 Maccabees 7: 28; nevertheless (a) is the sense in which Christian theists have usually understood the creation story. Thus Augustine (354–430) writes 'At the time of creation there could have been no past, because there was nothing created to provide the change and movement which is the condition of time.'[10] In this interpretation, the act of God first created the stuff of the universe *ex nihilo*, and then formed (and continually holds in being or sustains) the ordered universe. If God's sustaining power were withdrawn, the universe would collapse back into nothingness again. Islamic philosophers, on the other hand, have, with the important exception of al-Kindi, generally preferred meaning (b) in the Genesis story: Allah sustains by his will a cosmos which he has formed from the pre-existing and eternal chaos of matter.

From the initial concept of the universe as a divine creation, the typical and still familiar theistic answers to the cosmic questions evolve. In brief, they are: (1) God is the reason for the existence of the universe as a whole. (2) The stuff which the universe contains moves because God (as the first mover) set it in motion. (3) The ordered patterns and stable entities in the universe exist as a result of God's design or as an expression of his will. (4) At the very least, man is the concern of the Creator and Sustainer of all things, and each individual matters in the sight of God.

The irreconcilable divergence between classical atheism and the theistic system is now evident. In the first place the atheistic account takes the existent universe as a given, eternal, and ultimately inexplicable fact, and rejects as absurd the notion of creation *ex nihilo*; the theist, on the other hand, is scandalized at an inexplicable physical universe and explains it in terms of creation (generally regarded as creation *ex nihilo*) by an agent whom he calls God. Secondly, the atheistic account treats motion as a natural feature of bodies in space; the theist traces the origin of motion to the agency of God. Thirdly, the atheistic system regards the ordered processes which the universe manifests and the (relatively) stable entities to which these processes give rise as outcomes of infinitely numerous random movements of particles; the theist regards this as absurd: an almost perverse refusal to take the obvious course and explain cosmic order as the product of intelligent design and purpose. The final disagreement about the status of man follows from the differences already identified. I shall return to it in chapter seven.

It may well be that a preference for one or other of these profoundly different accounts of the ultimate origination of things is in the end decided by the possession of different intellectual or emotional dispositions. One genuinely rests content with the world itself; the other genuinely feels a need to look beyond the world in its quest for explanation. But this does not mean that the differences between atheist and theist are undiscussable, or that the differences are in all cases unresponsive to reasoned argument.

It has already been observed that the atomist (or classical atheist) is inclined to draw his questioning of nature to a conclusion at the point when he thinks he has reached its most general features: the existence of bodies in space, motion, the fact of natural order, etc. The theist carries the exploration one stage further; not to a further general feature of nature, but on to a different *kind* of explanation – the activity of an intelligent agent. The theist regards this move as not merely arguably better than resting content with the ultimately inexplicable brute facts of nature, but as rationally warranted by two arguments: one, the cosmological argument, drawn from the alleged logical need to terminate an infinite regress of explanations; the other, the design argument, drawn from an empirical analogy between the order imposed by man and the order discernible in nature. Both these arguments are eminently discussable, and atheist and theist can and do discuss them. We shall look at some of what can be said in sections iii and iv of the present chapter. But before doing so, the crucial notion of creation *ex nihilo* requires examination.

I have already indicated that Islamic philosophers generally shied away from the intuitively odd notion of creation *ex nihilo* (and they were following the consensus of Greek philosophy in doing so). The philosophical traditions apart, creation *ex nihilo* is odd for two reasons. One is because *creation* of a material body from *no* thing is never observed within the natural working of the universe. The other is because no intelligent agent has ever been known to bring about, or has ever experienced bringing about, the existence of a material body literally and totally from *no* thing. Put these two considerations together and you have a strong disposition to regard creation *ex nihilo* not only as something which does not happen, but as something which is impossible.

I say creation *ex nihilo* is never observed *within* the universe. There are two points here. One concerns the semantics of the verb 'create'. The other concerns what usage the facts actually warrant when recent astronomers and physicists speak of matter being 'created'.

In English the verb 'create' is transitive: it operates from a subject to an object. But when the *Shorter O.E.D.* specifies what it regards as the primary sense of the word, it makes explicitly clear that the only subject which the verb can normally take in this sense is God: 'Said of God: To bring into existence, cause to exist; especially "to form out of nothing" (Johnson)'. The various secondary usages, to create a garden, a work of art, a home, an obligation or legal bond, etc., will indeed have a human person, or personification, or institution, as subjects; but clearly these usages do not imply the production of any material body out of no pre-existing materials. Thus the primary notion of creation *ex nihilo* is semantically confined to activity which has a very special agent, God, as its subject. Secondary usages are confined to situations where *some* agent or personification acts to produce something (by re-using or re-forming pre-existent materials). Now it is evident that in the primary sense no *act* of creation is observed by the astronomer or physicist: what is observed is the *appearance* of an entity. When, for example, Joseph Silk writes, 'Other recent theoretical developments have led to some understanding of how matter behaves in the immense gravitational field surrounding a black hole, where spontaneous creation of particles can occur,'[11] he is committing himself neither to the view that the appearance of such particles is divine creation *ex nihilo*, nor to the view that some intelligent agent is involved in their production. Here, as in most other recent scientific usages, what is meant is that an entity which it seems proper to regard as a material object has formed where no material object previously existed (but where radiations, gravitational fields, and so on did previously operate). What is observed (or inferred) is the spontaneous appearance of a new material object. Whether such an appearance is a creation (*ex nihilo* or otherwise) is not a judgement which the scientific observer is able to reach *as a scientist*. What I am saying is that within the universe it may be possible to observe a new material body come into existence, but this is not to observe an *act* of creation, let alone an act of creation *ex nihilo*.

What about a human agent creating or bringing about something? Certainly human beings create, in the sense of bring about, prisons, children, symphonies, wireless sets and atomic explosions among countless other things. But as in the case of natural productions, and even more obviously, none of these things is a new material body created *ex nihilo*: such wonderful powers are not exercised by man even if God may exercise them. The point here is that even if we use the almost incredibly far-stretched analogy that some intelligent agent has the same relation to the universe that a man has to the things he produces, even if we use this analogy in order to try to grasp the notion of a created universe, it immediately breaks down for creation *ex nihilo*, which forms no part of the experience of man. For this reason, together with the impossibility of observing creation *ex nihilo* in physical nature, we have the strongest inclination which experience can provide to conclude that creation *ex nihilo* does not take place within the universe. Does this mean that such creation is impossible? Swinburne thinks not:

Some of the acts attributed by the theist to God are acts of creating *e nihilo* (i.e. not out of pre-existing matter); others are acts of moving, or changing the characteristics of, existing things. Creating *e nihilo* is not something which men are able to do, but it is easy enough to conceive of their doing it. I could just find myself able as easily to make appear before me an ink-well or to make a sixth finger grow, as I am at present able to move my hand. Various tests (e.g. sealing off the room and keeping its contents carefully weighed) could show that the ink-well or finger were not made of existing matter. Creating *e nihilo* is a perfectly conceivable basic act.[12]

I disagree. The examples given would not be regarded, I would venture to say would *never* be regarded, as examples of creation *ex nihilo*. Such a recondite possibility would scarcely occur either to an observer or to the supposed agent himself. The events Swinburne mentions would be regarded as tricks, or inexplicable freaks, or as pre-existing matter gathered into sensible forms in ways not understood: almost anything in preference to the repugnant notion that I brought things into being out of literally nothing. Certainly the tests Swinburne proposes would not satisfy the sceptic, although he might be satisfied if the entire contents of the universe could be shown to have increased in weight by just the weight of the ink-well and finger. Again, if Swinburne means by 'a perfectly conceivable basic act' one which is not logically self-contradictory, then indeed creation *ex nihilo* may be conceivable. All sorts of things may be conceivable in this sense although not possible in the actual universe we have. For example, it is conceivable that every physical body should *repel* every other body, or that entropy, the degree of disorder in a physical system, should continually *de*crease. But this is not what happens. It is conceivable that it should, but such a conception would count as a paradigm for what is meant by the impossible in our system. Perhaps we can agree that whatever is conceivable is not logically self-contradictory, but some of what is conceivable will be sheerly impossible, and it is in this light that we tend to regard the notion of creation *ex nihilo* in the physical universe.

A further consideration is that even if creation *ex nihilo* were *not* one of those conceivable acts which we have the strongest evidence which the nature of things can provide for supposing to be impossible, any candidate for such a creation would have to be established against the equally conceivable, but non-supernatural, possibility that it just happened *ex nihilo*. So, we may say, the universe is not infinitely old as the atomists thought: it started, B A N G! But if conceivability is to be the test of anything, it is just as conceivable, perhaps more conceivable, that the beginning of the universe simply happened *ex nihilo*: which would not be theism (God's act of creation) but atheism (it just occurred).

The sum of all this is that I am inclined to say that those who rejected the notion of creation *ex nihilo* had good, if not absolutely conclusive, grounds for doing so. The notion is recondite in the extreme, depends upon a far-fetched and broken analogy with human acts, is rightly regarded as impossible from within our experience of the universe, and would anyway have to stand comparison with the atheistic possibility that the new physical object just happened. But this does not mean that the way forward for the theistic system is now closed. One path leads to a typically Islamic theism in which God created the cosmos from a pre-existing chaos. Some versions of the cosmological argument would remain viable on such an assumption, and the design argument would be unaffected. Another path is for the (Christian) theist to insist that agent explanation of the natural world, including creation *ex nihilo*, is required by a version of the cosmological arguments which he holds to be valid.

(iii) *The Ultimate Origination of Things*

We are interested in evidence concerning the real existence of God. An important part of that evidence has always been argument to a divine origin of things (a) from the existence of the world, and (b) from certain exceedingly general features of the world.* Both (a), and *some* of the arguments which come under heading (b), have conventionally been termed 'cosmological arguments' by many writers on the philosophy of religion in the past century (recently, for example, J. L. Mackie did this). Kant, on the other hand, who actually devised the term, used it for the sole purpose of naming argument of type (a), and some people still carefully follow him in this (recently, for example, Richard Swinburne). As a result of this divergence, there is uncertainty about what 'cosmological argument' means, and ambiguity concerning precisely which arguments

* The word 'world' can mean all there is, the universe, or an ordered part or system within the universe. In this chapter it is used only as a synonym for 'universe'. I say that such arguments have *always* been part of the evidence for the existence of God or a god. They have, at least since the appearance of Book I of Xenophon's *Memorabilia* and Book X of Plato's *Laws* – which is as near to 'always' as philosophy can aspire.

it does or should refer to. Since this confusion infects the ways in which arguments for the existence of God are discussed, we must digress to consider the issue before returning to the main theme again on p. 59.

Argument of type (a) is a direct response to the first cosmic question (see above p. 48) which Leibniz, for example, put in the form 'Why is there something rather than nothing?' It is almost certainly Leibniz's account of this argument in the *Theodicy* (1710), the only account of it published during his lifetime, which Kant had in mind when he devised the term 'cosmological argument' in the *Critique of Pure Reason* (1781), describing it as argument which begins 'with a purely indeterminate experience, i.e. some empirical existent'.[13] Nevertheless other and subtly different versions of this type of argument had existed at a much earlier period, for example in the Third Way of Aquinas, not to mention in certain Jewish and Islamic philosophers and in the mind-twistingly sophisticated scholasticism of the *Opus Oxoniense* of Duns Scotus (*c.* 1266–1308). It is this type of argument which Swinburne calls a cosmological argument and characterizes as 'an argument to the existence of God from the existence of some finite object or, more specifically, a complex physical universe'.[14] It is this type of argument which Flew proposes[15] we should follow Kant in calling cosmological argument. I accept this proposal.

Argument of type (b) on the other hand (Kant's awkwardly named physico-theological argument) is a response to the second and third questions I set out on p. 48. The various arguments of this type focus attention upon certain general or very prevalent features of the world and seek to account for them. The arguments include (but the list is not exhaustive): (1) argument from the fact of motion to a prime mover, (2) argument from causal sequences to a first cause, (3) argument from the order in the natural world to an intelligent orderer, and (4) argument from the adaptation of means to ends in the natural world to an intelligent agent capable of imposing such adaptations. This is apparently clear enough. Difficulties begin when it is noticed that arguments (1) and (2) share characteristics with the cosmological argument properly so called which they do not share with arguments (3) and (4). In particular (1) and (2) are arguments which depend upon appeal to the unsatisfactory nature of an infinite regress of causes or movements. But the cosmological argument also depends upon the unsatisfactory nature of an infinite regress – regress to previously existing things in answer to the question

'Why is there anything?' Moreover regress arguments (1) and (2), although they start with a matter of fact or real existence such as things moving or causally related events, depend upon treating some general principle – 'every event has a cause' for example – as *a priori*. Again in much the same way, Leibniz's account[16] of the cosmological argument treats the principle of sufficient reason ('nothing happens without a *reason* why it should be *so* rather than otherwise') as *a priori*. In contrast arguments (3) and (4) do not appeal to the unacceptability of any infinite regress nor do they involve any *a priori* principle. Any generalization involved in them is entirely *a posteriori*.*

It is to take account of these factors that usage of the term 'cosmological argument' is quite often extended to cover both type (a) argument, and type (b) arguments of the regress variety exemplified by (1) and (2) above. The disadvantages of doing this are that it ignores the distinctive character of type (a) cosmological argument; it breaks up Kant's categories of argument for the existence of God without entirely removing the magisterial influence of his terminology, and it makes necessary an almost *ad hoc* subterfuge to prevent arguments (3) and (4) from being included among cosmological arguments.

The rather breathless footwork of such a usually clear-sighted writer as J. L. Mackie results from his attempts to accommodate these disadvantages. Writing with reference to what *he* calls cosmological arguments (i.e. type (a) plus what I am calling regress arguments from type (b)), he remarked:

> What is common to the many versions of this argument is that they start from the very fact that there is a world or from such general features of it as changes or motion or causation – not, like the argument from consciousness or the argument for design, from specific details of what the world includes or how it is ordered – and argue to God as the uncaused cause of the world or of those general features, or as its creator, or as the reason for its existence.[17]

---

* A term often glossed over by the eye without being grasped by the mind. In modern usage it is always contrasted with what is said to be *a priori*. An *a priori* principle or proposition is one that can be known to be true, or false, without reference to experience, except in so far as experience is necessary for understanding its terms. An *a posteriori* principle or proposition can be known to be true, or false, only by reference to how, as a matter of fact, things have been, are, or will be. (Adapted from *A Dictionary of Philosophy*, ed. A. Flew, London, 1979.) Other, but trivial, examples of philosophers' Latin for which literal translations avail little are *ad hoc*, meaning 'added on in any way that suits', and *de facto*, meaning 'from the fact of the matter'.

Quite apart from what Kant may have said, it is not really helpful to conflate argument from the fact that a world exists (whatever it is like) with argument from the general features which the world actually has, and then to declare that one of those general features – order – is disallowed on the alleged grounds that it is a 'specific detail'. (End of digression!)

For the purpose of discussion I am adopting Kant's category of cosmological argument. I propose to subdivide his category of physico-theological argument into two sub-sections: regress arguments and design arguments. Traditional arguments for the real existence of God (excluding the ontological argument) will thus be divided as follows.

Cosmological argument is evoked by the first cosmic question (p. 48 above). It is argument from the *existence* of the universe to a reason or explanation of the universe. In its strongest traditional form it involves appeal to the *a priori* unacceptability of an infinite regress of explanations or reasons.

Regress argument is evoked by the second cosmic question. It is argument from a general *feature* (usually motion, change or causation) of the universe to the origin of that feature. It depends upon the unacceptability of an infinite regress, the regress usually being regarded as *a priori* unacceptable.

Design argument is evoked by the third cosmic question. It is *a posteriori* argument from the order discernible in the universe, or from the purpose served by particular things, to an intelligent agent capable of imposing the order or purpose.

Having divided these categories of argument for the real existence of God a mite too decisively, I now have to retreat a little. None of the arguments at their first appearance, or for hundreds (or even thousands) of years after their first appearance, were classified or had names. They are woven through the history of philosophy and theology, sometimes with the names of particular persons attached, in the manner of themes, with variations which overlap. In what follows I shall try to state the theme of the cosmological argument in contemporary terms and to assess its significance as a reason for belief in God. I shall not attempt to follow out the various historical variations of this argument. This is partly because such a task would be lengthy, partly because it has already been carried out elsewhere by others.[18] But it is mainly because, in looking at the central theme of the cosmological argument, one is covering much of what has to be said about the variations, even those variations which spill over into regress argument. My final reason for restricting discussion in the present context is because intricate examination of each particular variation is not obviously relevant to what would *now* be significant in our quest for a foundation for reasonable belief in God (however much it may intrigue the professional philosopher).

I expressed the first cosmic question in three different ways:

(a) Where does the stuff which the universe contains come from?

(b) What is the reason for the existence of the universe?

(c) Why is there something rather than nothing?

In a limited sense question (a) is being answered by the cosmology which is a branch of astronomy. The best current hypothesis is that the universe as we are now able to observe it (i.e. the physical universe) has been expanding from a single beginning, 'the big bang', about twenty thousand million years ago. The hypothesis is subject to wholesale revision, for example in the light of the new possibility that all the visible material of the universe may exist in an invisible sea of neutrinos which, although almost undetectably small, may have *some* mass. If they do, then the mass of the universe may be inconsistent with the Big Bang theory. Nevertheless at the moment the Big Bang theory is the best scientific cosmology we have. Let us suppose that it, or some revision of it which preserves the notion of a beginning, is finally established as the best account we shall ever have of the origin of the observable universe, of its *start*. Have we then got an answer to question (a), or for that matter to questions (b) or (c)? I must reply, no – not in the sense in which they are usually asked. What we would have is the history of the physical universe back to an area of time (or perhaps even to an instant) when something happened beyond which nothing can be said to have happened because *all* that happens is, or is expressed in terms of, what was established by that first something. But although this takes us as far back as scientific knowledge can ever take us, in principle it takes us no further back than we have always been: namely, to some point in the history of the physical universe prior to which we know not what. All we have that is new is a longer history traced back to a unitary start. At that start (to whatever point it is traced) there remain the same enigmatic options: (1) Epistemological resignation – silence, the questions are meaningless, we close the book of our knowledge and plant our lettuces. (2) There was nothing, absolutely nothing whatever, just emptiness and the beginning happened *ex nihilo*. (3) We suppose that there was some earlier physical situation receding from us into infinity, unknown and unknowable because of the discontinuity of the big bang. (4) In the beginning was God – some power, no longer physical in our sense, which flung the stone that set alight the stars and drew the dawn upon the face of night. The first two are the agnostic or atheistic options. The third is indecisive. The last is the theistic or deistic option.

Rather than rest unsatisfied with these alternatives, let us try another track – the one by means of which Leibniz gave almost definitive expression to the main theme of the cosmological argument. Let us, he suggests, employ the 'great principle' that 'nothing takes place without a sufficient reason':

> that is to say that nothing happens without its being possible for one who has enough knowledge of things to give a reason sufficient to determine why it is thus and not otherwise. This principle having been laid down, the first question we are entitled to ask will be: *Why is there something rather than nothing?* For 'nothing' is simpler and easier than 'something'. Further, supposing that things must exist, it must be possible to give a reason *why they must exist just as they do* and not otherwise ... And although the present motion which is in matter arises from the one before it, and this in turn from the one before that, we are no further on however far we go; for the same question always remains. Thus the sufficient reason, which needs no further reason, must be outside this series of contingent things, and must lie in a substance which is the cause of this series, or which is a being that bears the reason of its existence within itself; otherwise we should still not have a sufficient reason, with which we could stop. And this final reason of things is called *God*.[19]

As well as in the late essay 'Principles of Nature and Grace, Founded on Reason' (1714) from which the above quotation is drawn, Leibniz expressed fundamentally the same argument with the same vigour and clarity on a number of earlier occasions, notably in the wonderfully succinct essay 'On the Ultimate Origination of Things' (1697):

> Now neither in any one single thing, nor in the whole aggregate and series of things, can there be found the sufficient reason of existence ... for what follows is in some way copied from what precedes (even though there are certain laws of change). And so, however far you go back to earlier states, you will never find in those states a full reason

why there should be any world rather than none, and why it should be such as it is.[20]

Leibniz's words 'we are no further on however far we go' and 'however far you go back to earlier states . . .' express exactly why it is that the Big Bang theory does not answer the first cosmic question in the sense in which it is asked: 'for the same question remains'. No physical or scientific answer could *ever* satisfy the question because such an answer would *always* refer to earlier physical states or more general physical laws about which the question could be asked again. The first cosmic question looks *beyond* the physical laws according to which those states change into one another.

It is important to understand that the words 'beyond', 'external', 'outside' etc. used in the present context *may* be intended to indicate some extension of space, but are more likely to be used as a somewhat vague (and possibly empty) metaphor or abbreviation to try to convey such a notion as 'of a different category or order of existence from the physical universe'. It is in this way that Leibniz uses these words. Whether they can be used in this way and still have any meaning will be considered below, pp. 115 f.

The discovery (if that is not, as yet, to give the Big Bang hypothesis too high a status) that the knowable physical universe may have had a beginning, and that this beginning does not answer the first cosmic question, has given a new piquancy to the objection of Leibniz and others that a regress of physical states does not explain 'why there should be any world rather than none, and why it should be such as it is'. But suppose, as most Greek philosophers thought, that the universe is infinitely old – that there really is an infinite regress of physical states. (In modern terms we might find, for example, that the expanding universe is a phase of an eternally pulsating universe somewhat in the manner of the Stoic cosmology.[21]) In that case there would be *no* physical state of the universe which was not explainable in terms of a preceding state together with the 'laws of change'. In the face of this possibility, Leibniz (and for that matter Swinburne[22]) would wish to say that *neither* the infinite series of states as a whole *nor* the laws according to which those states change, will have any explanation.

I accept the second but not the first conclusion. Certainly the laws of change will have no explanation. They will simply be the natural facts of the universe on the schema of classical atheism; *or* they will be explicable by reference to an external power on something like the theistic or deistic schema. But the infinite regress of physical states themselves will *always* have a sufficient explanation in the immediately preceding state in a universe which is eternal. It does not appear to me to make sense to talk about any sort of explanation (internal or external to the universe) of an *infinite* series of states considered 'as a whole'. No 'whole series' exists to be explained. If a real infinite series means anything, it means a series incapable of being gathered as a whole – whatever whole you take, there is limitlessly more. It is *impossible* to take such a whole, and yet every state has a sufficient explanation.

Let us try to get at this in another way.[23] Schematically, explanation of the present physical state of the universe, U_1, is given in terms of its previous state, U_2, together with certain laws of nature ('laws of change') which relate one state to another. (We may suppose U_1 and U_2 to last a finitely small instant of time.) Now the same type of explanation can be given of U_2, namely in terms of the laws of change and the preceding state U_3; similarly U_3 may be explained in terms of U_4 *and so on*. Now whether the *and so on* is finite (as the Big Bang theory might suggest) or infinite (as the Greeks supposed and as we may yet be forced to conclude) the actual laws of change are indeed inexplicable within the physical system. They just are as they are. But in the case of the succession of physical states, it makes a difference whether the *and so on* is finite or infinite. If it is finite, then there is a first state which lacks a previous state to explain it. If it is infinite, then there is no first state, i.e. no state which lacks a previous state in terms of which it may be explained. So in a temporally finite physical universe both the first state and the laws of change lack a sufficient explanation; in a temporally infinite universe only the laws of change lack explanation.

It should be noted that not all recent philosophers would agree with this conclusion. For example Richard Taylor argues in his important little book *Metaphysics* (New Jersey, 1963, pp. 91–2) that it is not plausible to suppose that the world as a whole is self-dependent given that each item in the world depends upon something outside itself for its existence. (Classical atheism would not grant this assumption since the world is composed of atoms and no atom would ultimately depend upon anything for its existence.) The world 'clearly depends for its existence upon something other than itself, if it depends on anything at all . . . And it must depend upon something, for otherwise there could be no reason why it exists in the first place.' Taylor then offers the alternatives: '(1)

that the world depends for its existence upon something else, which in turn depends on still another thing, this depending upon still another, *ad infinitum*; or (2) that the world derives its existence from something that exists by its own nature and which is accordingly eternal and imperishable, and is the creator of heaven and earth.' He then rejects (1) as impossible 'for it does not render a sufficient reason why anything should exist in the first place'. I agree that if the world has a finite history, its start either has a reason outside itself or is blankly inexplicable – a denial of the principle of sufficient reason. I do not agree that this holds if the world is infinitely old. In *that* situation there never existed any 'in the first place' which could lack a sufficient reason. Taylor's very words 'in the first place' deny the hypothesis of an infinitely old universe, and this gives him the excuse to say that at some stage it depends upon something other than its own previous state.

So I repeat: if the universe *started* at some remote but finitely distant time in the past, then both its existence and its laws of change lack a sufficient reason. If it never started, i.e. is infinitely old, then its existence at any time whatsoever is explicable in terms of its existence at an earlier time, but its laws of change lack a sufficient explanation.

Where are these ultimate sufficient reasons or explanations to be found? Leibniz is led to conclude:

> The reasons of the world then lie in something extramundane, different from the chain of states, or series of things, whose aggregate constitutes the world. And so we must pass from physical or hypothetical necessity, which determines the subsequent things of the world by the earlier, to something which is of absolute or metaphysical necessity, for which itself no reason can be given.[24]

But this is much stronger than the almost neutral alternative between natural fact and external power which we have so far encountered. Why *must* we pass on to something of metaphysical necessity? Because, according to Leibniz, the *a priori* principle of sufficient reason states that 'nothing happens without a reason why it should be so, rather than otherwise', and no reasons can be adduced from within the 'physical necessity' of the world for the laws of change (or for the whole series of physical states if that series is capable of being considered as a whole, i.e. if it had a first state a finite time ago). Therefore the reason must be sought from outside – 'and this final reason of things is called God'.

I do not think we can accept the force of this argument. What Leibniz establishes with unrivalled clarity is the insight that in the last resort explanation of the laws of change and of the existence of the physical universe (if the universe is of finite duration) cannot come from within it. What is not established is that it *must* therefore come from outside. There may indeed be *no* explanation. And if there were an outside explanation, there is no *a priori* necessity for there to be one. Why? Because the principle of sufficient reason terminates at the point of the last physical explanation. If it does *not* terminate there, but extends *a priori* to a further, external explanation – God – then one must ask, why does the principle not apply to *that* explanation? The only possible answer seems to be because it only holds within the physical universe. But if it only holds within the physical universe, then it cannot be used to insist upon an explanation *of* the physical universe from outside. Leibniz's beguiling device of referring to an 'absolute or metaphysical necessity' for which no reason can be given is a form of words which allows him to terminate the regress of sufficient reasons just one step beyond the point where *as an a priori principle* it has to terminate. We are led to feel that this new category of being, for which no reason can be given, excuses further applications of the principle, whereas the principle should never have forced us *a priori* to this new category. *If* the laws of change and the beginning of the physical universe are to have an explanation at all, *then* it must be in something which is different in kind from the physical universe: that is the acceptable conclusion of Leibniz's argument. But we are not obliged to accept that there *must* be such an explanation. As I have already said, there are a number of possibilities. There may be an infinite, but absolutely unknowable, physical pre-history to the Big Bang so that *every* physical state is preceded by *some* physical state and for one who could know these states there would always be a sufficient reason for any state. There may be nothing whatever before it. There may be an act of an outside force. But, it will be noticed, in this cluster of possibilities only one corresponds in any way with what might count as an explanation of the laws of change being what they are. If the laws of change are not to be taken as inexplicable natural facts, the only possibility seems to be to relate them to an external agent: to a power capable of making them what they are; the same outside force, perhaps, which began the series of physical states of things, if indeed it began.

There is, however, a further objection to this last possibility. Many philosophers would now argue that such a question as 'What is the reason for the existence of the physical universe?' makes no more sense than the question 'Where is the universe?' Since 'the universe' comprehends all there is, nothing is left by means of which an explanation can be given. I have much sympathy with this view of things and so, perhaps, will you, having been for a few pages submerged in the cosmological argument. But I do not think it is decisive. The question 'Where is the universe?' is manifestly absurd because location can only be specified relative to existent things within the universe. But 'What is the reason or explanation of the universe?' is somewhat different, since 'reason' and 'explanation' are being explicitly referred to something different in ontological category from the physical things of the universe. Certainly the universe comprehends all the physical things there are, but a 'being of metaphysical necessity' is not a physical thing. It may indeed be meaningless to postulate the existence of such a being, but at this stage such a conclusion is not self-evident. I shall return to it in chapter five when we consider arguments *against* the existence of God.

In conclusion: the main theme of the cosmological argument tries, but fails, to compel us to an external explanation of the physical universe in something which needs no further explanation. It succeeds in establishing that *if* an explanation is to be sought, *then* it must be sought externally to the laws of change or the physical states themselves; and it succeeds in indicating that one such external possibility of explanation would be a force or intelligence which we might wish to call God. But it remains for the design argument to give some actual probability to the possibility indicated by the cosmological argument which, of itself, does not establish the ultimate origination of anything.

After all that has been said about the cosmological argument, regress arguments may be dealt with relatively briefly in the present context since they follow the cosmological argument in one critical point – namely in holding that an infinite regress is unacceptable.

A typical regress argument proceeds as follows:

> Every physical event (or movement or change) in the world is caused by a preceding event (or movement or change). The regress of caused causes (or movements or changes) cannot be infinite. Therefore there must be an uncaused cause (or an unmoved mover or an unchanged changer), and this is what men call God.

The obvious objection to arguments of this form is the premise 'The regress ... cannot be infinite.' Perhaps it will be established that as a matter of fact the regress is not infinite, that it stops. But that is quite a different matter to use of an argument which depends for its force upon the *a priori* assertion that the regress of causes, movements or changes, *cannot* be infinite. There seems to be no more reason to reject the idea of an infinitely old universe than to reject the notion of an infinitely extended universe. Indeed most of us do now tend to accept in a vague way that the universe is spatially and temporally infinite, i.e. we tend to regard the Big Bang as a block in physical history, not its beginning. But there is a more precise reason why we should reject the *a priori* claim that an infinite regress of causes will never account for the present fact of motion, or of changes, etc. As I have already remarked, a real infinite series will be one such that any item in the series will have one earlier than it. In other words, there will *always* be a change to explain a change, a motion to cause a motion. The whole series does not hang on nothing, or start nowhere. *It does not start.* The worry about a chain of causes needing a start is only a worry if it is *not* an infinite chain, if it *has* a start. Furthermore the supposed uncaused cause is often little more than a verbal device for preventing us from asking what its cause is, and once that question is asked the same *a priori* reasoning which started the regress will continue it. Then again, if regress argument is successful, it provides no reason for us to arrive at a *single* first term: there may be multiple uncaused causes or unmoved movers. Even if, for reasons of intellectual economy, we restrict the possibilities to one, then a real doubt exists whether this one should be identified with God. I do not propose to follow this discussion further. It has been done elsewhere[25] and at no point takes us further than the cosmological argument has already taken us.

The conclusion so far is that if the existence of the universe, working in the way it does, is *not* to be accepted as a basic and inexplicable natural datum in the manner in which classical atheism accepted it, then an explanation can only be given in terms of a Being which is not of the physical universe at all. If that Being dealt with a pre-existing physical situation or chaos, we might be led to say 'In the beginning God formed the ordered universe out of chaos.' If that Being also brought into existence the first physical situation out of nothing, then we might want to say 'In the beginning God created the heavens and the earth.' However, at this stage, these are little more than empty possibilities, the latter made even a little more empty than the former in view of what was said earlier about the supreme peculiarity of creation *ex nihilo*. Let us now see what empirical content, if any, the design argument can put into either possibility.

(iv) *The Origin of Natural Order*

The third cosmic question concerned the origin of intelligible regularity and order in the natural world. From the beginning this question has evoked an argument of very different character from anything we have so far been examining. The design argument[26] does not depend upon any *a priori* generalization of the sort 'everything has a sufficient reason', or upon the unacceptability of an infinite regress, or upon a concept of God being so understood that it already includes the notion of real or necessary or eternal existence. Instead what we have is an *a posteriori* argument, subject to probabilities rather than certainties, and dependent upon analogical and inductive procedures which are used in scientific or ordinary-life situations.

Historically the design argument has had great persistence. There is a hint of it in Psalm 19. It is first recorded in philosophical literature by the Greek general Xenophon in his *Memorabilia* (c. 390 B.C.). Subsequently it had an almost continuous history up to the eighteenth century, by which period it was virtually a standard position for all Christian theists. It was subjected to a profound critical examination by David Hume in his *Dialogues concerning Natural Religion* (1779), and then, in the next century, to the apparently contrary evidence of Darwin's theory of evolution. As a result of these influences one version of the argument (usually called the *teleological argument*) suffered near extinction, while a second version (which I shall call the *regularity argument*) survived as the *a posteriori* counterpart of that aspect of the cosmological argument which focuses upon the *a priori* need to explain the laws of change. There is no short, standard, historically famous version of either the teleological argument or the regularity argument, but they evolve as follows.

It is everywhere observable – and more evident with every advance of science – that the physical universe, from very small things to very large things, functions according to what Leibniz called 'laws of change' (we call them 'laws of nature'). That is to say the workings of natural things are intelligible and predictable in terms of patterns and regularities which we can express in mathematical and natural languages. In a word: the physical universe is *orderly*. This is not merely to say that we impose order in virtue of the way we happen to perceive the world, but that there exists something real 'out there' which *is* regular and orderly and is therefore intelligible and describable. Now without asking in general terms where this order comes from, one might instead observe that at least *some* orderly systems have their order readily explainable in only one way; namely, it was imposed by us, by intelligent agents of very limited power. The more or less predictable workings of a steam engine, an atomic pile or a silicon chip are an inexplicable mystery in the nature of things unless we recognize what is obviously the case – that *we* made them. Now given that an explanation of order in certain things can only be given in terms of the activity of an intelligent agent of very limited power, could it be that natural order should similarly be explained in terms of an intelligent agent, but of vastly greater, possibly even of limitless power?

So the *regularity argument* runs as follows. Some things, human artifacts, have an order which is only explainable in terms of the activity of intelligent agents. Other things, natural physical objects, also display order both in their internal structures and in the ways they function relative to other physical objects. From the similarity of the order in artifacts and natural physical objects, it is inferred by analogy that the explanation of the order is, or is probably, similar in both cases; and hence that the author or authors of nature bear some remote analogy to the intelligence of man.

A somewhat narrower but historically important variation of this argument, usually called the teleological argument (from the Greek 'telos' meaning 'goal' or 'end'), was commonly given in terms of the useful and apparently purposeful adaptation of parts of living organisms to serve the ends of the whole organism,* but a version which might now look a little less dated is as follows.

Life on earth, particularly the more complex forms of life such as cats,

* This is the form in which the design argument is first recorded by Xenophon about 390 B.C. After observing the useful adaptation of particular organs in living creatures, he reports Socrates as saying 'With such signs of forethought in these arrangements, can you doubt whether they are the work of chance or design?' And again, having remarked the sexual adaptation of living things for the purposes of procreation he concludes: 'Undoubtedly these, too, look like the contrivances of one who deliberately willed the existence of living creatures' (*Memorabilia*, I, iv, 6–7). Cicero, writing about 45 B.C., reports something much closer to the regularity argument: having observed the definite and regular motions of the world, the natural inference is to 'a ruler and governor, the architect, as it were, of this mighty and monumental structure' (*De Natura Deorum*, II, xxxv). Apart from their intrinsic interest, I draw attention to these early statements of the teleological and regularity arguments to emphasize their intellectual independence of Judeo-Christian religious beliefs. The original appeal of the design argument does *not* depend upon looking for evidence to back up what is already firmly established theistic belief.

horses and human beings, depends upon the achievement of an exceedingly finely balanced combination of many factors, each of which has to operate within narrow limits of variation. (A great deal of evidence to support this assertion could be put in here, e.g. the critically important filtering processes of the upper atmosphere.) It is implausible to attribute this complex and delicate balance to chance. It is more credible that it has somehow been brought about for the purpose of permitting life: a purpose which we can only attribute to such an intelligence as we suppose God or the gods to be.

So the *teleological argument*, using part of Aquinas's Fifth Way as a useful short statement, runs as follows:

> We see that things which lack knowledge, such as natural bodies, act for an end . . . Now whatever lacks knowledge cannot move towards an end, unless it be directed by some being endowed with knowledge and intelligence . . . Therefore some intelligent being exists by whom all natural things are directed to their end; and this being we call God.

It will be immediately apparent that the crux of any such argument as this lies in the assumption that 'whatever lacks knowledge cannot move towards an end, unless it be directed by some being endowed with knowledge and intelligence'. Let us accept that things only have real purposes if those purposes are imposed by a knowing and intelligent agent. It does not follow from this that any inanimate things (or the parts of animate things which when separated would be dead things) which appear to us to have purposes actually have *real* purposes. The appearances of purpose may be explainable in other ways, and this is just what the nineteenth-century theory of evolution does, as Darwin was well aware. In a letter of 11 July 1861 to Julia Wedgwood he wrote:

> When I ask him [Asa Gray] whether he looks at each variation in the rock-pigeon, by which man has made by accumulation a pouter or a fantail pigeon, as providentially designed for man's amusement, he does not know what to answer; and if he, or any one, admits these are accidental, as far as purpose is concerned (of course not accidental as to their source or origin); then I can see no reason why he should rank the accumulated variations by which the beautifully adapted woodpecker has been formed, as providentially designed.[27]

And again in a fragment of autobiography written in 1876 he remarks:

The old argument from design in Nature, as given by Paley, which formerly seemed to me so conclusive, fails, now that the law of natural selection has been discovered. We can no longer argue that, for instance, the beautiful hinge of a bivalve shell must have been made by an intelligent being, like the hinge of a door by a man. There seems to be no more design in the variability of organic beings, and in the actions of natural selection, than in the course which the wind blows.[28]

But why does Darwin say this so confidently? Because if the theory of natural selection is correct, then the adaptation of a particular living organism to its environment, and of a particular part of a living organism to a use in that organism, will be the outcome of a natural elimination process, not of purposes knowingly directed by intelligence to any particular end. What is more, the elimination process (whether it is described in terms of random mutations or in terms of gradual changes which render certain organisms more appropriate than others in the prevailing balance of natural conditions) has apparently no more foresight of an end to be achieved than the moon has in drawing the tides after it. A similar readjustment of view will be effected when one considers the finely balanced complexity of atmospheric conditions which makes the life of higher animals possible on earth. Instead of saying 'this balance is so improbable that it must be the result of an intelligent purpose seeking to make life possible', one will say 'the prevailing life forms are those which the present atmospheric conditions happen to permit'.

The theory of evolution has thus involved a major change of view. Under its influence we have moved from a world in which real purposes are apparent, to a world in which apparent purposes are explainable in terms of the operation of non-purposive processes of elimination. But this change of view effects a transformation, and a weakening of the immediate force of the teleological argument, not its total destruction. What can still be said is that these apparently non-purposive processes are the mechanisms by means of which God has chosen to permit the eventual evolution of man (and man's happiness if he is careful with his inheritance). This conclusion is, however, far weaker than the old teleological argument. There are three reasons for saying this.

In the first place, under the old teleological argument, a failure to perceive a purpose in nature would have left an essential element out of the explanation – like trying to explain the existence of a long barrow on geological principles without reference to the purposes and activity of men. But the post-Darwinian perception of ends and purposes is an optional extra added on after everything has already received a sufficient explanation in natural terms. It is a way of looking at things, not an inference from the way things are.

Secondly, if we opt to see the evolutionary process as the mechanism by means of which God is working his purpose out, then we assume, in a rather arbitrary way, that *we* are the end and purpose of that process. But our own arrogant partialities apart, we ourselves may just as easily be an expendable stage on the way to some other divine purpose as far as purposes can be read into the theory of evolution. As far as the natural facts of evolution are concerned, it is pure prejudice to portray *our* intelligence as like to God's, rather than God's as like to something – we know not what – which will be the final end and outcome of the divine purpose being expressed in evolution.

Thirdly, if we are to see the processes of evolution as expressing a divine purpose whose end is in fact our existence and value as individuals, then one cannot but question the curiously long and painfully destructive process which has been used to achieve and maintain that end. As Hume observed almost a hundred years before the publication of *The Origin of Species*:

> Look round this universe. What an immense profusion of beings . . . You admire this prodigious variety and fecundity. But inspect a little more narrowly these living creatures . . . How hostile and destructive to each other! How insufficient all of them for their own happiness! How contemptible or odious to the spectator! The whole presents nothing but the idea of a blind nature, impregnated by a great vivifying principle, and pouring forth from her lap, without discernment or parental care, her maimed and abortive children.[29]

But there is no need to look round the universe. Look in your own back garden at the struggle for life between plant and disease, greenfly and gardener! More recently, in one of the few really effective articles on the design argument, Louis Dupré remarks in similar vein:

> Even if a compelling case could be made for the teleological view, the existence of a perfect designer would not necessarily follow. For to warrant such a conclusion the evolutionary process would have to appear *evidently* good. But who would claim this for a development in

which individuals and entire species are sacrificed? The end result is the outcome of a long and cruel struggle which left most of the participants dead by the roadside. From the victims' point of view at least there would be little perfection in the alleged ends–means relation of the present arrangement.[30]

In conclusion: the post-Darwinian teleological argument is of little account as *evidence* for the existence of God. We may on occasions feel surprise and delight that the history of the universe and the evolution of life on earth have resulted in such a splendid being as ourselves, living in such a beautiful world, so admirably suited to our existence. If such surprise and delight leads us to see the world as an expression of God's purposes we may not be wrong; but there is no evidence in the teleological argument to suppose that we are right in seeing it this way.

The situation with the *regularity argument* is different. As I have already pointed out, every extension of our knowledge of the orderly processes of nature, including their expression in the conditions which result in evolutionary selection, is an addition to the basic empirical fact upon which it relies: that nature is orderly in very many of its aspects. We are not presented with a random and unintelligible chaos, but with intelligible order. The second empirical fact upon which the argument relies is that the *only* instances of orderly objects or processes in which we can explain any part of the fact of order itself are instances where the part of the order we can explain is known to result from what has been done by intelligent human or animal agents. In short, order is apparent in artifacts and in natural physical objects. In the former case its presence is only explainable by reference to the activity of intelligent agents of limited power. This leads us to infer that since in the latter case its presence can be explained in no other way, it *may* also be explained by reference to the activity of an intelligent agent or agents, this time of very great or even of limitless power.

Before we examine the crux of this argument – the analogy between artifacts and natural objects – it is important to note its relatively limited value as a pointer to specifically theistic belief. If the regularity argument were valid, it would not direct us uniquely to one omnipotent, merciful and loving God who created all things and to whom individual human beings matter. The intelligence revealed in natural order may be one or many, active or inactive. Thus Hume remarks:

The world, for aught [the user of the design argument] knows, is very faulty and imperfect, compared to a superior standard and was

only the first rude essay of some infant Deity, who afterwards abandoned it, ashamed of his lame performance; it is the work only of some
dependent, inferior Deity; and is the object of derision to his superiors:
it is the production of old age and dotage in some superannuated
Deity; and ever since his death, has run on at adventures, from the
first impulse and active force, which it received from him . . .[31]

Perhaps a similar thought provoked the graffito 'God is alive and well but
working on a far less ambitious project.'

But the greatest limitation on the regularity argument is its failure to
give any pointer to benevolence or concern in the designing intelligence.
The regularities which we can express in the inverse square law (or in
any other scientific description of the world) are morally neutral. If we
argue from such regularities to an ordering intelligence, we seem to
arrive at some unconcerned agent with 'no more regard to good above ill
than to heat above cold'. The world as it is may perhaps be shown to be
consistent with belief in a concerned theistic God (this is the subject
matter of the problem of evil to be dealt with in section i of chapter six
below). But that is quite a different matter from inferring the existence of
a concerned theistic God from the morally and personally neutral fact of
order in the physical universe. Such a theistic inference is simply not
warranted.

The inference from the intelligible regularities of the world to an intelligent and powerful agent capable of producing such regularities depends
upon an analogy between order in artifacts and order in natural objects.
The analogy has to be strong enough to permit us to infer similar agent
explanation of the two species of order. Is the analogy strong enough?

It is much of the burden of Hume's seminal discussion of the design
argument (see note 26 to this chapter) that the analogy is not strong
enough. I have already attempted a more extensive exposition of his
arguments elsewhere [32] but his three main points concerning the analogy
are these.

First, the magnitude of the order and arrangement for which men (or
intelligent animals) are responsible is exceedingly tiny when set against
the magnitude of the order discernible in natural things: 'All the new
discoveries in astronomy, which prove the immense grandeur and mag-
nificence of the works of nature . . . become so many objections, by
removing the effect still farther from all resemblance to the effects of
human art and contrivance.' [33] Secondly, the explanation of order can be

traced to the activity of an intelligent agent in but a minute proportion of the examples of order which are known to us: 'Here we may remark, that the operation of one very small part of nature, to wit man, upon another very small part, to wit that inanimate matter lying within his reach, is the rule by which Cleanthes judges of the origin of the whole.' [34] Thirdly, we know from experience what sort of things intelligent agents produce:

> If we see a house, Cleanthes, we conclude, with the greatest certainty, that it had an architect or builder; because this is precisely that species of effect, which we have experienced to proceed from that species of cause. But surely you will not affirm, that the universe bears such a resemblance to a house, that we can with the same certainty infer a similar cause, or that the analogy here is entire and perfect. [35]

Furthermore, although Hume does not make this point, the order in artifacts is only partly agent-imposed. In any artifact, a watch for example, there is the order imposed by the human agent – the intersecting wheels, tensed springs, etc. – and the underlying facts of natural order employed by the agent: elasticity, communication of mechanical motion, etc. No such division of labour is apparent in any natural system. This observation does not destroy the analogy, but it makes it work harder. We are now comparing that *part* of the order in artifacts for which intelligent agents are responsible with the whole world of natural order which known intelligent agents employ or take for granted in their artifacts.

But the matter does not rest there. We may agree that the works of man bear a feebler analogy to the works of nature than a waxen taper bears to the sun. That, it may be urged, is not the main point. The main point is that we can identify two species of order in the universe: agent-imposed order and natural order. In the case of agent-imposed order we know for certain that any explanation of why it is there will be inadequate unless it refers to the activity of intelligent beings. In the case of natural order we have absolutely *no* explanation of why it is there, and there in such profusion, if we rest content with the descriptions of natural order given in the form of laws of nature, and natural order is at least open to the possibility that its explanation is similar to that of agent-imposed order. Yes, the sceptic replies, but a possibility is not any sort of evidence for the actual reality of that possibility. Agreed, but we are offered this possibility, and it seems to be the only way of coping with the third cosmic question, and it is supported by a little evidence, namely, the weak analogy with human artifacts . . . *and so on.*

I am afraid that 'and so on' covers a much longer and more intricate discussion than is possible within the confines of this book. Moreover it is a discussion whose final outcome I am unable to anticipate for you at the moment. I am simply uncertain what a thorough examination of the regularity argument might yield. At the end one might extract something like Hume's final conclusion 'that the cause or causes of order in the universe probably bear some remote analogy to human intelligence'.[36] But one might conclude with the Epicureans that order is a natural characteristic of existent things. Even if one did reach Hume's conclusion, it would be of very little religious consequence, as he himself points out: it affords 'no inference that affects human life, or can be the source of any action or forbearance'.

The curious and enigmatic force of the unresolved quest for an explanation of the order in the universe – a quest which sometimes seems to draw us on to a designing intelligence and sometimes to leave us satisfied with order as a natural fact of the universe – is perfectly caught in an anecdote from 1882, the last year of Darwin's life. The Duke of Argyll recorded in 1885 that he had said to Darwin that it was impossible not to construe a designer from the works of nature. 'He looked at me very hard and said, "Well, that often comes over me with overwhelming force – but at other times," and he shook his head vaguely, adding, "it seems to go away." '[37]

The ontological argument obliges us to think out more carefully what is involved in the affirmation that there is a God. If he really exists, then he could not not-exist, and he exists eternally. The cosmological argument establishes that if the physical universe is eternal, then the laws of change, if they have any explanation, can only be explained by reference to something of a different order of being from the physical universe. Alternatively it establishes that if the physical universe had a beginning, then both its beginning *and* the laws of change can only be explained by reference to an 'external' order of being. But the notion of a beginning to the physical universe, when it was created *ex nihilo*, is so enigmatic that most philosophical and some theistic traditions have rejected it. The teleological argument, inasmuch as it survives at all, invites us to view the world as if it and we represented the purposes of God, but the argument gives no good reason why we should view things in this way. The regularity argument, on the other hand, may give some real substance, however slight, to the schematic possibility set out by the cosmological argument: namely, that the laws of change are the product of an intelligence remotely similar to the mind of man.

The evidence in favour of the typically theistic response to the first three cosmic questions would thus appear to be weak, but not entirely negligible. The arguments seem to disclose a recurring and possibly coherent theme which is the only one available if classical atheism is unacceptable. The questions now are – in chapter four – is there anything in the immediate experience of man which seems to link up with the cosmic possibility of a God? And – in chapter five – whether, among other issues, the notion of another order of being, or of an invisible, all-pervading agent, is fundamentally *meaningless?*

4 THE EVIDENCE FOR BELIEF IN GOD: PRIVATE ILLUMINATIONS

An experience of awe and wonder at the world, a sense of encounter with the Great One, of breaking through to a living and terrible reality which lies beyond the mundane reality accessible to the ordinary working of the senses, of an ultimate union with what is holy and worthy of worship: these things, or things akin to them, are the reported experiences of men and women at almost all times and in almost all places from which records survive. They constitute what Rudolf Otto called 'numinous' experience.

It is this 'numinous' experience which often makes the religious person who is aware of it so impatient with philosophical discussion of the existence of his god. Long before he has struggled through the first few pages of sophistical hair-splitting he has said in his heart: *there is* a god. I know it. I have experience of him. If we cannot be sure that the handiwork of a god can be discerned in the structure and workings of the world or inferred from the existence of the universe as we know it; if cool analytic attention to the concept of a divine person indicates that such a concept may be incoherent; if his apparent intervention in history cannot be used as evidence to authenticate his revelation and make manifest his nature and agency: then none of this matters *provided* we have personal experience of the Divine breaking through to us. This personal experience, the religious man continues, does not depend upon arguments, inferences, thought-out decisions to interpret the world in a certain way, or hypothetical explanations of what is observed. It is thrust upon us as a direct awareness, as reliable and certain for the person who has it as meeting a familiar friend on a country walk, but of a depth and significance which is capable of illuminating and sustaining the whole of life, and, in certain remarkable instances, of illuminating and sustaining the lives of others through the establishment or revitalizing of a religion.

The enormous sense of inner authority and illumination which accompanies these experiences tends to produce an instinctive and entirely understandable reluctance to discuss them, or to have them made objects of scrutiny and analysis. Nevertheless this is what has to be done. We are now thinking *about* experience, not experiencing. But this is not to adopt J. L. Mackie's almost clinical iconoclasm: 'Though such people commonly do subjectively take their revelation as authoritative, this is no more than a sign that they are insufficiently critical.'[1] Taking a revelation as authoritative is not, in itself, a sign of being insufficiently critical. But the religious man in his thoughtful moments can ask, and the interested outsider should ask, certain questions about such experiences.

Can the various experiences of what people take to be the Divine be categorized in any way which might assist us in reaching an understanding of their significance? Do any of these experiences have a real object which lies beyond the experience itself, i.e. are they experiences *of* anything, or have they merely internal significance and importance for the person whose private experiences they are? These are the questions I shall try to answer in the second and third sections of the present chapter. But before doing so there are four preliminary issues which need clarification. These are: (a) How do we distinguish between what it will be convenient to call 'internal' and 'external' experience? (b) How should the terms 'numinous experience' and 'religious experience' be understood and how do they relate to each other? (c) To what use has numinous religious experience been put as *evidence* concerning the existence of God? (d) How should the new awareness or conviction resulting from numinous religious experience be distinguished from what John Hick calls 'experiencing-as'?

(i) *Clearing the Air*

(a) I have already implicitly used a distinction between 'public' and 'private' experience (the distinction can also be expressed as one between 'extentional' and 'intentional', 'objective' and 'subjective', or 'external' and 'internal' experience) but the distinction requires to be sharpened. Since all experience is in a sense private – it is experience within some person – I shall not use the public/private contrast. The extentional/ intentional contrast is unnecessarily technical, and the objective/subjective contrast is vague and overworked. I shall therefore distinguish between experience of an externally existing object and experience of an internally existing object.

By *experience of an externally existing object* I mean experience such that any other person rightly and possibly situated, with normally functioning senses, powers of attention, and a suitable conceptual understanding, will have the same or a closely similar experience. I shall call this *external experience*. (For example: 'Come and sit at my desk in the Rubrics and you'll *feel* the draught!' You came, and sat at my desk, and you did feel the draught: you positioned yourself correctly, you felt your feet and legs grow chill, you attended to that unpleasant experience, and you interpreted it by means of the concept 'draught' with which you were familiar.)

By *experience of an internally existing object*, which I shall call *internal experience*, I mean experience such that any other person rightly and possibly situated, with normally functioning senses, powers of attention, and a suitable conceptual understanding, will *not* have the same or a closely similar experience. (For example: 'Go down the garden and stand at the back of the wood shed at full moon and you will feel afraid: there's something there!' You do, and merely get cold. 'There's nobody there. It's just imagination!' You had situated yourself rightly, all senses functioning at full attentive alert, and you understood the concepts 'fear' and 'something there'.)[2]

The clearest cases of external experience are experiences of the normal sensible world around us. But even apparently odd cases can be subjected to the test. A mirage, for example, is experience of an externally existing object although the object is not what it seems to be or where it seems to be. Clearest cases of internal experience are dreams, daydreams, and emotions or pains whose causal objects are located in one's own body: you take them with you when you move, and no one else *can* be situated so as to experience them since no one other than yourself is your own body. But there are ambiguous cases. For example: most people who pass Gallows Hill on St George's Night have a powerful sense of being followed by an invisible and hostile presence; or, many people visiting the shrine felt the power of the god which infused the oracle. In these uncertain cases, the question will remain: do they have some elusive externally existing object or are they internally caused by the expectations, dreads, or even blood chemistry of the person claiming the experience? (It is such ambiguous cases which make the best ghost stories.) What will not do in doubtful cases is for the claims of the experiencer to decide the issue. Certainly *to him* the experiences feel like external experiences. But to everyone else the issue is genuinely in question just because the most straightforward criteria for an external experience are not properly satisfied. As we shall see, numinous religious experience is of precisely this sort.

(b) In *The Idea of the Holy*[3] Rudolf Otto devoted several chapters to analysis and description of what he called 'the numinous'.[4] Any paraphrase is unlikely to do justice to his seminal work, but here is an attempt: numinous experience is experience of the Holy, or Sacred, or Divine Other, accompanied by a sense of awe, wonder, terror, etc. The experience is *felt* as that of a powerful or living reality beyond the self rather than *observed* as such by any ordinary exercise of the senses.

In this account, the meaning of the word 'numinous' includes reference to an object experienced: the Divine Other, the Holy, etc. But in using the word we must not prejudice the issue which is of greatest consequence, namely whether numinous experience is experience *of* some sort of external object, however strange or unusual. By speaking of 'numinous experience' I therefore mean experience which *feels* as if it were experience of an external object. I leave open the question whether it *is* experience of an external object or not.

A similar restriction applies to the phrases 'religious experience' or 'experience of God'. Use of these phrases must not be understood to carry with it any commitment about whether the experience is *of* an external object since that is exactly what is under discussion at present.

Numinous experience will always be included within the wider and more commonly spoken of category 'religious experience' except in the cases where the numinous experience is received agnostically. I disagree with H. D. Lewis when he contends that the numinous experience cannot be so received. As we shall see later from examples, the numinous experience is not *uniquely*, as Lewis puts it, 'one of finding God in some way present in the world'.[5] The mistake of thinking that it is, is facilitated by the most important compendium of evidence and articulate comment ever put together on the subject. William James's *The Varieties of Religious Experience* (originally the Gifford Lectures of 1901–2) confines itself almost entirely to numinous experience which is numinous *religious* experience, i.e. to experience of what the subject takes to be the Divine. But as I have said, numinous experience can be received agnostically (as a directionless shiver of awe) and religious experience extends to a great number of experiences which are neither numinous, nor startling, nor unusual: e.g. sincere prayer, or corporate devotion, or the sense of quietness which may be found in music or words long associated with a religious observance. These are, if you prefer it, experiences within the religious life, but they are still a part of the totality of religious experience, even if they are unlikely to be set before the perplexed agnostic as *evidence* for the reality of the Divine.

It is then, in particular, the category of numinous experience taken as experience of God or of some god which challenges us with the claim: *this* is direct evidence for the existence of something Divine. I shall call numinous experience taken as experience of God or of some god *numinous religious experience.*

(c) The claim that numinous religious experience provides evidence for the external reality of what is experienced has no significant intellectual history prior to the work of the German Protestant theologian Schleiermacher (1768–1834). What he did was to put personal experience of God at the centre of the phenomenon of religion in such a way that it could function as a justification of belief for the believer, and as a challenge to the unbeliever. Thus he writes, typically, 'The common element in all expressions of piety is . . . the consciousness of being absolutely dependent, or, which is the same thing, of being in relation to God.'[6] Prior to Schleiermacher the various stages of what we are now calling numinous religious experience had either been understood as indicating one's standing in relation to a god whose existence was not in question (in Christian terms one's 'state of grace'), or rejected as a dangerous and arbitrary ground for belief. John Locke (1632–1704) puts this danger vividly:

> Reason is lost upon them, they are above it; they see the light infused into their understandings, and cannot be mistaken; it is clear and visible there, like the light of bright sunshine; shows itself, and needs no other proof but its own evidence; they feel the hand of God moving within them, and the impulses of the Spirit, and cannot be mistaken in what they feel. . . . They are sure, because they are sure. . . . But the question here is, How do I know that God is the revealer of this to me; that this impression is made upon my mind by his Holy Spirit, and that therefore I ought to obey it?[7]

For the most part Locke has in mind the religious experiences which are claimed to impart a doctrine, and his question 'How do I know that God is the revealer of this to me' implies his own pre-existing belief in God. He is in doubt about the revelation, not the revealer. But his critical stance needs only minor re-wording to apply to the less doctrinal, post-Schleiermacher, claim that numinous religious experience gives its subject direct access to the reality of what he takes to be the Divine. 'How do you know,' we ask, 'that what you *feel* as a relationship with God, or as a vivid awareness of the Divine, actually *is* a relationship with, or an awareness of, something which exists beyond and apart from your own private experience?' Even apart from the strong claim to know the reality of God by direct experience, a weaker position may be argued. It is this: the assumption of the external reality of what is experienced may be the best or only way in which the occurrence of such experiences can be explained. Just as the simplest way of explaining a person's claim to see a cat is by supposing that there is a cat to be seen, so the simplest way of explaining a person's claim to experience God may be that there is a God to be experienced. Both the strong claim that numinous religious experience gives direct knowledge of the reality of God, and the weaker claim that the existence of God is the simplest explanation for these experiences, require examination.

(d) In an influential article 'Religious Faith as Experiencing-as' John Hick argued that religious faith consisted in experiencing the events of our lives and of human history as something 'mediating the presence and activity of God': 'For there is a sense in which the religious man and the atheist both live in the same world and another sense in which they live consciously in different worlds . . . For one does and the other does not experience life as a continual interaction with the transcendent God.'[*] But such 'experiencing-as' is very different from (and Hick does not, although others might, confuse it with) the numinous religious experience used as a ground for asserting the external reality of its object. Hick's 'experiencing-as' is the *result* of adopting a religious faith; the numinous religious experience, at least when offered as a ground of assent, is a *reason* for adopting a religious faith. Furthermore experiencing life and history as the activity of God is not thrust unavoidably upon one by the nature of the reality experienced. It is optional in a sense in which experiencing paraquat as orange juice is not optional. The numinous religious experience, on the other hand, *is* apparently thrust upon its subject without the option. It is apparently more like experiencing an external object than like interpreting an experience in one way rather than another.

The questions now before us are: can numinous experience and numinous religious experience be usefully distinguished into experiences of various kinds? And then: can any of these experiences be justly taken as experience of an external object, or, at least, can they best be explained by supposing such an external object to exist?

(ii) *Varieties of Lighting*

Rather than describe a series of abstract categories, I propose to let differing examples speak for themselves. The ones I have chosen represent species of numinous experience which are distinguished by the character of what is experienced (a sense of the living power of nature, an encounter with or vision of a Divine Person, a feeling of dependence, etc.) and by the degree to which what is experienced is or is not specifically religious or specific to a particular religion. I have distinguished five species of experience. They are: numinous agnostic, numinous pantheist, numinous encounter, companionship experiences and dependency experiences.

Numinous agnostic. Unlike H. D. Lewis, I think there are experiences which are properly called 'numinous' but which are *not* taken as experiences of God or of any object which could properly be called the divine. Many people experience the shiver of fear or awe which is the kernel of the numinous experience when they focus their attention, in a real-life situation, upon the profound immensity of the universe which engulfs them. Albert Einstein gives a more intellectualized account of this experience:

> The fairest thing we can experience is the mysterious ... A knowledge of the existence of something we cannot penetrate, of the manifestations of the profoundest reason and the most radiant beauty, which are only accessible to our reason in their most elementary forms – it is this knowledge and this emotion that constitute the truly religious attitude; in this sense, and in this alone, I am a deeply religious man ... The individual feels the nothingness of human desires and aims and the sublimity and marvellous order which reveal themselves in nature and in the world of thought. He looks upon individual existence as a sort of prison and wants to experience the universe as a single significant whole.[9]

I appreciate that what Einstein is giving to us is an impassioned judgement rather than a direct report of a numinous experience; but it is not hard to imagine that something very like a numinous experience lies behind his writing, and hard not to imagine that for others essentially the same report could be of a numinous experience received agnostically. What we have in these cases is the hesitant, ambiguous inference of the design argument and the cold rational possibilities of the cosmological argument presented with the force of an immediate experience of nature or of the universe at large: but it is the wonder and immensity of the cosmic questions filling us with a shiver of awe and fear *without* an accompanying perception of anything which, without hopeless confusion of the issues, could be called God or god. The shading away of numinous agnostic experiences into something with a little more religious colour provides a very indistinct boundary with the next species of numinous experience.

Numinous pantheist. The awareness of nature as somehow alive, awesome, powerful, wonderful, and at times terrible, gives rise to the numinous experience at its least specifically religious. The awareness is most easily associated with Wordsworth. For example, in *The Prelude*, Book I, ll. 340–400, having taken a shepherd's boat 'by the shores of Patterdale' he describes how a great black rock seemed to rise up between him and the stars like a living thing, and how, afterwards, the sense of

> ... huge and mighty forms, that do not live
> Like living men, moved slowly through the mind
> By day, and were a trouble to my dreams.

In parts of *Tintern Abbey* the sense of a living other in nature is put even more directly:

> And I have felt ... a sense sublime
> Of something far more deeply interfused,
> Whose dwelling is the light of setting suns,
> And the round ocean and the living air,
> And the blue sky, and in the mind of man:
> A motion and a spirit, that impels
> All thinking things, all objects of all thought,
> And rolls through all things.

Such passages from *The Prelude*, *Tintern Abbey*, and other poems are too well known to need extensive quotation; but what Wordsworth describes with the indulgent self-reference of the Romantic is by no means uncommon in different ideological climates. There can scarcely be anyone who has walked the highlands of Scotland or the western seaboard of Ireland to whom the scenery is a matter of indifference, but some are more deeply moved. In lines written in 1963 'On the Sea of the Hebrides' the unknown poet seems to express a Wordsworthian experience of the living power in, or discernible through, nature. One reads:

> In such a place as this the very wind is like a prayer:
> Come unto me all that travail and are heavy laden –
> For I am the meeting of the land and the sea,
> I am the presence on the hills and in the far islands,
> I am the living air,
> I am the light beyond the light of the sun,
> I am the face hidden in the mist,
> I am the watcher at the threshold of the dawn.

This is the numinous, in Rudolf Otto's words, 'pervading the mind with a tranquil mood of deepest worship'. Apart from the second line, the feeling is not Christian, or even religious in any specific sense. There is a consciousness of some living power in nature which inspires awe and worship, and this is expressed through words which, in this instance, may carry overtones from some more ancient original. That is all.

I think it is useful to label experiences of this type numinous pantheist. They are numinous inasmuch as the senses of awe, worship, and *mysterium tremendum* are present although they are not focused upon any historically established god or interpreted within any particular metaphysic of the world, religious or otherwise. They are pantheist inasmuch as they are usually associated with nature, or with some awesome aspect of nature.

Numinous encounter. A third variety of experience is distinguished from the numinous pantheist experience in virtue of being expressed in terms of an encounter with what is taken to be a living agent – usually a god, seen or unseen. I will call these 'numinous encounter experiences'. They are important because this is the form of experience most usually associated with religious conversion or the gaining of a religious certainty (not necessarily Christian or theistic). I will give several examples.

One is in chapter VII of The Wind in the Willows. The source is fictional, but feels so genuine and so exactly fits Otto's classic description of the numinous, that one almost imagines the Rat and the Mole hiding between the volumes of Luther and Schleiermacher in Otto's library. It is before dawn one summer morning, and the two animals have been out all night looking for a lost baby otter when the Rat hears a distant piping:

> Breathless and transfixed the Mole stopped rowing as the liquid run of that glad piping broke in on him like a wave, caught him up, and possessed him utterly. He saw the tears on his comrade's cheeks, and bowed his head and understood ... 'This is the place of my song-dream, the place the music played to me,' whispered the Rat, as if in a trance. 'Here, in this holy place, here if anywhere, surely we shall find Him!' Then suddenly the Mole felt a great Awe fall upon him, an awe that turned his muscles to water, bowed his head, and rooted his feet to the ground. It was no panic terror – indeed he felt wonderfully at peace and happy – but it was an awe that smote and held him and, without seeing, he knew it could only mean that some august Presence was very, very near. With difficulty he turned to look at his friend, and saw him at his side cowed, stricken, and trembling violently. And still there was utter silence in the populous bird-haunted branches around them; and still the light grew and grew ...
>
> 'Rat!' he found breath to whisper, shaking. 'Are you afraid?'
>
> 'Afraid?' murmured the Rat, his eyes shining with unutterable love. 'Afraid! Of *Him*? O, never, never! And yet – and yet – O, Mole, I am afraid!'
>
> Then the two animals, crouching to the earth, bowed their heads and did worship.

Kenneth Grahame's description relates the numinous encounter experience fairly closely to the pagan god Pan, and just such a pagan encounter, this time with the god Asclepius, is described by Aelius Aristides (*c.* 117–181)

> It was like seeming to touch him, a kind of awareness that he was there in person; one was between sleep and waking, one wanted to open one's eyes, and yet was anxious lest he should withdraw too soon; one listened and heard things; one's hair stood on end; one cried and felt happy; one's heart swelled, but not with vainglory. What human being could put that experience into words? But anyone who has been through it will share my knowledge and recognize the state of mind.[10]

The god is the kindly god of medicine, and Aristides is the first successful hypochondriac of whom we have any record, but neither fact puts his report in a worse light as evidence than the theistic reports to which we may feel more sympathetic.

The final examples of numinous encounter experience are specifically Christian, or interpreted as such. The first, and most famous, is St Paul on the road to Damascus:

> Now as he journeyed he approached Damascus, and suddenly a light from heaven flashed about him. And he fell to the ground and heard a voice saying to him, 'Saul, Saul, why do you persecute me?' And he said, 'Who are you, Lord?' and he said, 'I am Jesus, whom you are persecuting; but rise and enter the city, and you will be told what to do.' The men who were travelling with him stood speechless, hearing the voice but seeing no one. Saul arose from the ground; and when his eyes were opened, he could see nothing; so they led him by the hand and brought him into Damascus. And for three days he was without sight, and neither ate nor drank.
>
> (Acts 9:3–9)

The momentous consequences of *that* encounter are still with us. But apart from its importance, it has the unusual feature of being reported as an external experience. The men who were with him *heard the voice*. A more typical numinous encounter experience (typical inasmuch as it felt like an external experience but whether others would judge it so is an open question) is quoted at length by William James from the report of an anonymous clergyman:

> 'I remember the night, and almost the very spot on the hill-top, where my soul opened out, as it were, into the Infinite, and there was a rushing together of the two worlds, the inner and the outer. It was deep calling unto deep – the deep that my own struggle had opened up within being answered by the unfathomable deep without, reaching beyond the stars. I stood alone with Him who had made me, and all the beauty of the world, and love, and sorrow, and even temptation. I did not seek Him, but felt the perfect unison of my spirit with His. The ordinary sense of things around me faded. For the moment nothing but an ineffable joy and exultation remained. It is impossible fully to describe the experience. It was like the effect of some great orchestra when all the separate notes have melted into one swelling harmony that leaves the listener conscious

of nothing save that his soul is being wafted upwards, and almost bursting with its own emotion. The perfect stillness of the night was thrilled by a more solemn silence. The darkness held a presence that was all the more felt because it was not seen. I could not any more have doubted that *He* was there than I was. Indeed, I felt myself to be, if possible, the less real of the two.'

The writer continues to explain the significance of his experience thus:

'My highest faith in God and truest idea of him were then born in me. I have stood upon the Mount of Vision since, and felt the Eternal round about me. But never since has there come quite the same stirring of the heart. Then, if ever, I believe, I stood face to face with God, and was born anew of his spirit. There was, as I recall it, no sudden change of thought or of belief, except that my early crude conception had, as it were, burst into flower. There was no destruction of the old, but a rapid, wonderful unfolding. Since that time no discussion that I have heard of the proofs of God's existence has been able to shake my faith. Having once felt the presence of God's spirit, I have never lost it again for long. My most assuring evidence of his existence is deeply rooted in that hour of vision, in the memory of that supreme experience, and in the conviction, gained from reading and reflection, that something the same has come to all who have found God. I am aware that it may justly be called mystical. I am not enough acquainted with philosophy to defend it from that or any other charge. I feel that in writing of it I have overlaid it with words rather than put it clearly to your thought. But, such as it is, I have described it as carefully as I now am able to do.'[11]

A fundamentally similar experience, communicated to him by a retired Cornish mining engineer, was quoted by the B.B.C. Religious Affairs Corrrespondent in the 'Today' Programme on 27 March 1982:

'I am no plaster saint. I live very much in the world. But what I have told you now is the first time I have ever told anybody . . .' I was able to write back to him, assuring him that even his reticence was typical of something which is far more common than most people suppose. Quoting his letter, this is how it happened one afternoon thirty-four years ago:

'I suppose I had nodded off. For I woke up with the sun streaming down on my face – just enjoying doing nothing in particular, listening to the birds singing. Suddenly, I became aware of a strange mixture of fear and uplift entering my mind, and sat there deeply puzzled for some minutes. Finally, it became so insistent that I had to find out what it meant.

'I walked up the passage to my bedroom, went down on my knees, and asked. As I did so, the Glory of the Universe shone before me. I was blinded by the dazzling white light. In my heart, I flung my arms before my eyes, because I knew that man could not look upon God and live. I was both terrified and yet uplifted – I can't explain it – I was shattered. And then I knew I was a nothing. All my conceit and personal esteem vanished.'

The letter continues: 'So great and awful was the Holiness that stood before me that I feared lest it should ever happen again. But it completely changed my life. When I hear men in their folly say "You can't prove that there is a God," I reply "You wait until He takes half a step towards you, and you are left in no doubt."'

'Why this happened to me,' writes my correspondent, 'I cannot understand. It may have been to arm and stiffen me for what was coming: for my world was about to collapse about my ears.' He then describes the sudden death of his father and the long, painful death of his mother, from which he emerged with what he calls 'the inner revelation of the fact of personal resurrection' which has left him 'doing my best to bring comfort to those who are breaking their hearts over the bodily death of their loved ones.'

(reproduced by permission of the B.B.C. and Gerald Priestland)

Clearly numinous encounter experiences are of great consequence to those who have them. Notice the subsequent impatience with arguments and evidence, but notice also that as well as being related to theism, or even specifically to Jesus, the encounter may have pagan objects.

Companionship experiences. Apart from numinous pantheist and numinous encounter experiences, there are also what I shall call companionship experiences (I am not inventing this terminology but adapting it from usages previously suggested).

At its most straightforward the companionship experience is the simple, sincere, sense of non-aloneness which is a normal experience in Christianity and a perfectly familiar one in other theistic religions. The Jew experiences the sense of a sustaining presence which is always and everywhere with him:

> If I take the wings of the morning
> and dwell in the uttermost parts of the sea,
> even there thy hand shall lead me
> and thy right hand shall hold me.
>
> (Psalm 139)

The presence will sometimes be felt strongly, sometimes less strongly; and it may be withdrawn:

> How Long, O Lord? Wilt thou forget me forever?
> How long wilt thou hide thy face from me?
>
> (Psalm 13)

Likewise for the Christian: Jesus promises that he will be with us even unto the end of the world – a promise which the Christian experiences as fulfilled in his daily life as well as more dramatically in moments of disaster or despair. The experience is not, it must be emphasized, one which fills up the gaps and failures in life, or satisfies an unwholesome sense of sin, or comes with the force of St Paul's encounter on the Damascus road. The experience is rather of a deep, continual, sustaining presence in the normal and healthy Christian life.

Now described in these terms, the companionship experience is perhaps better regarded as an experience within the religious life than as a variety of numinous religious experience to which appeal may be made as evidence of the reality of its external object (God, Jesus, or other manifestation of the Divine). But the companionship experience can be used as evidence in two ways. One is when the companionship experience becomes so strong that it moves into the category of numinous encounter. The other is when the general sense of companionship, or of *relation to* a Divine Person, is used to argue that an interpersonal relationship implies *two* persons: in this instance the human person and the Divine Person. Thus for there to be a companionship relation, a Divine Person must exist.

Dependency experiences. A group of experiences which become, at a certain level of intensity, numinous religious experiences, are what we may call dependency experiences. These take many forms. One is the sense of contingency or metaphysical dependence: that the world and all sensible things are transient shadows, insubstantial and brief existences held in being by another reality which to Plato (in some of his works) appeared as the world of real forms, and which to the theist appears as God. Indeed, for the Christian and Muslim, cosmological arguments are probably suggested by this feeling of dependency, albeit that as arguments they have a claim to validity quite apart from the feelings which may commend or suggest them. Another form of dependency experience is the sense of moral dependency: the sense that what I do or refrain from doing of my own choice is answerable elsewhere. This is not belief in a retributive immortality, but the old Jewish sense of a moral dependency *now*, of being answerable to a God from whom certain deeds or thoughts can separate me *now*, or put me into what the Christian calls 'a state of sin'. I shall return to the importance of moral dependency in chapter seven.

In what follows I shall make few references to dependency or companionship experiences. At an intense level they both tend to be subsumed into one of the earlier categories; at low intensity both are experiences *within* the religious life rather than evidence for the reality of the object of worship.

It is, of course, possible to distinguish further categories of (possibly) numinous experience. Mystical experience which comes as a sense of union with or loss of the self into the divine other can be so distinguished (James's clergyman's report comes near to this). But its distinctive quality (a sense of union *with* X rather than awareness *of* X) does not require the mystical experience to be treated separately as *evidence*. I mention two further possible categories (which may occur to you) only to dismiss them. These are aesthetic and psychic experience. I suppose 'aesthetic experience' must mean something like the intense thrill which is sometimes caused by the perception of great music, paintings, buildings or literature; in older language, a sense of the sublime. Whatever qualities a sense of the sublime may have, its evidential value is quite different from the numinous religious experience. The sublime experience is seldom, if ever, claimed to provide evidence for the existence of an external object other than its own overt cause; and if it were, its object would not be a religious object. The same applies to the psychic experience. However quaint or frightening or beyond the normal it may seem, it is seldom used as evidence about the reality of any worshipful object. At worst it is the paraphernalia of the spiritual quack, at best it is an indication that not all the natural processes of the world are fully understood. Either way it is irrelevant to our present concerns.

(iii) *The Significance of the Numinous*

The question one wishes to ask immediately is whether numinous religious experience is experience *of* God rather than merely a self-imposed creation of the person claiming the experience. I wish – and so will you – that this question were simple enough to answer in isolation. But it is not. It presumes answers to four somewhat narrower questions which can be expressed in terms of the distinction between external and internal experience. The questions are:

1. Can any actual numinous religious experience be identified *with certainty* as experience of an external object?
2. Can any numinous religious experience be such that it *may* be experience of an external object?
3. Since the answer to question 2 will be yes, then: Is the possible external object God, or a god; always the same thing, or many things?
4. Is the reality attributed to God such that it matters whether God is experienced as an external or as an internal object?

Let us deal with the last question first, since the answer to it will indicate the degree of importance which attaches to the other questions.

If we ask what sort of reality was usually attributed to God in the two or three thousand years of theistic history before it occurred to the Tillichs, John Robinsons and Don Cupitts of the present century that practically everyone else may have made a mistake, then an approximate answer, of the type I set out in chapter one as the historical and continuing bedrock of Jewish, Christian and Islamic belief, can be given. God is an eternal, invisible, universal, ever-present and limitlessly powerful and knowing agent; the maker and sustainer of all things, who manifests justice, love and mercy to mankind. Now this concept evidently makes God the most tremendous independent reality anyone could ever begin to apprehend. Such a God not only exists *independently* of all other entities for all time whether or not I or any aspect of me or thee exists, but I and all other things exist only because held in being by such a God. But although God is said to exist independently, it is evident that he is not *directly* experienced as an external object in the way in which many independently existing things can be experienced. I emphasize *directly* experienced because the existence of some independent things, for example atoms, can be inferred from the experience we have of other things: just as the existence of God might be (but is not easily) inferred from order in the world. But at the moment we are concerned with experience, not inference. Now if God, understood as an independent existence, were only to be directly experienced as an internal object, how would this affect the *evidential* value of such experience?

The fundamental feature of internal experience is that it is not of independent objects, but of objects whose existence depends upon us. My dreams, fears, pains, hopes, loves, itches and daydreams exist because I have them. It is incontrovertible evidence for the existence of my love (of God or of Diana) if I truly say that I experience such love. But the existence of such love (unlike the existence of God or of Diana) begins and ends with me and my experience of it. It is manifestly absurd for me to say to you 'Last night I dreamt that I dwelt in marble halls – let's go and look for them!' My internal experience of marble halls is not evidence for me, let alone for you, which could justify a search. At most, other people might look for the causes of such experience (it was the cheese I ate at supper) not for the object experienced (the marble halls). The same holds for direct experience of God. If all numinous religious experience (i.e. numinous experience taken by its subject as experience of God or god) is internal experience, and if this interests other people at all, then it should interest them in seeking for the causally predisposing factors for such experience, not for the (internal) object of the experience. But, it may be said, experience of God is a common (internal) experience. Unlike the dream of marble halls, many people have it and can communicate with each other about it afterwards. To which I reply: this is exactly what one would expect if there were general causes operating to produce broadly similar internal experiences of this sort. That there *are* such general causes – common emotional and psychological states, common cultural and religious expectations, etc. – almost every social psychologist will affirm, and these general causes alone are sufficient to account for the common forms which an internal experience of God may present. But perhaps the independent reality of God is itself the common cause of these internal experiences of him: the cause of the experience and its object are alike. Even this will not do. The causally predisposing factors for an internal experience need not be in the least like the experience itself. Indeed it is hard to think of any internal experience which is, or is itself like, its own cause. Malarial delirium need not be like a malaria germ; a headache is not like a glass of Cockburn's '55.

The sum of all this is an answer to question 4 above. God is usually taken to be an independent existence, indeed THE independent existence.

If direct experience of God is used as *evidence* for the independent existence of God, then the experience must actually *be* what it always *feels* as if it is: an external experience. The only independent existents which might be inferred from internal experiences are their causes, not their objects; and the causes of internal experiences are not the same as their objects.

Before using this conclusion to sharpen our discussion of the vital issues posed in questions 1 and 2, I must apply it to three suggestions, namely, that experience of God *is* God; that experience of God is self-authenticating; that experience of God is an 'I–thou' encounter.

Some commentators have tried to say that numinous religious experience is not *of* God, but *is*, is identical with God; the having of such experience just is the existence of God.[12] I find such suggestions difficult to understand. They appear to make God into an internal experience and nothing more. But this 'god' would not be God at all. Such a 'god' would not be an agent, and could no more create and sustain all things, raise the dead or answer prayers, than a sore finger or a look at Edinburgh Castle could grow a potato. Moreover the religious believer does not have faith in an experience *per se*, but in what he takes to be the object of the experience, and, furthermore, the object of what he takes to be an *external* experience. A worshipper offering praise to the glory of God on high is not doing the religious equivalent of kissing himself.

It is often claimed that numinous religious experience is 'self-authenticating', meaning something like 'carries with it its own unchallengeable authority' or 'warrants the existence of its own object'. Certainly such experience is accepted as authoritative for the individual to whom it comes at the time of its coming. But this is not to say that it ought to have authority over anybody else, or even over the subject who has it when he stops to think. The only sort of authority an internal experience can have is in giving to the experiencer the right to declare whether he has the experience or not, and what it is. As soon as it is argued that the experience *feels* (authoritatively) like an external experience and therefore is one, two further arguments follow. One is that you cannot declare an experience to be external merely because you feel (authoritatively) that it is: an external experience must be one whose object others, rightly positioned etc., can also experience. The second argument is that if the experience turns out after all to be an *external* experience, then claims to self-authentication are not acceptable. The sophisticated reasons for this are set out in an article by R. A. Oakes,[13] but in brief: even external experience does not guarantee (in the absence of other checks) against all error, mistake or deception concerning its object; and the certainty that it is an external experience does not guarantee that it is so if the usual criteria fail to apply or cannot be operated. Once again Locke's point holds: you cannot plead as a *reason* for your certainty the fact that you are certain.

The third suggestion is that experience of God is an 'I–thou' encounter. The usefulness of this suggestion depends upon numinous religious experience actually being external experience. If it should turn out to be an internal experience then the entire theology of the 'I–thou' encounter between God and man goes to pieces, and with it goes any sort of argument from a reciprocal God–man encounter relationship. The case has already been argued judiciously, and I believe definitively, by Ronald Hepburn,[14] but the salient features are these. In *I and Thou* (English translation first published in 1937) Martin Buber distinguished between 'I–it' relationships of the sort 'I told him to cut the grass', and 'I–thou' relationships of the sort 'I know him deeply as a person; we meet soul to soul'. Both relations are possible between human persons; only the latter relation is possible between a human person and God, and such an encounter, such a meeting, is at the heart of the phenomena of religion.

Leaving aside the question whether such a meeting is indeed at the heart of religion, the critical issue is this: can one encounter a bodiless person in such a way that you can be sure, and can have a right to be sure, that you are in fact encountering such a person (having an external experience) rather than merely imagining such an encounter (having an internal experience)? The arguments revolve around bodily existence as a pre-condition for attaining an 'I–thou' relationship with *any* person, and I must refer you to Hepburn for this. But as far as we are concerned the important thing is to identify the numinous encounter as an external experience. If any encounter could be so identified, the evidential value would be very great. If none can be so identified, or only ambiguously, then encounter experience and the theology based upon it will be of very little account. I may internally 'encounter' the person of God in my experience, but this simply means that it feels that way to me in virtue of my internal experiences, and it would feel that way to me if I merely imagined the encounter, or if God were no more than the culture-conditioned fiction which Don Cupitt seems to want to substitute for the real thing in *The Leap of Reason* (London, 1976).

So, having argued that our concept of God demands that he be an independent existence and hence that the evidence of direct experience must be the evidence of some external experience, I now turn to the first question: can any actual numinous religious experience, taken as an experience of God, be identified with certainty as experience of an external object? To which I reply – no.

There are several rather dull practical reasons for this bald negative. The first is that actual accounts of such experiences usually come from people who were alone at the time of the experience (James produces dozens of such accounts). In such cases no one else was rightly positioned to check whether the experience was external or not. Furthermore, when there have been other people present, whatever was experienced has very often passed unnoticed by the other or others: 'I saw John standing there with a curiously abstracted expression on his face, apparently gazing into the sunset over the island. When we moved on up the hill to pitch tent he was very reticent for a while and it was only years later that he told me what he had experienced.' The effect of these matter-of-fact observations is to cast a strong *suspicion* into one's mind that a critically disinterested person might never get himself rightly positioned etc. to have a numinous experience as an experience of God because such experiences maybe never are external. Even in Kenneth Grahame's beautifully imagined example the Mole 'understood' his companion's awe rather than exactly shared his experience. Paul's experience on the Damascus road is a challenging exception inasmuch as others are reported to have heard the voice. The sceptically minded will at once object with doubts about the precise reliability of all the details reported.* But suppose several people shared the experience, not a vague feeling of awe or encounter, but something specific: for example, a vision of the Virgin Mary accompanied by awe and exultation. Again the sceptic can ask: was there anyone there who was disinterested enough *not* to be subject to the expectations or religious enthusiasms which would sufficiently explain what was experienced without supposing an external object? Even if the experience were specific enough and external enough to be identified by the sceptic (together perhaps with a certain shiver of numinous awe) his first recourse might well be to question its interpretation. Is it a natural phenomenon, a coincidence miracle (see p. 141)? My point is not that any of this proves that numinous religious experience could not be external experience of God. I only seek to show that ordinary earthy scepticism can always find grounds – often very good grounds – for *doubting*

* Compare Acts 9:7 with Acts 22:9 and 26:13 and observe and carefully compare the differences.

whether an actual experience, which claims to be an experience of God, is an *external* experience.

If it is objected that no one having a numinous encounter or a numinous pantheist experience really expects others to have the same or a closely similar experience when rightly situated etc., then two things need to be said. One is that you cannot admit that something has all the marks of being an internal experience, and at the same time try to use it as if it had the evidential authority of an external experience. The other is that if you insist that what fails the ordinary criteria for being an external experience is, nevertheless, experience of an external object, then if you are to interest other people you have to give reasons, not just why it is possibly experience of an external object, but that in fact it is so, and no such reasons are usually forthcoming.

I have so far argued that no actual religious experience can be identified beyond reasonable doubt as an external experience of the sort which would be evidence for the external reality we normally take God to be. That was question 1 on p. 93, but what of question 2? Is it the case that *some* religious experiences *could* be experiences of an external reality without us being able to be *certain* that this is so?

The considerations which tell against admitting such a possibility are: the solitary character of so many such experiences; the frequent failure of such experiences to show up as external experience when there are other people present; and the well documented causally disposing factors which could account for such experiences without having recourse to the existence of an elusive external object.

Against these must be set the following: First, that the person who misses out on such experiences, either all the time or when others are claiming to have them, may be deficient as an observer, like someone who is colour blind or partly deaf. Secondly, that the object of such experience may be able to choose to be experienced by certain persons at certain times. Thirdly, that a distinctive characteristic of the numinous religious experience is that it is *felt*, and felt strongly and confidently, as experience of an external object and, unlike vivid dreams etc., the confidence of there being an external object is not modified by reflective consideration afterwards.

The first suggestion is that a person who either never has a numinous religious experience, or does not have one when he is in the presence of someone else who does, is like someone partly blind or deaf. This is weak and implausible. Why? Because unlike one suffering from a deficiency in the operation of one of the senses which makes him, as it were, sub-standard as an observer, the person to whom the numinous religious experience does not come has nothing ascertainably missing in his physical and mental make-up. It is not even the case that he has normal perception in any particular channel of perception in which the person who has the numinous experience is detectably *more* proficient as a percipient. It is a physical fact about me (I believe it is rare) that I can hear the very high-pitched squeaking of bats when they fly, for example, in the old ash tree in the field by my house. My wife cannot. She has more or less normal hearing. But what I exceptionally hear *can* be heard by a few others, and the physical fact of what I hear can easily be confirmed by careful experiment. The squeaking of bats is an external experience, not 'noises in my head' (or perhaps bats in the belfry). But the case is quite different if I claim to experience God. I am not exercising any ascertainable sense (or any ascertainable extension of any sense) which you have not got, and my wife's (unjustifiable) scepticism: 'You're just imagining hearing bats' would be entirely apt, if more iconoclastic, were she to say 'You're just imagining an experience of God'. But surely there are experiences open to some and not to others which do not depend upon the senses? To me Berlioz's *Romeo and Juliet Symphony* is beautiful almost beyond the possibilities of the world; to you it is an aimless noise. Truly we differ in what we can experience. But I *know* my sublime experience is an internal feeling and not evidence for the exist-ence of anything in dispute. We both agree about what exists: in this case the music. We disagree about the value of the music. But the sceptic and he who experiences God do not disagree about the value of what exists. They disagree about what exists.

The second suggestion, that the object of a numinous religious experi-ence (God or some god) may be able to choose who shall have the experience and when, is like saying that I have the power of making myself invisible to certain people. When two or three of you are gathered together and only one of you can see me, that is because I choose to reveal myself to that person. He is indeed having an external experience of me in the sense that I am an externally existing object although it seems to the rest of you as if he is having an internal experience. Clearly the ordinary human who can make himself invisible at choice will be greeted with the scepticism appropriate to a pantomime demon. But if God is the everywhere present, invisible, all-powerful agent we take him to be, then it is entirely possible that he may only permit some people, on some occasions, to have an experience which is of him. Such an experience will be experience of an external object which does not fulfil the normal requirements for such an experience. Hence those who do not have it will presume it to be an internal experience. However, it will be noticed that this possibility does not permit experience of God to crowd in as evidence for his existence. If we have grounds other than the experiences themselves for believing that God exists, then his selective revelation of himself would account for the solitary and frequently unshared experiences which people have of him. On the other hand, if we do not have other grounds for believing in his existence, then it will remain a more simple and obvious explanation of the selective experiences if we take them to be internal, and caused by social and psychological factors.

Finally, it is said that the numinous religious experience is felt confidently as an external experience, and this confidence is not modified by subsequent reflection as is usually the case with typical internal experiences such as dreams or illusions. Indeed reflection over long periods often strengthens the confidence that the experience was significant and external: look at the report of James's clergyman or the B.B.C.'s Cornish mining engineer, not to mention St Paul or Aristides. There are two points which need to be made here. In the first place no sensitive commentator would wish to deny that these experiences are influential and significant for their subjects, and that the significance is abiding, especially when it forms a part of (or is interpreted within) a religious system. But the main point is not whether these experiences are of abiding significance or 'make a difference' to life. It is whether they actually are external experiences of some kind which could provide evidence for the independent existence of their object. And concerning this, the abiding and confident feeling of externality is insufficient, especially when what is experienced seems to others like an internal experience readily subject to causal explanation. In the last resort one can do little better than embellish again Locke's observation: confidence that you are right, which cannot be justified to other people, cannot justify itself.

From all this I must conclude that however much one may doubt that numinous religious experience ever gives direct experience of an external object, nevertheless the *possibility* remains that it could, not as an external experience which satisfied all the criteria for such an experience, but as experience of an external object selectively revealed; but is such a possible external object God or a god, one thing or many things?

It is often said that the feature of numinous religious experience which most clearly distinguishes it from delusional experience (drug, dream or disease induced) is that the object of the experience is common enough from one person to another for the experiences to be compared and found to be the same or similar. But when this contention is examined it is found to be true under two conditions only. One is when the object of the experience is very specific or interpreted very specifically. The other is when the object is very vague indeed. Let us look at these before drawing our conclusions.

The numinous religious experience may be, or be interpreted as, an encounter with Jesus, a saint, the Virgin Mary, Pan, Asclepius, Diana (or any pagan deity); as a vast and vague 'Other' which the Christian identifies as God and which the Hindu seeks as Brahman; or it may come as the overwhelming sense of a vast power in nature, or be received as an almost totally agnostic shiver of numinous awe. But such agreement as there is (and it evidently can be found within confined categories) need not be explained in terms of the existence of a common external object which is anyway in conflict with the common external object of some other category. The explanation which most readily offers itself is in terms of causes which include the beliefs, expectations, and fears of the subject.

The point is this. Even when we discount all the identifiable conditions in which illusions, dreams, deceptions and mistakes occur, and focus, not upon the experience of the sick or those subject (by their own choosing or otherwise) to exceptional emotional pressures or life privations, but upon the experience of the normal and healthy person, then one influence is likely to remain which disposes him or her to have or to interpret numinous experience in a particular way. That influence is the cultural and religious environment of the person; the possession of one world view rather than another, or at the very least, familiarity with, or concern with, one system of ideas rather than another. Now there is ample evidence to show that numinous religious experiences are frequently received as, indeed are normally articulated by means of, the religious forms, symbols and figures with which one is familiar, and these may be as incompatibly different as a feeling of union with the god at a Dionysian festival on an Aegean island, or a vision of the Blessed Virgin Mary in a Dublin suburb. To put it baldly: one encounters what one has been brought up to expect to encounter. This, not the independent existence of multiple and incompatible external objects, seems to account for the similarities of what is reported as the object of religious experience within a given community, and for differences between communities with differing world views.

But if we turn to the other extreme and seek for a lowest common factor in all numinous religious experience, then a different and much weaker result is achieved, but one which is not explainable in terms of cultural or religious predispositions. William James expressed it thus: 'The only thing which it [religious experience] unequivocally testifies to is that we can experience union with *something* larger than ourselves and in that union find our greatest peace.'[15] But even this goes a little too far. It is not proven[16] that this union is an external experience, although the subject strongly feels that it is. The most we can say is that it is *possible* that something neither Christian nor Jewish, neither Hindu nor Pagan, may at moments become accessible to normal men and women in certain numinous experiences. This something is usually experienced as the religious forms and symbols with which one is familiar and which will therefore be glaringly incompatible with the religious forms and symbols of different cultures. But in certain numinous pantheist experiences, in which the element of cultural interpretation is at its lowest, the awareness of IT may become very strong without being mediated through any conventional religious symbols. If you ask what this IT is, I can only reply I do not know. Perhaps it is the thrill of awe and fear which is our natural response to the vast emptiness of the universe. Perhaps it is our response to something which we dimly discern so that we try to speak of it as I AM: the light beyond the light of the sun, the face hidden in the mist.

This is the sum of our conclusions. To be good evidence for the existence of God, direct experience must be external experience. But no direct experience of God can be decisively identified as external experience. The most that can be admitted is that on the assumption of God's selective revelation of himself, some religious experience may be experience of an external object. This makes religious experience consistent with, rather than evidence for, the existence of God. But the evidential value of religious experience is further diminished because of the variety of divine objects experienced. It is only in terms of a very vague and general description that a common object can be identified, and even then the independent existence of this vague object is not necessitated by the experience. If claims to direct experience of God constitute poor evidence for his existence, can we adopt the weaker position: the assumption of his existence is the simplest way to account for religious experience? We cannot adopt this because the simplest and most obvious way to account for all these apparently internal and culture-conditioned experiences, with their different particular objects, is in terms of predisposing causes.

Let me, however, add one thought which might put these conclusions in a different light. If there were a God – an invisible, all-permeating, intelligent force operating as an agent throughout the universe and to whom man matters as a tiny, pale reflection of himself – if there were such a God, how could his presence be made accessible to man except by means of a powerful numinous experience which most men are only capable of receiving through the myths and images of their particular beliefs?

5 ARGUMENTS AGAINST BELIEF IN GOD: EXTERNAL SCEPTICISM

The arguments and evidence so far considered give some vague indications that belief in God or some god may not be altogether groundless. But that is not the end of the matter. Hostile evidence has to be taken into account. Part of such evidence comes from within theistic belief in the familiar antinomies between God's goodness and human suffering, and between divine omnipotence and moral responsibility. These will be considered in the next chapter. The immediate concern is philosophical and popular scepticism from *outside* theistic religions about their central belief in God. The focus of this scepticism is whether it makes coherent sense to suppose, or even to talk about, the existence of anything corresponding to such an extraordinary description as that normally given of God (see above, p. 24).

In this chapter I shall deal in a rather summary manner with three such sceptical issues. Each of them represents a more or less sophisticated philosophical expression of the general, lay, scepticism which feels instinctively that nothing can be known about the existence of God and that the discussion of such a subject is futile. The first section is concerned with the surviving influence, such as it is, of the harshly anti-metaphysical logical positivism of the nineteen twenties and thirties. The second examines the particular question whether it is coherent to suppose that anything could exist which combines being able to act as an agent or person with having no body and no location. In the third section, I am concerned with the possibility which we must all sense at certain times: that, as Hume put it, 'our line is too short to fathom such immense abysses'.

(i) *The Relics of Positivism*

A significant part of the analytic and linguistic philosophy of the twentieth century has regarded talk of God, along with most other 'metaphysical' language, as meaningless. But the original source of this attitude was not sceptical philosphy. It was over-enthusiasm for the methods, or supposed methods, of successful science. Everyone could agree (and can still agree) that the sciences have been extraordinarily successful in answering questions about the way the world works. They have also, in practical terms, brought home the goods to a staggering extent; sometimes, as we now know, very nasty things indeed concealed with the goods, but the goods none the less. Now the scientific questions have been answered, and the goods provided, without reference to God or to any aspect of religion. The belief may therefore be engendered, and was engendered among certain intellectuals between the World Wars, that the scientific picture of reality is the only picture which is possible, and that scientifically answerable questions are the only questions which it is significant to ask. Sigmund Freud (1856–1939) clearly intended to adopt this position. In 1927 in *The Future of an Illusion* he wrote 'scientific work is the only road which can lead to a knowledge of reality outside ourselves'.[1] Again, in the final sentences of the book, he remarks 'Our science is no illusion. But an illusion it would be to suppose that what science cannot give us we can get elsewhere.' At about the same time as Freud was writing, thinking of this type was adopted with almost evangelical fervour by a group of philosophers, scientists and mathematicians known as the Vienna Circle. In the distorting compass of a single paragraph their programme – logical positivism – was as follows.

All meaningful propositions are in one or other of two groups: statements (tautologies) of logic or mathematics such as '$2 + 2 = 4$' or '$\sim(p.\sim p)$', and statements of fact such as 'that cat is black'. The test of whether a non-tautological statement was a statement of fact was provided by the verification principle. It declared that a proposition was factually significant or meaningful if and only if some observation could lead one to reject it as false or accept it as true. If no actual or theoretically possible observations were relevant to deciding whether the proposition in question were true or false, then the proposition must be a pseudo-proposition, i.e. a proposition in form, but factually insignificant or literally none-sense; although perhaps having emotive significance for the persons using or hearing it.

The results of applying the verification principle to the statement 'God exists' can be anticipated. No straightforward observations are relevant. God is not like a smut on a window sill, a remote astronomical object, or even a gravitational force whose existence can be inferred by observation of its effects. Therefore it is factually insignificant to declare that God exists. The clever arrogance of the youthful A. J. Ayer in *Language, Truth and Logic* (originally published in 1936) has never been bettered in its expression of the logical positivist position:

> [The theist's] assertions cannot possibly be valid, but they cannot be invalid either. As he says nothing at all about the world, he cannot justly be accused of saying anything false, or anything for which he has insufficient grounds. It is only when the theist claims that in asserting the existence of a transcendent god he is expressing a genuine proposition that we are entitled to disagree with him ... The point which we wish to establish is that there cannot be any transcendent truths of religion. For the sentences which the theist uses to express such 'truths' are not literally significant.[2]

Unhappily the embargo upon taking seriously the factual claims of theism was itself taken far too seriously for far too long, particularly by those at the margins of philosophy who remained unaware of the deep trouble in which the verification principle rapidly found itself.

The principle is unsatisfactory for internal and external reasons. The internal reasons are, among others, that it proved impossible to give a satisfactory definition of what constitutes an observation statement, difficult to agree upon a formulation of the principle, and difficult to defend the principle against itself: it was neither a tautology nor a factually significant statement according to its own terms. The external reasons centred on one point. The principle, in its usual formulations, excluded far too much. Not only religious and metaphysical propositions but the propositions of morality and aesthetics among others became factually insignificant according to its standard.

The discovery that verification was too strong to use as an acceptable criterion of meaning led some philosophers (following in the wake of Sir Karl Popper's identification of falsifiability as the main requirement of a scientific statement of theory) to suggest instead that if a proposition is to have meaning it must be *falsifiable*. I do not want to trace the history of this suggestion and of its eventual demise, but one item in the history, a conspicuously powerful challenge to religious statements from their alleged *lack* of falsifiability, is important for our purposes. In a celebrated short article, originally published in 1950 but reprinted many times since, Antony Flew threw down the challenge thus:

Now it often seems to people who are not religious as if there was no conceivable event or series of events the occurrence of which would be admitted by sophisticated religious people to be a sufficient reason for conceding 'There wasn't a God after all' or 'God does not really love us then.' . . . Just what would have to happen not merely (morally and wrongly) to tempt but also (logically and rightly) to entitle us to say 'God does not love us' or even 'God does not exist'? I therefore put to the succeeding symposiasts the simple central question, 'What would have to occur or to have occurred to constitute for you a disproof of the love of, or of the existence of, God?' [3]

The dilemma is that religious statements are either meaningful and falsified by some event or observation; or they cannot be falsified and are meaningless.

In the symposium of which Flew's challenge is a part, neither of the distinguished respondents grasped the central nettle and argued that unfalsifiability does not, of itself, decide whether a statement is meaningless. But consider the following examples. (a) In the year of our reckoning 4004 B.C. the world, together with all evidence which we presume to be traces of earlier periods, came into existence *ex nihilo* as an act of divine creation. (b) At some time in the future there will be born a man who will live a thousand years. (c) On Hallowe'en, if and only if no observation is being made, the face of the gorgon from the temple of Sulis Minerva in the museum at Bath smiles. None of these is falsifiable by any observation which can be made. Certainly we feel that they are very peculiar statements, and our instinctive response may well be to reject them – they are *too* odd to be true. But they *seem* to make sense, and there is nothing to justify overruling what *seems* to make sense by legislative declaration that unfalsifiable propositions are meaningless. Of Flew's two propositions, I would be inclined to say that 'God loves us' has some of the appearances of being false, not meaningless, from the evidence available (but of that more in the next chapter); while 'God exists', even if unfalsifiable by event or observation, has *some* claims to make sense of what would otherwise be totally mysterious, namely, questions about the origin of the universe, and about the source of some of the experiences we were examining in the previous chapter.

In the late fifties logical positivism as a serious philosophical programme was dead. But the anti-metaphysical prejudice which it engendered was not dead. As far as the philosophy of religion is concerned, deference to this prejudice showed itself in a number of ways. Several philosophers, notably John Hick,[4] argued that certain religious statements which *seemed* to be making factual claims, for example concerning the existence or activity of God, *were* making factual claims, even when judged according to the verification principle. Such religious statements were in principle verifiable, but only, according to Hick, in rather outlandish ways – for example, after death. A far commoner (and more fruitful) response to the anti-metaphysical prejudice of philosophers (and, it must be said, the decay of belief in 'traditional' religion in the secular world urged theologians in the same direction) was to interpret statements about God in almost any way *except* as the factual statements which they appear to be. Thus the existence of God, instead of making a difference to the reality of the world and *therefore* to what we should do or hope, became, among many other suggestions, 'really' a behaviour-commending locution, an affirmation of moral values, an embodiment of ultimate personal commitments, or an affirmation of 'the unconditional authority of religious categories in a person's life'. One of the best worked out responses of this type, that associated with the name of D. Z. Phillips and generally labelled 'Wittgensteinian Fideism', has been cut to pieces by the recent criticisms of J. L. Mackie.[5] But without following the details of such criticisms, we may note that almost all reconstructions of what the believer 'really' means when he affirms belief in the existence of God suffer from one overmastering defect.

The defect is that the great majority of Jewish, Christian and Muslim believers at the present day, and in the past, would not recognize what they are now told is their 'real' meaning in affirming belief in God, as what they actually *do* mean in such affirmations. From first to last, whatever else theistic religions have affirmed about ways of life, or moral priorities, or ultimate social or personal concerns, the central affirmation has always been that the ultimate nature of the world is of a sort which is *different* from what it would be if no God existed. The existence of God, in something like the sense set out on p. 24 above, is something which the believer holds to be a significant truth about the reality of things; a truth from which the rest of his commitment to religion follows, and which if judged false would invalidate the central reality of his belief.

In saying this I am not suggesting that the numerous discussions[6] of the meaning of religious language which went on in the late fifties and sixties were worthless. Far from it. Many perceptive suggestions were made, and the result has been a far more detailed awareness of the possibilities of religious language than would otherwise have been the case. But the central questions 'Is there a God?' and 'What is he like?' were largely avoided in anything like the sense in which ordinary people ask them; the avoidance stemming from the preconceptions (a) that such questions were naïve and meaningless if regarded factually, and (b) that it was the business of philosopher and theologian to defuse this situation by suggesting what the believer 'really' meant in his formulas.

In the seventies the suggestion that verification should be a test of meaning weakened to being little more than a salutary critical suspicion that if *nothing whatever* was allowed to count as evidence against the truth of a proposition, then perhaps it would be better to regard such a proposition as insignificant rather than false. At first almost imperceptibly, then explicitly, the movement was away from discussion of religious language, and towards, first the coherence of what is believed, and then its substantial truth. Thus in *The Coherence of Theism* Swinburne is able to reject verification *in toto* (pp. 22–9), while someone like J. L. Mackie, fundamentally hostile to theism, was able to sweep aside[7] the whole subject of the meaning of religious language by directing his readers to Swinburne's excellent discussion of coherence. But there is at least one possible incoherence which cannot be swept aside. It remains an area of philosophical dispute as well as a puzzle which catches something of the layman's sceptical suspicion that *there could not be* anything which fitted the description of God given by traditional theism. I refer to the description of God as a bodiless agent or person (a 'spirit') able to act everywhere.

(ii) *Eternal God and Coherent Person*

On p. 24 above I offered the following as a minimum common statement of what God is understood to be in the Judaic, Christian and Islamic religions:

> There exists one God who is (a) creator and sustainer of all things; (b) omnipotent, omniscient and eternal; (c) an agent able to act everywhere without a body, and (d) morally concerned with mankind.

Item (a) was dealt with in chapter three, as was item (b) in part. Item (d) will be examined in chapter six, section i. The present concern is item (c).

The nub of the problem is set out by Antony Flew in his challenging book *God and Philosophy*:

When we turn to the positive terms in the definition we are at once in difficulty. For the crucial ones are all essentially personal: not only is God required to be in general personal; he is also, in particular, to have a will and, as maker and preserver, to be an agent [and to be good, wise and powerful] . . . but . . . Being an agent, showing willpower, displaying wisdom are so much prerogatives of people, they refer so entirely and particularly to human transactions and human experience, that it becomes more and more forced and unnatural to apply the relevant expressions the further you go down the evolutionary scale. To try to apply them to something which is not an animal at all cannot but result in a complete cutting of the lines of communcation.[8]

The question is this. Even if the only agents we can observe have bodies, and the bodies, moreover, of humans and of a few other higher animals, is it coherent to suppose that there could be an agent without a body, and an agent, moreover, able to act everywhere without a body? Swinburne is inclined to answer yes, and I shall return to his affirmative shortly. But first note how excessively peculiar the notion of a bodiless omnipresent person or agent actually is.

In an ordinary but not particularly deceptive view of the matter, a person or agent, such as I am or you are, consists in a publicly observable body, more or less in working order, and a private mental apparatus of thoughts, pains, inclinations, sensations, etc. From observation of others and experience of ourselves we learn, not only that most of what we can achieve, directly or indirectly, depends upon control over our own bodies, but also that damage to, or interference with, the body brings about concomitant changes in the mental apparatus. Concussion all but cuts out the mental person. Serious illness disrupts, and bodily death, on a commonsense view, terminates the mental person whose body it was (at least we do not sympathize with the late lamented on their gout or sleepless nights or social disappointments). Now leaving aside the acutely complicated philosophical question[9] raised by supposing that mental persons *in general* survive the death of bodily persons, is not a ghost a trace or aspect of some bodily person which remains active in a particular place and able to achieve certain limited tasks after the destruction of the bodily person?

Very well. Let us concede (despite the ambiguity of the phenomena and the frequently questionable veracity of the evidence) that it makes sense to suppose that there could be instances of persons, who once had bodies, who remain able to carry out very modest tasks (such as being 'experienced' by cats or dogs, or frightening people, or causing a candle to go out) after the demise of the body. Even this modest concession would be resisted by many people, but what we are asked to suppose in the case of God is vastly more strange. We are asked to suppose that there could be an entity which never had, and does not now have, a body of any sort through which it can carry out its intentions, but which can, nevertheless, everywhere and anywhere at once will and achieve anything which it is logically possible to will or achieve. But surely, on the face of it, this supposition is incoherent? We are being asked to combine the characteristics of having actions and intentions, which (as Flew points out) are almost always understood in relation to what higher animals directly or indirectly attempt through their bodily mechanisms, and always from the point of view of a particular place, with the characteristic of acting everywhere without a body. Such bodiless universal action sounds, at first description, more like an operation of gravity than the work of an intelligent agent. What would it be, we may ask, for an entity whom we have deprived of a location to *will*, and for that same entity whom we have also denied the possession of the recognizable means of carrying out a will, to *act*? If I may again borrow Hume's phraseology for my (quite similar) purpose: we must be far removed from the smallest tendency to scepticism to suppose that we have not strayed into a fairyland long ere we reach this stage in our philosophy.

The arguments which Swinburne employs in *The Coherence of Theism* to try to show that 'it is coherent to suppose that there exists a person without a body who is present everywhere' are too lengthy to do justice to here, but a skeletal outline of his position is as follows. A coherent statement is one which it makes sense to suppose to be true (p. 12) and whose constituent words have a meaning (p. 36). Persons are entities which satisfy (putting it very roughly) descriptions appropriate to bodies and descriptions appropriate to consciousnesses (pp. 100 f.). God does not satisfy any description appropriate to a body-person except that he can move any part of the universe as a basic act. 'A basic act of an agent is one which he performs without having to perform some other action in order to do it' (p. 103). For example, moving my own arm is a basic act; moving yours by my taking hold of it is not. On p. 105 Swinburne describes the characteristic of being able to move things other than your own body as a basic act, while at the same time losing dependence on the mechanical well-being of your own body. He concludes 'Surely anyone

Kansas School of Religion
At the University of Kansas
Smith Hall, Rm. 109, Library
Lawrence, Kansas 66045-2164

can thus conceive of himself becoming an omnipresent spirit. So it seems logically possible that there be such a spirit.' The remainder of his argument (pp. 106–25) concerns the question whether a disembodied spirit can be identified.

Swinburne's position is carefully argued and limited in its objective. He is not here saying that a disembodied omnipresent spirit – God – actually exists, but that it is coherent to suppose that such a spirit exists, such a supposition *makes sense*. Flew's conclusion is that it makes no sense.

I suspect that in this issue we are close to one of those ultimate points of disagreement which are difficult to shift by argument. Some people can make no sense of themselves thought of as persons in the manner in which God is spoken of as a person. Others think they can make sense of such a supposition. But let me leave this subject with two final thoughts which may explain why I find myself in the former category.

One is the complete loss, for an omnipresent bodiless entity, of any point of view, any *centre* relative to the world. I do not think it is merely a failure of my anthropocentric imagination that I cannot grasp what it would be like to be a conscious agent everywhere at once. Conscious agents (men, cats, dogs, ghosts and Greek gods) act from a point of view of the universe. They even have a point of view of their own bodies where a body is present. God, *ex hypothesi*, does not. If I imagine myself able, as a basic act, to turn the moon round on its axis so that you could see the other side of it from earth, I would inevitably conceive of myself seeing the moon from *some* point of view. The supposition of a sight, or an awareness, which embraces *all* points of view, is not just omniscience, it is dispersal of the agent. It might be like seeing myself from my own fingertip *and* from everywhere else on my own body simultaneously. *I* cannot make much sense of even that degree of dispersal of my centre of consciousness, let alone understand a dispersal which embraces every view of everything in the universe. But perhaps I am just unimaginative.

My second problem with the notion of a disembodied omnipresent agent takes the above a stage further. The basic acts which a person can perform are movements of his own body. Now if God is an omnipresent spirit which moves any part of the universe as a basic act, this must surely mean, if the analogy with a human agent is to hold in any way at all, that the universe is identical with God's body. If we really have to think in this way in order to make sense of the supposition that God is an omnipresent agent disconnected from any normal body, then two things go wrong. The first is that, once again, control over the body implies a centre of consciousness from which the body is directed. An equal dispersal of consciousness over the whole body, like life in a lump of primeval protoplasm, may indicate a living thing in some weird way, but it is not a *person*. So if we are hooked on this strange idea that the universe is to God what a body is to man, it seems unavoidable to ask: how does the directive centre of consciousness relate to it? *Where* is God's mind? The second worry is that if God's embodiment is the universe itself, and *its* movements are *his* basic acts, then it would appear to be absurd to speak of God *creating* heaven and earth. Heaven and earth *are* God. All the talk about God being the explanation of the fact of order or the reason why there is anything at all would then be a theistic fantasy. The universe *is* the eternal, self-explaining necessity we take God to be. But this supposition is identical in all respects that I can understand with the central thesis of classical atheism that the physical universe and its movements are the ultimate realities (see above pp. 49–51). Thus, in the end, it turns out that to believe that God is an omnipresent spirit able to move any part of the universe as a basic act is no different from the atheistic belief that the universe is an eternal, ultimately inexplicable, natural fact. God's agency no longer operates on, or explains, all that is. All that is, simply *is* God.

(iii) *The Unfathomable Abyss*

There can be no doubt that logical positivism, particularly in its weaker forms, gave intellectual expression to a mood of incredulity about the possibility of making sense of religious statements – a mood which still prevails. That is probably why theologians, and philosophers well disposed to religion, went to such inordinate lengths, not to challenge logical positivism, but to show, in one way or another, that religious claims could either accord with it, or elude its force by being understood in their 'true', non-factual, character. Similarly the particular problem of a dispersed, disembodied, agent catches hold of a mood of contemporary scepticism which feels, not that religious claims are *false*, but that somehow it is all beyond our ken anyway; maybe there is something there, but thinking about it gets us nowhere:

> Myself when young did eagerly frequent
> Doctor and Saint, and heard great Argument

About it and about: but evermore
Came out by that same Door as in I went.

The feeling that the right response is 'to sit down in quiet ignorance of
those things which, upon examination, are found to be beyond the reach
of our capacities',[10] and that the existence and activity of God is one of
these things, can look for rational justification in only two directions.
One is from the failure of two and a half thousand years of philosophical
debate, religious experience, and scientific development to bring us any
nearer to a conclusion than Xenophon and Plato appeared to be at the
beginning. The other is from some theory of knowledge or language
which could show in a generally acceptable way *why* certain speculations
are beyond our understanding or intrinsically vacuous. Let us look at the
second possibility first.

The suggestion is that some account of what constitutes meaningful
discourse, or some account of what knowledge is, or some account of
where the limits of our understanding can be drawn, will give effective
rational backing to the commonsense feeling that conclusions about God
are beyond our ken. Logical positivism was itself a less than fortunate
example of the first of these enterprises. But there could be better. Many
people would be willing to concede that if a statement is to convey meaning,
then normally the nouns (and, in a much more sophisticated and indirect
way, the adjectives and verbs) in the statement must be empirically
locatable. I must be able to point to, or indicate by means of a description
which employs familiar words, what object or situation is referred to by the
noun 'blictri' if you are to begin to understand such a statement as
'Weezabelle loves blictri'. (Since you have not been introduced to her
before, I also need to tell you that Weezabelle is the name of my cat.) Now
without following this, or any other, theory of knowledge or language
through the philosophical complexities with which it would invariably be
surrounded, it is permissible to suggest two general conclusions.

One is that it is by no means obvious that even such an empirically
grounded account of meaningful language would exclude talk of God. No
one but a fool (or perhaps one of the first Russian cosmonauts who is
reputed to have sent back to earth the message 'I see no God around up
here') is going to pretend that 'God' can be given meaning by pointing to
the thing or situation which the word indicates. Nevertheless the words
used to describe God, words like 'powerful', 'agent', 'everywhere', 'merciful', 'without body', etc., *can* be grounded in empirical situations even if,

as in the present case, they are combined to form a unique description or used in an unusually extended or analogical way. One may very well want to say, 'I don't believe that anything corresponds to your description of God.' But that is quite different from saying 'I don't have the slightest comprehension what your description of God means.' The description may be difficult to grasp. It may contain hidden incoherencies. But the difficulties are not so great nor the incoherencies so evident as to justify abandoning hope before one has even commenced the quest.

A second general conclusion from the philosophical fortunes of theories of meaning or knowledge is that no one is likely to be able to produce (at least no one has produced) an account of meaning or a theory of knowledge which provides an acceptable decision procedure in marginal cases. Hume tried,[11] with some grossly implausible results, and both he and his successors are at their best when they are arguing with reference to the meaning of specific words or phrases (like 'bodiless omnipresent agent') rather than dogmatically employing a general theory to exclude some utterance as meaningless. So I say again: however strongly one may feel that certain theological or metaphysical (or for that matter political or scientific) formulations have lost their footing in the real world, it is far from evident that *any* general criterion of meaning or possible knowledge could be used to show that they actually are the nonsense which one might feel them to be.

If general theories of meaning are dubious as appeal courts, how can we deal with a particular case? In chapter three, partly on Leibniz's account, I several times used a formula which suggested that God might be 'of a different category or order of existence from the physical universe'. Does this formula convey a meaning or is it merely a grammatically correct but empty form of words? To me it has some of the feel of the bogus fantasies which masquerade as metaphysical insights in American cult religions; but let us indulge a science fiction whimsy for a paragraph – not to establish what might be true, but to establish what could make sense.

Suppose that certain things which we call realities of the physical world exist alongside certain other realities which are realities of – let us say – a mental world. Only one manifestation of such parallel worlds is known to us, namely the human brain and its related consciousness. Thus the bio-chemical lump with its detectable electro-chemical functions is the physical reality which you could observe. My thoughts, fears, anticipations, etc., my consciousness, is the mental reality, and no observer's knowledge of the physical reality can ever give direct access to or awareness of the mental reality which is also there. Now suppose that such parallel worlds were not confined to brains, but extended to certain highly general features of the physical world – gravitational or electro-magnetic forces perhaps. Suppose that what we detect as the physical reality of electro-magnetism were also the mental reality of some vast consciousness. Just as it would be theoretically possible for an altogether alien intelligence not familiar with biological life forms to investigate a human brain without recognizing its parallel reality as a consciousness, so we could become familiar with the physical processes of electro-magnetism without realizing that it was the physical parallel of a mental world – God's consciousness.

Very well: I don't like this idea either. Sensational metaphysics without an iota of empirical evidence in support are snares for the gullible, not paths to reasoned truth. But the point is simply that of trying to *make sense* of the notion of a different order of being and here, I think, we have it: a physical order of being which we all know, and a mental order of being which gives a *possible* sense to Leibniz's talk about a being of metaphysical necessity, or to God as 'external' to the physical world.

If general theories of meaning do not lend much reliable support to the feeling that talk of God is beyond our ken, what of the other depressing factor: failure to reach any agreed conclusions despite two and a half thousand years of thinking and arguing about God's existence and activity?

In the first place it is not true that *no* progress has been made since the beginning in our understanding of the evidence which bears upon the existence of God. It is apparent, for example, that Hume's grasp of the design argument is both clearer and more sophisticated than the grasp of those whom Cicero is reporting in *De Natura Deorum*. It is also apparent that in this century we have acquired a better comprehension of the evidential possibilities of religious experience than was achieved at earlier periods. It is also apparent – and I hope most of this book is an illustration of this – that it is possible to think carefully and coherently about issues which on some views may appear to be beyond our ken. The problem which some people find depressing is not that we make *no* progress, but that our progress always seems to leave the central issue, the real exist-ence of God, uncertain and a matter for the new judgement of each individual. But, of course, that is exactly what one would expect if the world were in fact the creation of an intelligence which intended to leave

us to our own judgements, and free of the crushing and distorting knowledge that he was in fact as we suppose him to be.

I do not want to argue that the nice balance of evidence is itself
evidence for the existence of a God nicely balancing the evidence. It may
be that there is no God, and that contrary hints are just a sample of those
seductive ambiguities which, on a much lesser scale, draw men on to
search for the Loch Ness Monster. But my point is that if there were a
God who permitted real human freedom (see p. 132), and did not want
slavish worship from human beings, then the lack of decisive evidence
about his existence would be something we should expect, not something
that should vex us. The conclusion should not be: no one can decisively
prove that God exists (or does not exist); *therefore* forget the subject. It
should be: knowledge is not permissible if there really is a God; *therefore*
each person must think the thing out for himself and reach his own
decision. All that one man can do for another is to draw the evidence,
and some thoughts about it, carefully to his attention.

But, someone may protest, if in the end each person's belief or lack of
belief in God depends upon a fine balance of evidence which may tip the
person's belief one way or the other almost at random (or be decided by
causes not reasons), why bother to think about it at all? Surely the
matter can be left to social influences, or to the grace of God, or whatever?
I can only reply – no. There are three reasons for this clear negative. The
first is simply a value judgement which I invite others to share although I
do not propose to defend it here. The judgement is that it is vastly
preferable that a man or woman possessed of the most sophisticated
physical thing known in the universe – a human brain – should try to
use it to decide critical issues rather than resign them to the chance
influence of causes. Secondly, the process of thinking out belief in God or
a god has the useful, even salutary, effect of making one aware of what is
involved in such a belief: and some of what is involved is indeed, as Flew
remarks, of the most intimate human concern. Finally, I do not think
that the evidence about the existence of God is all that finely balanced. I
think that an impartial view tips to one side. What I said above was that
the issue is uncertain, not that it is absolutely indecisive.

The conclusions of this chapter are: that no general theory of meaning is
likely to establish in an acceptable way that the central factual statements
of theism are meaningless; that there is at least a suspicion that the
notion of a dispersed, disembodied agent or person is incoherent; and

that if there is a God, our failure to reach generally agreed conclusions about his existence is what we should expect. But for many people it is not external scepticism, or any general science-motivated disenchantment with religious claims, which constitutes the real objection to theism. The real objections come from within. Theism is intrinsically incredible.

6 ARGUMENTS AGAINST BELIEF IN GOD: INTERNAL DILEMMAS

The arguments for the existence of God are indecisive. The evidence from religious experience is ambiguous. The coherence of the theistic concept of God is in some doubt. These things we have seen. But the problems for theism as a reasonable belief do not stop with the weakness of the evidence in its favour or with the external objection that its central proposition may be meaningless. Jew, Christian and Muslim alike bring problems upon themselves from within their beliefs. The most insistent of these is the problem of evil. Another concerns moral freedom and responsibility. A third concerns divine acts (miracles or answers to prayer) taking place within the order of nature. To the thoughtful believer these constitute difficulties which in one case, the problem of evil, may loom large enough to destroy faith. To the non-believer they provide additional reasons for rejecting any form of theistic religion. In what follows I shall look in outline at these three problems, pressing each of them home at the point which constitutes the gravest objection to theism. That atheism in its turn is not without difficulties will become apparent in the next chapter.

(i) Evil and Malformations in Creation

The word 'evil' carries with it the notion of an active and morally depraved agent: a notion which the O.E.D. gives as the primary sense, remarking as it does so 'now little used except in literary English'. (Presumably 'little used' because two centuries of the social sciences have so eroded our confidence that rational agents are fully responsible for anything they do that we are now shy of even *speaking* of someone as 'morally depraved' rather than as operating under some causally excusing category such as 'misguided' or 'unfortunate'.) The word 'suffering', on the other hand, refers, among other things, to the state of any sentient being (human or animal) which is hurt (mentally or physically) *either* by the activity of evil agents *or* by the processes of the natural world. The suffering occasioned by these two sources is usually distinguished by the terms 'moral evil' and 'natural evil'.

Moral evil is *unnecessary suffering caused by the free actions of rational men and women.* The word 'unnecessary' is an important qualification. The dentist who treats a diseased tooth causes some suffering, but it is suffering which, with his limited powers, is necessary if he is to deliver one from the far worse misery of the untreated abscess. Similarly the words 'free' and 'rational' impose qualifications upon the notion of moral evil. It is not a *moral* evil of my doing if I am physically compelled to inflict suffering or if my sanity is so impaired by disease that I do not have any rational grasp of what I am doing, or if I inflict suffering by blameless accident.

Natural evil is *suffering imposed on sentient beings by the processes of the natural world independently of the free actions of any human agent.* Earthquakes, tempests and many, but not all, diseases are examples. Note that even if all human agents were morally perfect in the sense that none ever freely caused unnecessary suffering, the evil occasioned by some of the workings of nature would remain untouched. Note also that the distinction between moral and natural evil is not in all cases immediately apparent. The person who ignorantly lags the pipes in his home with blue asbestos causes himself and his children an unpleasant death years later. It is a natural evil that blue asbestos causes a fatal disease. A moral evil would only be involved if the person knew this when he installed the stuff, or if he could reasonably be expected to have found out at the time. The spread of deserts in certain parts of the world – North Africa for example – looks like a natural evil. However, if it could be shown that it was the result of centuries of avoidable folly and conscious exploitation of the land by human beings, the spread of the deserts would be a moral evil. But despite these and many other cases which require care before being categorized, the distinction between moral and natural evil is serviceable enough to be of vital assistance in discussing the problem of evil.

The problem of evil (or, if one wishes to lay the emphasis on the recipient rather than on the origin, the problem of suffering) is generated for its devotees by any religion in which the God is held to combine omnipotence, omniscience and perfect moral goodness – in short by any theistic religion. 'Omnipotence' means being able to bring about anything which it is logically possible to bring about. (Although 'with God all things are possible' (Matthew 19:26), not being able to bring about the logically *im*possible is not a restriction on omnipotence since the logically impossible is not a characterization of anything. It is a non-thing: a mere syntactically correct form of words which gives and takes away sense in the same context.) 'Omniscience' means knowing everything that it is logically possible to know.* (If God knows everything it is, for example, not logically possible for him to think of something he does not know.) What should be understood by 'perfect moral goodness' is, however, less easy to indicate briefly. This is due to the existence of differing accounts of what morality and goodness are. Without following these accounts into a long digression, one can pick up a general *negative* requirement for perfect moral goodness – or for that matter even quite moderate moral goodness – from the definition I have already given of moral evil. Apart from whatever positive criteria are settled upon for perfect moral goodness, any agent which displayed perfect moral goodness would most certainly *not* freely inflict unnecessary suffering or allow others to inflict unnecessary suffering which the agent had the power to prevent.

The problem of evil, as it affects religion, is simply the observation that the world contains a very great deal of suffering which one would expect a perfectly good moral agent armed with omnipotence and omniscience to do away with or rather, as creator, never to have put here in the first place. Augustine (354–430) is reputed to have put the problem with formal succinctness thus: 'Either God cannot abolish evil or he will not; if he cannot, he is not all-powerful; if he will not, he is not all-good.' Hume also expresses it with classical brevity:

> Epicurus's old questions are yet unanswered. Is he willing to prevent evil, but not able? then he is impotent. Is he able, but not willing? then he is malevolent. Is he both able and willing? Whence then evil?[1]

Even if one's religious credulity gags at such theological technicalities as omnipotence and omniscience, when one reverts to the more familiar

---

* My statement in the text is simplistic but sufficient for present purposes. For a full discussion see Richard Swinburne, *The Coherence of Theism* (Oxford, 1977), ch. 10. For complex reasons, which I cannot reproduce here but with which I largely agree, Swinburne arrives at what he calls an attenuated understanding of omniscience: 'P is omniscient if he knows about everything except those future states and their consequences which are not physically necessitated by anything in the past; and if he knows that he does not know about those future states' (p. 175). In ch. 12 Swinburne rejects (and again I agree with him) the Neoplatonist thesis that God is outside time rather than eternal in the sense of always did exist and always will exist. In the second part of this chapter I shall employ an account of omniscience which is closely similar to Swinburne's. But while acknowledging the excellence of the light which he has shed on this subject from start to finish, I do not explicitly discuss further what he has to say since my purposes are somewhat different from his and are, perhaps, best not confused with them at this stage.

biblical notions of an Almighty who is also the wise, loving and merciful Father of mankind, the problem remains. How could all the misery against which good men strive be permitted in a world created and sustained by such a being as we suppose God to be? Surely there can be no such God as Christians worship?

As might be anticipated, two and a half thousand years of theistic worry about the problem of evil – beginning with the Book of Job – have produced a large crop of attempts to resolve the issue in such a way as to reconcile belief in an almighty God who is just, loving and merciful with the experienced suffering of humanity. I propose to outline some of these attempts before focusing upon what I believe to be the intractable core of the problem.

1. *Suffering is justly distributed among the sentient beings of this world.* This is the line taken by those who come to comfort Job in his miseries, and Job is half inclined to concede that man cannot be pure in the sight of his Maker; but he recovers himself and asks: 'Make me know my transgression and my sin' (13:23) and complains, 'The tents of robbers are at peace, and those who provoke God are secure' (12:6). And Job is surely right. The problem of evil exists because the affairs of the world are as they are, because we are subject to precisely the sort of moral inconsequence which is expressed with such melancholy perfection by the writer of the Book of Ecclesiastes: 'Again I saw that under the sun the race is not to the swift, nor the battle to the strong, nor bread to the wise, nor riches to the intelligent, nor favour to men of skill; but time and chance happen to them all' (9:11). It is this experienced situation, coupled with the contents of Jewish or Christian or Islamic belief about God, which *constitutes* the problem of evil, and the experienced reality will not go away simply by being denied.

2. *Suffering is God's way of trying the worth of those free and independent agents he permits to exist.* There are two reasons for rejecting this solution. First, the concept 'trying the worth of' will not fit many, perhaps most, of those who suffer: children, animals, those of unsound mind or feeble determination for example. Secondly, and conclusively, the notion of inflicting suffering in order to see how people react, what sort of character stamina they have, is morally repulsive. If practised by a human agent it would be regarded as criminal or lunatic. If attributed to God I do not see how it could be regarded in a less reprehensible light. Such a defence does not solve the problem of evil; it makes it more acute by making God explicitly fail the negative requirement for moral goodness.[2]

3. *Mundane suffering will be made good in the (post-mortem) totality of things.* But this will never do. Not only is belief in a personal survival after death when heavenly felicity or hellish misery could put things right not an essential part of theism (notably the Jews in much of their history rejected it); but such post-mortem experiences could *never* put things right. If a human agent makes some ghastly moral error he may repent and try to recompense his victim, but recompense cannot take away or justify the suffering already inflicted. With God the situation is worse. With God the notions of error and repentance have no place; and if mundane suffering is such, or in any part such, as God could have prevented but did not, then *no* eternity of cakes and sweets will remove the moral imperfection of him who could have prevented the innocent suffering but did not do so. The innocent suffering stands for all time as innocent.

4. *Suffering is the unavoidable outcome of the existence of such free, responsible, rational agents as men and women are* (and a world containing free rational agents is better than any world which does not contain such free agents). Usually known as the free-will defence, this amounts to saying that if human beings are to have and to exercise significant freedom, i.e. if we are to be what we are rather than be mere puppets of God, then an unavoidable by-product of such freedom will be the actual existence of suffering resulting from morally wrong decisions and actions. God could have created different beings, but given that he created *us*, or caused *us* rather than some other possible creatures to come into existence in the history of his universe, then suffering, as a result of our freedom, unavoidably came with us.

The free-will defence has a very long history and is still a subject of lively debate. J. L. Mackie and Antony Flew have argued that 'If God has made men such that in their free choices they sometimes prefer what is good and sometimes what is evil, why could he not have made men such that they always freely choose the good?'[3] Others have replied that significant freedom requires that men actully choose evil on some occasions (despite the curious circumstances that presumably God himself will always freely choose the good and that no evil choices would ever be exercised in Heaven after the Fall of Satan and hence the immortal life of God and of the Christian would allow no significant freedom). Whatever we make of all this, and of the more impassioned replies to the free-will defence such as Dostoevsky's cry that freedom is not worth such a price,[4] it is still necessary and permissible in the present context to by-pass the entire discussion. It is necessary because lack of space forbids me to pursue this fascinating and complex topic. It is permissible because even if the final outcome (and at present there is no final outcome) were ever so favourable to the free-will defence, this would *only* justify the existence of moral evil. The whole world of natural evil would remain entirely unaccounted for and apparently existing in a manner flatly incompatible with theistic belief.

5. *The existence of certain first-order evils is a necessary condition for the existence of certain second-order goods* (and a world containing first-order evils together with second-order goods is better than a world which only contains first-order goods). The point being made is that secondary goods such as compassion for the suffering of others, or stoicism and bravery concerning one's own suffering, can only be elicited, can only come into actual existence, if the world already contains such primary evils as pain, starvation and the illness of loved ones. It does not matter whether these primary evils are natural evils like disease or famine, or moral evils like war and personal violence. In both or either cases a 'better' world results because secondary goods are brought into existence through the existence of primary evils.

I think this suggestion has little to recommend it for the following reasons. (a) It is difficult to see why a world of *potentially* compassionate and brave men and women would be worse than a world in which their compassion etc. was *actually* realized. In other words one doubts whether the actual existence of secondary goods is worth the price. (b) Primary evils do not only bring into existence secondary goods. They also bring into existence secondary evils. War and natural calamity may bring people closer to each other in terms of personal regard, compassion, understanding or friendship; disease may sometimes be ennobled by the sufferer's heroism. But another response – looting and savage self-preservation in war and calamity, acute self-absorption and sordid lethargy in disease – these may equally be the response. It is no good saying that it is precisely the different responses which make the whole process worth while (they show up the saints and sinners) because that returns us to the rejected notion of God trying the worth of his creatures. Furthermore it seems strange that an omnipotent agent equipped with perfect moral goodness should seek to elicit on occasions *my* second-order worth by allowing *you* to be tortured. (c) Even if there were no problem of second-order evils, there is little or no chance of second-order goods being elicited among large sections of those who suffer or observe primary suffering in others. I refer to animals, most young children, those of unsound mind and to those whose mental make-up is such that they cannot help being of feeble determination. (d) If primary evils are to be justified because a world containing them together with secondary goods is *better* than a world containing only primary goods, then this involves the unacceptable consequence that if good men substantially eliminate primary evils – conquer disease, overcome starvation, and end wars – then they have actually made the world a *worse* place than it was, since the opportunity for the exercise of secondary goods (even among those from whom it is possible to elicit such responses) is now greatly diminished.

6. '*Now we see in a glass darkly; but then face to face*' (1 Corinthians 13:12). I give this tag to the position which allows that while some suffering may be explained, nevertheless cases remain – particularly deriving from natural evil – which we *now* cannot reconcile with what we believe about God. But when we see clearly, perhaps in a moment of divine insight or, for the Christian, at the general resurrection on the Last Day, all will be seen to be in true accord with the power, wisdom and loving kindness of God. The position is a way of accommodating both the fact of evil and one's religious belief about God without offering any present reconciliation. But if thought about, the position is unsatisfactory on several grounds. Quite apart from wondering why the moment of divine insight has apparently never taken place in such a way that it can be communicated to anyone else, one may ask two questions. First, why should those who suffer now and find no justification for it in the life with which they are familiar, presume that all will be or could be justified by a view of things in some possible future existence with which they are totally unfamiliar? Secondly, if we say that all will be reconciled when we see face to face, then surely this means that we can go on maintaining the wisdom, goodness etc. of God *whatever* we experience in this life? Now while acknowledging the demise of logical positivism (see above p. 106), it is still strange to make apparently important assertions which lead us to expect certain consequences (e.g. that there will be no unnecessary suffering inflicted by the natural world) and then to say that the assertions stand as true *whatever* the consequences we actually discern. God is almighty, wise and good *regardless* of anyone's experience to the contrary. Similar unease applies to a variant of the 'glass darkly' view which one might call the 'his ways are not our ways' move. (The tag is not biblical, although Romans 11:33 comes close to the sentiment.) But this time it is even worse. To take this view means that when we believe God to be good, his goodness need not be manifest in anything *we*

would call good. We can *describe* what he does or brings about in terms which in all ordinary circumstances would describe the actions of a malevolent or morally neutral agent, but we will still *call* him good. The potentiality for pernicious moral confusion in such double-talk is evident. We can be left praising in God what we would condemn in any other free moral agent. At the very least we are entitled to ask, as Hume asked in conjunction with his statement of the problem of evil which I quoted above, 'In what respect, then, do his benevolence and mercy resemble the benevolence and mercy of men?' The implication is clearly, on this view, not at all; and that implication does not solve the problem of evil. It destroys the crucial theistic position that God is morally concerned with us and our world.

7. *The universe operates according to general laws and this is better than any possible alternative.* The argument is associated with part of Leibniz's (1646–1716) in the *Theodicy* (1710). It is that the more or less predictable and orderly universe which we have is in two senses better than any other possibility: (a) it is better that it should operate according to general laws than be continually subject to special acts of providence which would make it difficult for us to conduct ourselves in accordance with properly arrived-at expectations about the consequences of our actions etc.; (b) taken as a whole, the universe is better with the general laws it actually has than it would be with any other possible set of general laws. Given that we agree with both (a) and (b), then it would seem to follow that the particular misery and distress which results to individuals from the operation of the general laws of the universe as they are at present is a necessary part of what is still the best of all possible worlds.

The argument is the most interesting we have so far encountered but it is not compelling. Concerning (a) it will be remarked that if general laws are a part of the best of possible worlds, it would have avoided a great deal of suffering if the general laws which actually operate had in all respects been more quickly and more thoroughly accessible to us. We simply did not know, and could scarcely have found out in 1346, that certain rodents carried totally invisible objects which caused the Black Death. We do not yet (1983) know precisely which things cause cancers and why (i.e. in accordance with what general laws) these enormities occur. Furthermore, it is by no means apparent that if general laws are to guide our actions and expectations satisfactorily then *no* particular acts of a benign providence are permissible. Our medical theories and provisions are not set in disarray because serious illness can sometimes spontaneously regress. Our knowledge of the earth is not set at nought because an earthquake misses a major city which might have been its target. Concerning (b), the simple response is that we don't know, and can't know, whether the presumption is true. We do not even know all the general laws of the universe we have, or know that we have stated correctly or at their most general those laws which we at present discern, let alone know what other possible universes, operating according to different general laws, would be like. All we seem able to say at present is that if *we* were armed with omnipotence, omniscience and perfect moral goodness – or simply with more substantial measures of power, wisdom and benevolence than most of us at present enjoy – we are much inclined to feel that we could put a few finishing touches, make a few trifling alterations, which would alleviate much natural evil without either upsetting the economy of the universe or producing a race of lotus-eaters.

Now at this stage let us make more concessions to the theistic position than are actually justified. Let us agree that each of the suggestions for reconciling the fact of evil with the power and goodness of God is successful for *some* category of evil. Some suffering is retributive, other suffering is refining, or a necessary by-product of the activities of imperfect free rational agents, or a result of the operation of general laws, or, to take possibilities I have not discussed, informative, biologically useful, or a spur to action. Having conceded all this, the question is: can we still identify *any* suffering which according to ordinary understanding and common sense remains clearly unjustified and such that an omnipotent and omniscient agent *could*, and an agent possessing perfect moral goodness *would*, remove? I think the answer is yes, a whole category which I shall shortly explain; but one trivial, useless, and utterly superfluous cause of suffering can make almost the whole point by its very triviality.

The common cold is widely and randomly distributed among the earth's populations. It is a mild, debilitating misery which neither refines character, nor is a product of human freedom. The responsible virus could cease to exist without any alteration of the general laws of the universe. The sight of a cold is more likely to provoke wry humour or a desire to vacate the vicinity than to elicit the second-order good of sympathy. It is uninformative, biologically useless, and a spur only to filling the coffers of pharmaceutical companies and distillers in our attempts at vain cures. A great deal of useless, petty misery would have been avoided in the history of man if the common cold virus never had existed. So why is it here, in a world allegedly the product of an almighty, wise and loving God? If any attempt is made to justify the existence of the common cold (on all but one ground) I would reply: smallpox has, belatedly, been put out of existence by man's efforts, and surely no one would want to say that any sentient being in the universe is worse off as a result. But if it is better now to have a universe without smallpox, then it would always have been better to have had a universe without it, and the same applies to the common cold. If man, by his own efforts, can make better the universe for sentient beings without subverting the challenge of life or the moral order, and without rewriting the general laws of the universe, then one can only wonder why God has not done as much. The one ground on which the common cold might be justified is as a spur to medical research. But are we really to justify the ways of God to man by means of such a manifestly superfluous triviality? Medical research would have plenty with which to occupy itself without the existence of *that* cause of useless, petty misery.

In section iv of chapter three I drew attention to two aspects of the problem of evil. One aspect arose from the design argument and is what I have elsewhere called the Inference Problem of Evil: given that we are arguing dispassionately from the world and its characteristics to a creator of the world and his (or perhaps we should say its) characteristics, what might we arrive at? Hume is inclined to suggest, rightly I believe, that if the inference to a creating agent were followed out in a disinterested way we would arrive at something morally neutral and quite indifferent to human and animal life: 'The true conclusion is, that the original source of all things is entirely indifferent to all those principles, and has no more regard to good above ill than to heat above cold, or to drought above moisture, or to light above heavy.'[5] But the other aspect of the problem of evil – the Consistency Problem, the problem we have recently been examining – does not depend upon a more or less probable *inference* to God's existence and character; it already assumes God's existence and character and seeks for ways, of the sort we have been discussing, in which that assumed character might be shown to be *consistent* with certain intractable facts of the world. Now the most intractable category of facts is not the general laws of the universe or the results of human freedom, but *malfunctions of nature*: natural processes, as it were run to disease or riotous excess – the massive earthquake which destroys all things indifferently, the volcanic eruption which suffocates an entire population, malformations at conception or birth which are not a product of moral evil, the destructive excess of normal body cells run to cancer, unusual droughts or frosts which render large parts of the earth and all the rest of the known universe unfit to sustain life. It is this category of natural evil, when nature turns against life, that presents the strongest possible evidence against the activity of an almighty, wise and benevolent God. Perfect moral goodness equipped with omnipotence and omniscience would not permit such breakdowns. But since such breakdowns do occur, and since they cause incalculable suffering to individual persons (not to mention animals), the most straightforward conclusion would surely be that there is no such God as the theist believes in. All other things apart, the apparently in-built capacity for our natural environment to turn against us and itself (not to mention such purely gratuitous and pointless miseries as the common cold) present, as John Hick concedes at the end of his seminal discussion, 'a real mystery, impenetrable to the rationalizing human mind'.[6] Hick attempts to make a positive religious virtue of such mystery. But it is hard to see how the agnostic, or the religious person himself under the pressure of very great suffering, can be expected to distinguish between what is legitimately mysterious in religion and what plainly falsifies or makes a nonsense of his belief.

(ii) *Freedom, Responsibility and Foreknowledge*

In the circumstances it may have felt like a welcome respite but, with due hindsight concerning philosophical and theological controversies, the diversion adopted by some of the weaker spirits among Milton's newly fallen Angels seems more like an extension of their torments:

> Others apart sat on a hill retired,
> In thoughts more elevate, and reasoned high
> Of providence, Foreknowledge, Will and Fate –
> Fixed fate, free will, foreknowledge absolute –
> And found no end, in wandering mazes lost.

And yet, for purposes to do with the philosophy of religion, the main outline of the problem is capable of being stated relatively simply. It is that in traditional Christian (and other theistic) belief, two apparently incompatible assumptions are made. *One* is that God is both almighty, and omniscient in the sense that he knows everything that it is logically possible to know. *The other* is that man is a morally responsible agent; but a morally responsible agent has to be a free agent in the sense of one who is conscious of what he is doing and is able to act otherwise if he so chooses. Now for Milton's Satan, puzzling over his condition (e.g. in Book IV of *Paradise Lost*), the problem is absolutely intractable because he *feels* free, and responsible, and able to choose to continue his rebellion, and yet he *knows* that it is all somehow hopeless because God really is almighty, and really does know the outcome of all things in advance including the fact of Satan's rebellion and its failure. But Satan need not be quite so depressed. Upon further consideration what he would find is a theologically embarrassing dilemma, not a personal impasse. The dilemma is as follows.

It certainly is within the bounds of logical possibility for an omniscient agent (God) to know in the present the future course of whatever physically necessitated events there are; after all, within our limitations, we have a semblance to knowledge of that sort ourselves. Hence, to the extent to which the choices of human agents are physically necessitated events, they are already known to God and foreseen by him at the creation of the world; but to that extent they are not free. On the other hand, to the extent to which the choices of human agents are not physically necessitated by past events, they are free; but their outcome is not known to God. To opt for the first horn of the dilemma by assuming the extent of physical necessitation to be total, or at least that it extends to human choices, is to deny moral responsibility to human beings and to place the responsibility for moral evil upon God as the creator of the whole system (he who freely creates something and knows what it will do, and what will be done with it, is accountable for all that happens). To opt for the second horn of the dilemma preserves human moral responsibility at the cost of assuming that God freely permits (i.e. chose to, but did not in any sense have to choose to permit) the existence of intelligent agents who are such that he really does not know what they will do when they act freely. It was perfectly possible for God not to create such agents, and it remains perfectly possible for him to put them out of existence at any time, but while they remain in existence it is logically impossible for him to know all that they will do while they remain free agents.

So perhaps Satan should not despair. Either he is genuinely a free agent, worthy of punishment but with the possibility of surprising God by his choices; or he is a mere physically necessitated automaton, programmed to feel free, whose 'rebellion' and other activities are a creation of the Almighty which cannot justly, or even meaningfully, warrant punishment: either Satan has a chance, or God is horribly unjust.

But what is meant by a 'physically necessitated event' and what is meant by saying an agent is 'able to act otherwise if he so chooses'? All of us, in a rather haphazard way, employ the lay notion of something being physically necessary and the correlate notion of something being physically impossible. Similarly we all understand, or think we understand, what a free choice is. But more needs to be said and the reader will perhaps forgive a difficult digression for two paragraphs.

I would suggest, but only as a minimal characterization for present purposes (it would not be sufficient for a monograph in the philosophy of science!), that a physically necessitated event is one which can be accurately predicted from a universal nomic generalization of the sort we call a law of nature, together with a knowledge of the present or past state of the system to which the law applies. Now it may be argued that, notwithstanding our vast confidence in science, as far as human beings are concerned we may never hit upon, or be able to know for certain that we have hit upon, a perfectly accurate statement of a law of nature: our predictions are not in all respects accurate, and they are far from complete. But with God the situation is very different. The religious supposition is that God created both the initial conditions and the laws of nature themselves and therefore knows exactly what they are and exactly what situations they will give rise to except when they are influenced by the (very minor) free agents he permits to exist. Hence my confident assertion that an *omniscient* agent like God knows the future course of whatever physically necessitated events there are. I employ the somewhat cautious form of words 'whatever there are' in order to allow for the possibility that not all physical events are necessitated. It is quite possible that God did not physically necessitate the whole system but left parts of it, or certain functions of it, in a state of randomness (a concept which I take to be intuitively clear or explicable elsewhere).

The notion of 'being able to act otherwise if one so chooses' is, at one level, a clear and obvious condition of being a free and responsible agent. Obviously an agent literally forced to act by the physical constraints of his situation cannot exercise a choice to act otherwise and is not free. But at a deeper level the demand of freedom is that the choice itself should not be subject to physical necessitation. In cases where we suspect that the choice is subject to such necessitation, for example because we suspect that the person is under the influence of drugs or hypnotism or (much more dubiously) because we suspect that his upbringing or environment inhibits certain otherwise legitimate choice possibilities, in these cases we excuse such persons from (full) responsibility for their actions. Their choices were not *entirely* the expression of themselves as free agents. This is not to say that free choices have to be non-necessitated in the sense of being random. A random choice is not the choice of a free rational agent. It is, except when consciously undertaken by such a means as the toss of a coin, the act of a species of lunatic: that is to say, of one whose actions happen any old how, and not as the free expression of his character, of what he is in himself. So a free choice is one exercised in accordance with the character the person is. But it is also a choice which is felt to begin, and somehow does begin, in the person: in his own being the free agent is an autonomous initiator of his actions and *that* is what makes his choices free and responsible and not subject to physical necessitation so that even God cannot know what they will be.

I am fully aware that in the above paragraph I am at odds with a recent tradition of philosophy which argues that so long as an action is physically unconstrained and 'in character' then there is no need for the agent to be an autonomous initiator of his own choices. The view which I am advocating is expressed with typical clarity by Richard Taylor in his book *Metaphysics* published in 1963. He writes (p. 50):

> The only conception of action that accords with our data is one according to which men – and perhaps some other things too – are sometimes, but of course not always, self-determining beings; that is, beings which are sometimes the causes of their own behaviour. In the case of an action that is free, it must be such that it is caused by the agent who performs it, but such that no antecedent conditions were sufficient for his performing just that action. In the case of an action that is both free and rational, it must be such that the agent who performed it did so for some reason, but this reason cannot have been the cause of it. Now this conception fits what men take themselves to be; namely beings who act, or who are agents, rather than things that are merely acted upon . . .

Taylor goes on to point out that this view is not without difficulties, and I agree with him. Nevertheless, without arguing the matter at length here, I do think that something like this account of agent-freedom is required both by what we feel ourselves to be, and by what responsibility and accountability require us to be. We feel, in depth, that at least sometimes our choices are initiated by us as uncaused causes. *I*, like Faust, freely sign the bond. I am thus morally accountable to other men *and* to God (if he exists). But I would not be morally accountable to God if he had not freely allowed me to be an agent, able, sometimes, to choose without physical necessitation, and therefore able to do things which God did not know about in advance.

I now return to the dilemma that *either* human agents have free choices and God does not know what they will be *or* God has complete omniscience and human agents do not have free choices, thus absolving them from responsibility for what they do. In grappling with this, Christian theologians and philosophers have resorted to all manner of complex and implausible contortions in an effort to have it both ways – to say that God's omniscience extends to a knowledge of human actions *and* that such knowledge does not preclude human freedom and responsibility. I do not propose to follow their contortions here except for a brief look at one example.

It is sometimes said that God's knowledge is 'outside time', or held in an eternal 'now', so that our past, present and future are all simultaneously apparent to him.[7] Our choices really are free from physical necessitation in our time sequence, but they are already known to God because of the way he comprehends our time sequence.

The suggestion is unnecessary and obscure. With the exception of a few late phrases, one in John 8 : 58 but mostly in the Book of Revelations, the Bible uniformly speaks of God and of his relation to our world in terms which only make sense if man and God participate in the same reality of time and change: God's forgiveness operates from present back to past events and on into future situations; going out and preaching the gospel is a present instruction leading into the future; the Second Coming, the Day of General Resurrection, is unequivocally in the future . . . 'the Lord *will* descend from heaven . . .' (1 Thessalonians 4 : 16). Unlike its assumption that God is a unique, almighty, wise and invisible agent, the language of the Bible does not assume that God is 'timeless' or 'out of time'. These are notions which come into Christian theology from some of the less fortunate speculations of second-century Neoplatonism.[8]

'Timelessness' is, I would suggest, one of those deceptive concepts which at first seem able to convey some dim and mystical sense, and then acquire a verbal function in a metaphysical system without first being critically scrutinized. Very well, let us say God is timeless. This, we are told, means that our past, present and future is all one in his immutable (unchangeable) and eternal present. But because the notion of *some* time is irremovably conveyed by the words 'his . . . present', what is being said is that one time instant, an eternal now, for him, makes simultaneous all our time instants. But if, 'in the sight of eternity', all our time instants are simultaneous, then there really are no past and future instants of time. Our experience of time and change is an impossible illusion since really all things are at one time and are therefore motionless.[9] Such a conclusion would be at variance with every item of our experience and every category of our understanding. Yet it is the consequence of one of several possible theological accounts of timelessness.

You are apparently being asked to imagine or conceive successive events, not in a state of movement and progression, but somehow frozen and simultaneous. Perhaps it would be like seeing all the frames of a roll of cinema film set out in front of you at once. But they would not be perceived successively, or related in a before and after by the celluloid strips, because that would be to perceive them as a result of a temporal sequence. They are perceived simultaneously but without *any* temporal relation to each other. But you now see nothing *happening*. There is literally nothing before or after anything else, just an eternally static exhibit, and if *all* events were presented in this way, there would be no events: everything would just exist, stuck and immutable, and what would have to count as knowledge would be similarly static. So the concept 'timelessness' not only contradicts and makes unreal our categories of time and motion, but also makes it logically impossible for the timeless percipient to conceptualize change: if God is timeless in this sense he could not even *understand* us, let alone make us free agents or bring about temporal events.

I do not wish to suggest that the account of timelessness I am criticizing is the only one available or even that it is the best. But I do want to suggest that it is typical in throwing up peculiar and far-fetched results which even if coherent are unlikely to be persuasive. Little wonder that some of the Fallen Angels were tormented with attempts to reconcile foreknowledge and freedom!

The philosophically occult notion of a timeless God is typical of the labyrinthine extremities to which theology has sometimes gone in its efforts to combine God's foreknowledge with human responsibility and freedom. But there are at least two simpler expedients: one corresponding to each of the horns of the dilemma.

What I might call the social democratic view concedes that once God had created genuinely free agents distinct from himself, it was no longer logically possible for him to know the outcome of their choices with certainty because *that* knowledge was precisely what he had given away in allowing such agents choices which were not physically necessitated by past events. By his own free concession, however shrewd and well-informed his predictions, we *could* surprise him. Now although something like the social democratic view has been adopted by a number of theologians,[10] it has not found the same favour as the alternative which ultimately issues in the baleful doctrine of predestination. The alternative, let us call it the justified sinner view, accepts that God's omniscience extends to our choices. Hence follows the doctrine of predestination and election: the theology which accepts that God knew, in the strong sense of infallibly decided, who were to be the Elect and who the Damned 'before the foundations of the world were laid'.[11] I call this 'the justified sinner view' because carried to its logical conclusion it is just that. It excludes us from being significantly free agents and informs us that God has already chosen some and damned others in the light of his foreknowledge of our actions. It was James Hogg, 'The Ettrick Shepherd', a contemporary of Sir Walter Scott, who gave the logic of this theology its most horrific literary embodiment. In his solitary masterpiece *The Private Memoirs and Confessions of a Justified Sinner* there is a profoundly disturbing double view, by observers and from within the Justified Sinner, of what is ambiguously religious insanity or satanic possession. In one place the Sinner reasons perfectly in accordance with the belief that God really has an omniscience which includes all we do:

> The more I pondered on these things, the more I saw of the folly and inconsistency of ministers, in spending their lives, striving and re-monstrating with sinners, in order to induce them to do that which they had it not in their power to do. Seeing that God had from all eternity decided the fate of every individual that was to be born of woman, how vain was it in man to endeavour to save those whom their Maker had, by an unchangeable decree, doomed to destruction. I would not disbelieve the doctrine which the best of men had taught me, and towards which he made the whole of the Scriptures to bear, and yet it made the economy of the Christian world appear to me as an absolute contradiction.[12]

The Justified Sinner's reaction to an advocate of the social democratic view is also illuminating: 'And then he was alleging, and trying to prove from nature and reason, that no man ever was guilty of a sinful action, who might not have declined it had he so chosen! ... What horrible misconstructions!'[13]

The reader may conclude that, although it impinges on secular philosophical questions about responsibility and predictability, the problem of reconciling God's omniscience with man's sense of significant freedom is more properly a private theological dispute than a philosophical problem which should influence reasonable belief. I agree, but it is a theological dispute which is capable of leading into such a thicket of absurdities that it sheds doubt upon the enterprise which gives rise to it. The theist, in order to hold on to his belief, has to choose (perhaps freely) between the social democratic view about which he tends to be uneasy because it admits such a possibility as Satan taking God by surprise, the justified sinner view with its unacceptable and, we feel, unrealistic consequences, and a variety of immensely complicated and highly improbable attempts to have it both ways.[14] More succinctly: either Satan has a chance, or God is unjust, or the believer is 'in wandering mazes lost'. The agnostic may well feel tempted to let him stay lost.

(iii) Miracles and Divine Acts

If the proverbial man in the street (perhaps now a person in a car?) thinks about miracles at all, he (it?) is inclined to ask whether there have ever been any; did they once happen in Palestine a long time ago; do they ever still happen? The theist – in this context particularly the committed Christian – may feel obliged to answer, or be enthusiastic about answering, 'yes' to all three questions. He may even, but this is less likely, regard his 'yes' as providing resounding evidence about the existence, character and purpose of God. The philosopher, on the other hand, is more inclined to ask what is *meant* by a miracle; and a consequence of one very common answer to his question can be that if a miracle has ever occurred no one will be able to know that it has. This consequence, together with other sceptical implications of the philosophical inquiry, can so fuel the doubts of the late-twentieth-century person concerning divine interventions that a request for belief in miracles can itself become almost an embarrassment to the theist.

A seminal definition of what is meant by a miracle is that given by David Hume (it is close to a reportive statement of the traditional religious concept): 'a transgression of a law of nature by a particular volition of the Deity, or by the interposition of some invisible agent'.[15] If we adjust

Hume's statement to take account of more recent philosophical and theological refinements, a statement which would now command reasonably wide assent is:

> *Miracle*: an event of religious significance, brought about by God or a god, or by some other visible or invisible rational agent with sufficient power, *either* in violation of the laws of nature (the 'violation concept') *or* as a striking coincidence within the laws of nature (the 'coincidence concept').

In the commentary which follows, I shall principally devote attention to the two concepts of miracle. It will become apparent that there is a general problem concerning the occurrence and identification of divine acts, whether these are classified as miracles, answers to prayers, or in any other way as particular acts of Providence.

The initial requirement, religious significance, is critically important. A pointless prodigy called into being by a magician is not even a candidate for being regarded as a miracle,[16] nor is an unexplained freak of nature occurring in a context which is religiously neutral. But the calling down of fire by Elijah to consume the sacrifice and establish the authority of God (1 Kings 18:20–40) did have religious significance, especially for the unfortunate priests of Baal; so did the raising of Lazarus from the dead by Jesus and, most important of all, so did the Resurrection itself. It is easy to see that these events, if they took place, had very considerable religious significance. It is more difficult to give a general characterization of what religious significance is. At its broadest, an event with religious significance will be one which confirms or illustrates a moral or metaphysical teaching within or in connection with a religion, or is at least clearly in accord with what we believe God's character to be.

An event is 'brought about by God or a god' if any explanation which can be given of the event would be essentially incomplete and unsatisfactory without reference to the agency of God or a god. Thus the turning of water into wine (John 2:1–11) may be inexplicable without reference to God as the agent which caused it. In a similar way any explanation of the carefully cut yew-hedge growing now in my garden, if it avoided reference to the purposeful activity of a moderately intelligent agent (me in this case), would be essentially incomplete. In more general terms: events are sometimes explicable by reference to natural processes, sometimes by reference to the free activity of agents. Miracles are events not explicable by reference to natural processes, and of such a character that no exercise of natural power by a known human or animal agent could bring them about; hence 'brought about by God or a god'.

The phrase 'by some other visible or invisible rational agent with sufficient power' is cumbersome and apparently superfluous. It allows for the theoretical possibility (which is of very little practical interest in a quest concerning the reasonableness of belief in God) that the spirit of a dead person, or an angel, or even an unusual corporeal being could, by itself, bring about what we would, on other grounds, want to call a miracle. The phrase also permits such a usage as 'Jesus worked a miracle'. This is normally taken to mean that Jesus invoked the power of God to work the miracle, but some people may wish to say that he himself alone was the active power and agent.

The violation concept: 'in violation of the laws of nature'; but what counts as a violation? I have already used the term 'law of nature' in association with notions of accurate prediction and nomic (i.e. law-like) generalization. Again informally, I would define a law of nature as a statement in the form of a nomic generalization about 'what happens in a regular and predictable way'.[17] A particular observed event is predictable – subject to physical necessitation – if it falls under the working of a law of nature which has not been amended *ad hoc* in order to include the particular event in question. But a particular observed event will be unpredictable – *not* subject to physical necessitation – if it comes under any one of three possible headings: if it is the result of activity within the natural powers of such free agents as human beings (it may be a well-informed probability that I will choose to do X rather than Y, but my free choice makes it logically impossible for you to be certain that I shall do X); *or* if it is random in the sense of being one of a class of events which are recognized to be in principle unpredictable (like the history of the movement and position of a particular electron); *or* if it is outside the scope of any extant statement of the laws of nature. Now an unpredictable event which is a violation of the laws of nature will be one which is (a) not the result of the natural powers of a known free agent, (b) not random, (c) not within range of any extant statement of the laws of nature, and also (d), outside the range of any possible restatement of the laws of nature. When such an event has religious significance and is therefore attributed to the agency of God or a god, then it will satisfy the violation concept of miracle. Let us call such events *violation miracles*.

But something is wrong with condition (d). Why should an event not within the range of any extant statement of the laws of nature be taken to be outside the range of any possible restatement of those laws? The observation that Mercury was not precisely where it should have been according to Newtonian calculations on successive perihelions (the point in a planet's orbit when it is nearest the sun) was not an indication that Mercury was outside the range of any possible restatement of the laws of nature. It was an indication that the extant laws were not quite right, i.e. it was an instance which falsified the extant laws (the further distinction between falsifying and modifying instances need not concern us). So how should we distinguish between an event which violates and an event which falsifies a law of nature? One suggestion is that a law of nature will be violated by a counter-instance which is not experimentally repeatable. The observable perihelions of Mercury repeat themselves, and very unexpected experimental results such as the Michelson-Morley experiment of 1881 (concerning the velocity of light in the supposed interplanetary aether) can be repeated. But the turning of water into wine (taking St John's account to be a factual report rather than a symbolic story) cannot be repeated. But again this will not quite do. All we are completely justified in saying is that we have not been able to repeat it. It may indeed be experimentally unrepeatable, but it is just possible that no one has yet been able to reassemble all the natural conditions which would constitute repeating the 'experiment'.

A useful complementary distinction between an event which violates, and an event which falsifies, a natural law is suggested by Swinburne among others. It amounts to saying that we are justified in taking an event to be a violation of the laws of nature if it is inconsistent, not just with an isolated or minor area of what we take to be the laws of nature, but with pretty well our whole scheme of things: 'We have to some extent good evidence about what are the laws of nature, and some of them are so well established and account for so many data that any modification to them which we could suggest to account for the odd counter-instance would be so clumsy and *ad hoc* as to upset the whole structure of science.'[18] Thus, for example, it was a worry to physicists and astronomers to find that Mercury was turning up in not quite the expected place. But the observation was not a shock to *all* the sciences as well as to our commonsense faith that certain things just cannot happen. On the other hand that a person who was truly a man should go through the post-mortem processes for forty-eight hours and then be alive in his physically ascertainable body is not only at variance with all ordinary experience; it is a violation of virtually all that is known in the biological sciences.

In summary, a strong candidate for an event which would satisfy the violation concept of miracle would be one (a) not within the natural powers of a known free agent, (b) not within an area which we recognize to be subject to randomness, (c) not experimentally repeatable, (d) inconsistent with a wide area of the extant laws of nature and of any thinkable reconstruction of them, (e) at variance with all common experience of the world, and (f) occurring in a context which gives the event religious significance.

Again, without raising any question about the historical precision of the records, the Resurrection would be a supremely suitable candidate for a violation miracle inasmuch as it satisfies in full all the criteria (a) to (f). On the other hand accounts of faith healings are much weaker candidates. There is evidence that healing may sometimes be within the powers of some agents and hence criteria (c) and (e) are not clearly satisfied. Our ignorance concerns the manner of operation and the nature of the power the faith healer has, and the suspicion must be, not that the laws of nature are being violated, but that some as yet unformulated laws are operating.

It will, of course, remain possible for the determined sceptic to say that an event which strongly satisfies all the criteria for a violation miracle is simply evidence that we have not got *all* the laws of nature set out correctly: don't attribute it to a supernatural agent, go back to the drawing board! But I think that even the most sceptically-minded will have their scepticism stretched to the point of incredulity by such a let-out. The substantial doubt concerning an event which strongly satisfied criteria (a) to (e) is not that after all at some time it might be shown to fail (d), but rather, *did it really happen?*

In his famous chapter on miracles, from which I earlier quoted the definition, the main line of Hume's argument is to the effect that when an event is reported which is unusual enough to satisfy such conditions as (a) to (f) above (Hume attends mostly to (d) and (e)), then if you are wise – if you proportion your belief to the evidence – you will require much more and much stronger evidence than when an ordinary event is reported. In short, the more improbable the event, the more you will look suspiciously at the evidence.

I have examined Hume's argument in considerable detail elsewhere.[19] There is much to agree with in it. In particular Hume is quite right to say that if I read or am told that real water has been directly altered into real wine, that genuinely dead men have become alive again, or that a man has successfully fed five thousand people and finished up with more leavings than there was food to start with, then I would subject such reports to a far more critical survey than when I read in Caesar's own account of an unexpected attack on his troops by the British 'the outposts stationed before the gates reported to Caesar that a cloud of dust, greater than occasion warranted, could be distinctly seen in the direction taken by the legion'.

Hume's argument is mainly directed at *reports* of miracles (i.e. at the form in which the evidence for miracles is presented to most people) but his doubts can be extended to include the evidence of my own experience. If I had seen the cloud of dust, I would have unhesitatingly reported it afterwards and expected to be believed. Dust is common enough, and large groups of men will put plenty up into the air in the right conditions (55 B.C. must have been a fine summer in South Britain). But if I tasted water, and then was offered a glass of such water *and it was wine*, what would I think afterwards? I *might* accept at face value what had apparently happened. I would be much more likely, as a critical and usually cautious person, to wonder if I had been tricked. Was it chemically wine? Had I really been attending properly? Perhaps I was caught up in the emotional circumstances of the moment? Well, anyway, no one will believe me afterwards!

The point is that, conceptual difficulties in the criteria for a violation miracle apart, the more strongly the candidate miracle satisfies all the criteria, the more sceptical, and the more justifiably sceptical, we become about whether the event ever happened at all, and this, much more than the conceptual difficulties, accounts for the sort of lay scepticism about violation miracles which I attributed at the start of the discussion to the average person in a car. It is not that unrepeatable violations of natural law cannot happen, or that it is always possible to defer identifying an event as one. It is rather that if there really were such a law-violating event, we could not realistically expect others to believe us when we told them, nor, retrospectively, could we give uncritical assent even to the remembered evidence of our own senses.

A problem of a very different type holds for what I have called the *coincidence concept*: 'a striking coincidence within the laws of nature'. It is easy enough in these cases to admit what happened. The problem is to find any place for an act of God.

R. F. Holland's example[20] is well chosen and frequently cited: an express train stops a few feet from a child whose toy motor car has become stuck on a level crossing. The train stops because the driver fainted from medical causes whose origins were totally unconnected with the child and 'the brakes were applied automatically as his hand ceased to exert pressure on the control lever . . . The mother thanks God for the miracle which she never ceases to think of as such even when she learns the real manner in which the train stopped.' For brevity I shall refer to cases of this sort as *coincidence miracles*. They are obviously coincidences, but in order to be thought of as miracles, they must have religious significance. What is it for a coincidence to have religious significance?

In attempting to answer this question it might seem that coincidences should be divided into two sorts: those in which the significance is given by the specifically religious context (e.g. a preacher calls for a sign of God's wrath at an unjust man and a fork of lightning strikes the man, killing him), and those in which the significance comes from the event being strikingly in keeping with the known or supposed character of the deity although it takes place in a non-religious context (e.g. Holland's train, or, more obscurely because of the polytheism involved, the python which seized Laocoön, in Virgil's story, outside Troy before the walls were breached). But while it may be more easy (for some people) to 'see' the hand of God in the specifically religious context, what is being 'seen' is in both cases the same: namely, an improbable event strikingly consistent with what a god or God might have brought about given the nature which we suppose him to have. ('Improbable' because without this qualification the coincidence would not be notable and to 'see' in it the hand of God would not be to see it as a miracle but to read all and any events equally as acts of God.)

It is often said that 'If an event is explainable on purely natural grounds then this is sufficient to show that it is not a miracle. And sometimes the believer will have to revise his opinion as to whether or not an event is miraculous in the light of later discoveries and explanations.'[21] But in the light of the two concepts of miracle this needs to be modified. An event once thought of as a violation miracle may be reclassified as a coincidence miracle by the believer. For example, if it were discovered that the darkness at the sixth to ninth hour (Matthew 27:45) could be explained as an eclipse, the event might still be thought of as a remarkable coincidence with profound religious significance although no longer a violation miracle. The difficulty here is that regarded in this way the

miracle has ceased to be resounding evidence for the existence or character of a god capable of producing it and has become instead the sort of
action which would be characteristic of a certain sort of god if there were
one. It is no longer that the agency of an invisible being is the only and
obvious answer to the question how the event took place, but that the
agency of an invisible being appears to be a possible and additional way
of viewing an event which is already fully accounted for as part of the
orderly course of nature. The event is no longer an act of god whether
you like it or not as a violation miracle would be. A coincidence miracle
is an act of god if you choose to see it that way. What might justify
seeing a coincidence as an act of god?

Suppose the event starts its life as a coincidence without a specifically
religious context (like Holland's railway train). To be seen as a miracle it
must be in character with the sort of god believed in. Thus in Christianity,
the event would be *in character* with God if the train stopped before it
reached the child. If the train stopped on top of him, far from seeing in it
an act of God, the Christian might see in it the agency of a Satanic spirit
or one of those puzzling tragedies which contribute to the problem of evil.
The secular man would see in it nothing but good or bad luck: sometimes
things turn out remarkably well, sometimes remarkably badly, and that's
just the way the world is. The same considerations apply to a coincidence
(e.g. an eclipse at the Crucifixion) within a specifically religious context
except that the coincidence may now seem altogether too strange to be
subject to the same sceptical nonchalance.

But in calling a coincidence a miracle, the religious man may well
want to say more than: seen through his eyes, with his beliefs, it seemed
like a miracle to him. He may want to say it would not have happened
but for God. God contrived it in the way in which I contrive the meeting
of two friends, not in the way in which two friends happen to meet
without the design of themselves or of other persons. Now in order to say
this it must be possible to give a coherent account of what it would
actually be for God to *act* in a coincidence rather than just be 'seen' in it.

One possibility is that in tracing the antecedent history of a religiously
significant coincidence one would come across a physically necessitating
event which was itself an obscured violation miracle. But where do we
find evidence for this? Where do we even start looking for the evidence?
In the case of Holland's train, I am at a loss. But take another example: in
the plagues of Egypt one might give an account of the plague of boils
starting with the mutation of a virus and then of someone drinking Nile

water and so on. If the plague was a *miraculous* coincidence, somewhere in the account room must be left to say: at *this* stage nothing more of interest would have happened had it not been for *this* event which is a violation of the laws of nature of the sort which must be attributed to the agency of God (i.e. is not 'merely random' and is not a candidate for a falsifying instance of a law etc.). But of what event in the history of the plague could it be said: *this* could only be the work of God? Of the mutation? Of the inclination of the man to drink that particular mouthful of dirty water and no other? But an inclination to drink is in no way peculiar for a human being and the mutation may either be accepted as part of the 'merely random' in nature (like the direction in which an electron leaves a nucleus) or (possibly) explained in terms of solar radiations, themselves explainable in terms of sunspots, and so on. My point is that in seeking to explain a natural coincidence there is no reason to suppose that at any stage we will come across a violation of natural law at which point God's responsibility displays itself. If overt violation miracles are all but incredible, it seems a thin line of defence to presume them to be where we cannot identify them at all.

Alternatively it might be said that the whole course and working of nature was originally set in motion by a God with the foreknowledge that at certain stages coincidences of events would take place which would lead some people (e.g. the child's mother in Holland's example or the witness at the Crucifixion) to see in them the special activity of God. But if this were so, then men would be deceived in thinking of special events as brought about by God and revealing his nature and purpose because all that happens would equally be brought about by him. A coincidence miracle would no more or less be brought about by God than would a shower of rain over an empty sea: *everything* would be a miracle.

Nevertheless the mother of the saved child, still opting for the miracle rather than the secular coincidence, may insist that the event is an act of God in just this sense: it was divinely preordained within the orderly concourse of things that her child should be saved. This is in keeping with the moral nature of God and it is appropriate to give thanks. But this insistence would then face the general challenge: are morally good coincidences more conspicuous and numerous than morally disastrous coincidences of the type: the train came to rest on the child (or just passed nonchalantly over him)? Clearly if the numbers or strength of morally advantageous coincidences exceed coincidences at variance with the character we suppose God to have, then there might be evidence of his general agency in designing the world. But in the absence of such evidence one may well again conclude with Hume 'That the original source of all things . . . has no more regard to good above ill than to heat above cold.'

There is another possibility: that in a miraculous coincidence God arranges things in the way in which I might arrange the meeting of two friends or in which I might arrange stones and mortar to divert a stream of water when it floods. This does not imply that I arranged the whole scheme of things nor does it imply any violation of the laws of nature at any stage. Could God (or any god) act in a coincidence in this way? The difficulty is that if he did it would probably look like a violation miracle. The movement of, say, a coffin from A to B is not mysterious if it is known that someone moved it, but if it *just moved* (as it would presumably look if a god moved it) it would appear as an event contrary to the laws of nature. In reported coincidental miracles even of the most awesome type (e.g. the darkness at the sixth hour) there appears to be no place for the sort of violations (or at least gaps in its antecedent history) we would look for and expect if a mighty and invisible agent (in some respects akin to a human agent) had been at work. This difficulty is decisive in coincidences whose histories involve only inert nature (floods, thunderbolts, earthquakes, rainstorms, etc.); less decisive in events whose histories involve living things. There is no philosophical absurdity in the supposition that Juno guided the python with invisible hands towards Laocoön and it might be that human inclination is such that it can sometimes be guided without the guide being noticed: 'I could have gone the usual way but I suddenly felt like taking a short cut home in my car which avoided the blind corner where the landslip had taken place.' It will, however, be noticed that we have not explained how God can act in the majority of coincidence miracles without either turning them into obscured versions of violation miracles (which we have no reason to suppose that they are) or turning everything that happens into an act of God which does away with any *particular* act of Providence.

To sum up: we have a strong inclination to regard violation miracles with scepticism. It is always theoretically possible to hold that they will be subsumed within some better or more complete statement of natural law; when this position is at its weakest because the purported miracle strongly satisfies all the criteria for the violation concept, sceptical doubts about the actual occurrence of the event are rightly at their highest. With coincidence miracles the converse holds. There is usually little difficulty in accepting evidence that the coincidence took place, but the only criterion being applied, religious significance, is weak and optional. Attempts to strengthen it by finding a place for a particular act of God in the history of the coincidence are generally unconvincing. Moreover coincidences which are strikingly consistent with the supposed concerns or nature of God have to be set against coincidences which are strikingly inconsistent.

A consequence of these conclusions is that the evidential value put upon miracles by the theist has changed. In eighteenth-century apologetics and earlier, almost to the beginning of the Christian era, miracles were generally regarded as resounding evidence for the authenticity of the Christian gospel. They were events which *did* happen, and which could not have happened without divine intervention. The position now, appeals to the truth of the Resurrection apart (see footnote on p. 147), tends to be that miracles are consistent with what we might expect if there were a god of a certain sort. It is evident that 'could not have happened if there is no God' is very different from 'could happen if there is a God': the latter is merely an apology for asking people to believe the improbability of a miracle; the former is a proof of God's existence and activity. In this difference we can see how secular scepticism has reduced a significant proof of God's existence to a slightly embarrassing obstacle to belief.

It will be observed that all I have said about acts of God which are miracles applies also to most acts of God which are answers to prayer. Without following out logical conundrums arising from trying to combine God's foreknowledge of physically necessitated events with answers to my prayer that the physically necessitated event will not be as God always knew it would be, without following that path to vexation, it will be seen that an answer to prayer, where the prayer is a petition that something will or will not happen, can only take four forms. One is as an intervention by means of a violation miracle. The second is by means of a coincidence miracle. The third is by divine direction of random events. The fourth is by divine direction of or influence in a person's mind (the mind of the one praying or the one prayed about). The first two are subject to what has already been said. The third is highly restrictive because of the remoteness from normal human concerns of areas where randomness is recognized. The fourth is suspect because it brings back worries about the divine puppet-master. The implications of these observations cannot be followed here. I mention them merely to underline that scepticism concerning miracles is likely to spill over to other particular acts of Providence.

The annoying thing is that having written the three sections of this chapter, I do not feel I have solved anything. But that is the whole point. I have been examining problems which arise *within* theistic belief. One, the problem of evil, is almost insoluble on any coherent theistic view. Another, the problem of responsibility, is a hideous thicket for theologians which is largely of their own making. The last, miracles and particular acts of Providence, combines conceptual difficulties with scepticism about whether certain events took place as described.* I now turn to the limitations of atheism as a metaphysic of existence.

---

* I remarked above (p. 141) that the better an event satisfies the criteria for a violation miracle, the more dubious we are likely to be about whether in fact it ever happened. Scepticism with regard to the Resurrection of Christ is the most important case in question. The Resurrection is, and always has been, the crucial miracle for Christianity: 'if Christ be not risen, then is our preaching vain, and your faith is also vain' declares St Paul (1 Corinthians 15:14). But the evidence for the Resurrection consists in the reports of near-contemporaries and the early credence given to those reports. From the beginning, doubts have focused either upon the accuracy of the reports (this is what worried Thomas, John 20:25), or upon their interpretation (this is the way out for the Muslim, see the Koran, 'Women', verses 156–8). More recently, but still well before modern biblical criticism got into its Anglo-Germanic stride, the *reasons* for having doubts about the evidence had been thoroughly aired by some of the English deists. Writing in 1748, towards the end of the controversy they provoked, Hume gave an incisive and abiding expression to their scepticism in the chapter 'Of Miracles', His discussion of evidence is for the most part carried on in very general terms and has to be read carefully in order to discern the extent to which it is really directed at the Resurrection story itself, but the crucial point for Hume (and it remains the same for us) is whether the evidence for the Resurrection is good enough to persuade a reasonable person that an event *as strange as that* and *with the significance attached to it* could have taken place. Clearly Hume thinks the evidence is not good enough. In this he is probably the forerunner of much tacit modern scepticism which exists quite apart from philosophical worries about the concept of miracle. But my point above is that scepticism about the evidence is at its strongest when the requirements for a violation miracle are best satisfied. In the light of this, the resounding sarcasm of Hume's conclusion is unsurprising: 'So that, upon the whole, we may conclude, that the Christian Religion not only was at first attended with miracles, but even at this day cannot be believed by any reasonable person without one.'

7 THE LIMITATIONS OF ATHEISM

We saw in chapter five that there are reasons for concluding that the root concept of God in theistic religions may be incoherent. The refinements of analytic philosophy are not the leading chit-chat of the bus queue or the coffee table, but at least in this matter the conventional scientific wisdom of the modern world seems to accord vaguely with the findings of the philosophers. Belief in God is somehow muddled or wishful thinking. It is pre-scientific or overtaken by more relevant knowledge. It is an embarrassing anthropocentric myth surviving from the infancy of mankind because we lack the vigour to deny it outright. The evangelical fervour of the Marxist urges mankind in a similarly secular direction; to plunder Nietzsche's slogan for another purpose – God is dead now that man (at least Communist Party Man) has taken control of his own (and other people's) destiny through the direction of society.

Even the believer, but there is nothing distinctively modern in this, can be shaken in his faith by the appearance that his God may have no concern with the suffering of individuals. So atheism, often politely muted as agnosticism or disguised as sheer indifference (except at birth, marriage, and of course death), is the implicit philosophy of our time. Is it a philosophy free from difficulties? I think not. Moreover the difficulties apply not only to the full-blown classical atheism I described in chapter three, and to its modern secular–scientific developments, but also to what I have called personalist reappraisals of theism which seek to retain the language of theism while evacuating the language of all reference to 'incredible' realities which lie beyond the actual feelings, needs and social commitments of mankind.

In this chapter I shall look principally at two difficulties for atheism. Whether they are fundamental objections or merely limitations will appear later. One concerns the status of morality. The other, and more serious, concerns a metaphysical and utilitarian failure of atheism. Before I turn to these it will, however, be useful to indicate some of the confused and confusing overlaps of morality and religion.

(i) *Morality and Religion*

It is evident that a significant part of almost all religions is concerned with conduct: with what men and women should and should not *do* (or even think of doing). It is almost equally evident that rules of moral conduct are frequently observed and enforced without any clear reference to religious belief. From these contrasting observations, both of which are correct, arise two strikingly different attitudes to morality. One regards morality as depending upon religion to such an extent that destruction of religious belief would at best leave morality without any foundations and at worst would lead to a world in which anything was permitted. The other regards morality as autonomous: something which exists as a coherent and justifiable entity quite apart from religious belief, although religion will probably be admitted at the end of the story either as a useful auxiliary to the secular morality (when the religious injunctions are seen to be the same as, or to support, the secular moral code) or as a useless or even mischievous source of what David Hume called 'frivolous species of merit' (when the religious injunctions have no co-relative in the secular morality or actually contradict the rules of the secular morality).

If I ask which of these two attitudes is closer to the truth, I am asking the complex question: how are religion and morality actually related? Among other possibilities, this may be answered in terms of an *historical, logical* or *motivational* relationship. Let us look at each of these, paying particular attention to the second.

The *historical* associations of morality and religion are so strong and obvious that one would be forgiven for concluding that the two are, *de facto*, inseparable in any real-life situation. Not only, for example, do the Ten Commandments contain the best known set of moral laws in the history of the Western world, but the books of the Old and New Testaments, as well as many of the chapters of the Koran, abound with recognizably moral precepts and rules, as well as with merely ritualistic instructions. Nor was the case significantly different in Pagan religion, where what was pious and what was right were virtually synonymous.[1]

The historical influence of religion upon morality, particularly in theistic culture, is probably the most significant single factor which gives rise to the assumption that morality somehow 'depends upon' religion in the sense that any valid morality has to be derived from religious belief. This *logical relation* of derivability is, however, far from clear. For one thing the derivability might hold in reverse. Religion may depend upon morality. Taking this possibility into account, the relation of derivability between morality and religion could hold: (a) if the terms and concepts of ethics ('evil', 'good', 'duty', etc.) had to be defined by reference to religious concepts ('God', 'divine will', etc.), or *vice versa*; (b) if moral rules or precepts ('keep promises', 'love your neighbour', etc.) had to be derived from religious statements ('God is merciful', etc.), or *vice versa*.

(a) Among recent philosophers, and to a somewhat lesser extent among theologians, there seems to be a measure of agreement to the effect that religious concepts are in fact sufficiently independent of ethical concepts for both religion and morality to exist without either subsuming the other. Apart from possible commonsense observation, the reasons for this conclusion lie mainly in consideration of what is usually called the 'Euthyphro Dilemma'. Plato (*c.* 428–348 B.C.) put the dilemma into the mouth of Socrates thus: 'The point which I should first wish to understand is whether the pious or holy is beloved by [all] the gods because it is holy, or holy because it is beloved by [all] the gods' (*Euthyphro*, 10a). Socrates opts (quite emphatically by his unemphatic standards) for the first horn of the dilemma. According to this view, religious concepts do not *define* ethical concepts. They *affirm*, at least in the sort of religion with which we are generally familiar, or *further reveal* what is involved in the ethical concepts. For example: we recognize, or discover, or have revealed to us, the highly significant fact that God is good. We do not have to discover what God is in order to find out for the first time what is meant by 'good'. From this it follows that *some* concept of good is logically independent of and prior to the discovery of God's character, and a similar conclusion applies to other ethical concepts such as 'bad', 'duty' and 'ought'. I emphasize *some* concept of good, because it remains open to anyone committed to the moral importance of religion to say that while human beings first (historically) asserted the goodness of God in terms of, say, tribal customs and values which were the archetypal moral concepts, nevertheless, subsequently, those moral concepts were greatly clarified and enhanced by particular revelations of God's moral nature. To which the secular moralist could retort that such clarifications and enhancements had in their turn to undergo the humanizing influence of many hundreds of years of social and personal experience before we could attain the sophisticated hybrid moral concepts of today's world.

On the other hand, if the second horn of the dilemma is chosen, the meaning of the word 'good' will be defined in terms of what God is, and will have no legitimate use or meaning prior to that discovery. Furthermore, the sentence 'God is good' will no longer commend, praise or inform. It will simply affirm analytically that God is what he is. But since what God is defines what is good, and since 'illegitimate' senses of the word 'good' are likely to co-exist with the religious sense, the way will be open for a divorce between 'good' thus defined by reference to God, and 'good' as defined by the non-believer by reference to some secular norm, human welfare, for example. At best such definitions might overlap in large measure so that the same characteristics were valued as good in the religious and secular senses. But at worst there could be divergent and competing moral orders: the religious, in which the concepts were defined by reference to God; and the secular, in which the concepts were defined by the needs of mankind (or whatever). Of these two possibilities the latter has generally held in the history of theistic religions. When it is joined by the wish of the believer to *inform* the world that his God is good, just, merciful, etc. in senses of those words which the secular world can understand in something like its own terms, we have the main reasons why even the believer has generally preferred the first horn of the Euthyphro Dilemma. The second horn can in the last resort only be made credible by the assumption (all too readily assumed) that although God's will *defines* the concept 'good', nevertheless the most sensitive and sophisticated secular concepts of goodness just happen to cover, or can be coaxed into covering, much the same activities as the religious concept.

(b) Similar comments apply to the suggestion that moral rules and precepts must be derivable from religious statements. It now seems clearly false to say that there could be no moral rules independently of religious propositions: 'you shall not steal' is invested with the fear of the Lord God in Exodus 20:15, but it is inconceivable that independently of that revelation human societies could not have recognized (and had not already recognized) the usefulness of discouraging stealing, and hence could not have formulated and enforced a moral prohibition of it. 'You shall keep your promise' is not one of the Ten Commandments although promise-keeping is clearly highly valued in the Old and New Testaments. But again it seems to us ludicrous to suppose that in the absence of its relation to the Covenant of the Lord no such moral rule could ever have evolved from recognition of what is convenient in social communities and what is useful between individual persons.*

But if the independence of certain moral rules from religious sources is as obvious as I am suggesting, why has it usually been regarded as a matter of such significance that 'You shall not steal' should be part of the Law delivered by God amid the thick darkness of Mount Sinai? The answer, I think, is not that, after all, the existence of such a rule *depends* upon the Sinai revelation, but that such a revelation gives the rule a force and *authority* over individuals far exceeding anything which could be attained by humanistic recognition of its advantages. The revelation makes what is otherwise a socially useful convention into a *commandment* for such as believe in the revelation. I shall return to the question of authority in the second section of this chapter, but at present it is sufficient to note that additional authority given to a moral rule by a religion is not the same as the rule depending upon the religion for its existence. The authority which a rule has and the motives and reasons which an individual may have for observing it are one thing; the valid existence of the rule – the usefulness to society and to individuals of what it enjoins – is another.

In a real-world situation in which secular morality can and does exist independently of any religion which itself involves a morality, any one of four situations could hold. (a) The demands of the religious and the secular morality coincide for all practical purposes. (b) The demands of the religious morality include, but go beyond, the demands of the secular morality: as when the latter forbids murder while the former adds that you should not even feel anger against someone who harms you. (c) The demands of secular morality go beyond those of the religious morality: as when Shelley's Prometheus suddenly cries in *defiance* of God, 'I wish no

---

* I take it to be true that it seems to *most* of us that moral rules can and do exist and are enforced independently of their relation to the will of God. But not all of us will take this view even now, and at an earlier period the dominant strand of Christian moral philosophy took a quite different one. Thus George Berkeley in *Passive Obedience* (1712), section 71, clearly regarded divine law-giving as a necessary part of morality, and in the previous century John Milton in *Christian Doctrine* is even more emphatic: 'If there were no God there would be no distinction between right and wrong; the estate of virtue and vice would entirely depend on the blind opinion of men . . . unless conscience or right reason did from time to time convince every one, however unwillingly, of the existence of God . . .' My points in the text are that as a matter of fact most of us do not now take this view, and that as a matter of the right understanding of the relations of morality and religion it is a mistaken view whenever it is held.

living thing to suffer pain.'[2] (d) The demands of religious and secular morality diverge, even to the extent of contradicting one another: as when the secular morality encourages or is indifferent to 'artificial' methods of contraception, while the religious morality regards such methods as a moral depravity.

It is in large measure the excessive attention which institutional religion has focused upon (b) which is responsible for the suspicion that when secular and religious moralities diverge (as in (d)) it will always be in the direction of permissiveness or corruption in the secular morality. The secular morality can permit 'wrongs' – abortion, lustful thoughts, etc. – which the religion forbids, or the secular morality can acquire anti-humanitarian characteristics of the sort seen in Stalinist Russia, or can be corrupted by political or social dogma in a way which the religious morality would have the authority to resist. But we should observe here what will have to be said again later: that the very wording of such criticisms implies the existence and force of some non-religious morality X by the standards of which it can be seen that religious morality is in some sense *better* or more effective than secular morality. But what is this morality X? I shall argue later that it has something to do with what are judged to be the best interests of humanity (in some sense of 'best' yet to be explained). At this stage I will simply say that covert appeal to a morality X lying behind actual religious or secular moralities is yet another indication that the first horn of the Euthyphro Dilemma is correct, namely, that what is good is beloved by the gods because it is good: morality is independent of, and logically prior to, the moral claims of religion.

I have so far been considering the logical relation between morality and religion in the form of morality being derived from, or depending upon, religion; but Kant and certain other writers have argued that the relationship holds in various ways in reverse: religion depends upon or is derived from morality.

In the *Critique of Practical Reason* (1788)[3] Kant argued that the greatest good for man is the combination of perfect moral righteousness *and* happiness. Since the former does not guarantee the latter in this world, therefore man's greatest good necessitates immortality. Such immortality is an inseparable practical postulate of an unconditionally valid moral law and, according to Kant, the moral law *is* unconditionally valid. A second practical postulate is therefore the existence of a God able to provide such an immortality. Religion thus springs from morality and is the recognition of all duties as divine commands. The argument does not feel right, but what is wrong with it? Picking up a hint of C. D. Broad's:[4] the desirability of man's greatest good as his ideal or goal does not entail the actual realizability of his greatest good. My striving to bring about a perfect garden in competition with greenfly, slugs, wind, frost and my own occasional folly, in no way requires the actual existence of any perfect garden. Similarly, striving for moral rectitude and happiness does not necessitate an actual achievement of both or either in perfection, and if Kant's first 'postulate of practical reason', immortality, is not necessitated by the nature of morality, then neither is his second, the existence of God. But further, if, as seems likely, we do not fully accept Kant's account of morality as an unconditional law valid in virtue of its form, but look for its sources in, for example, the convenience and ease of social relationships, then it is simply absurd to use morality as the premises upon which to build the actual existence of that most awesome of all entities, God. *We don't think like that about morality* is all we really need to say here.

Perhaps Kant's derivation of religion from morality, combining as it does a peculiar ontological status for the moral law with an unexpected argument for the existence of God, is unlikely to find many advocates in the late twentieth century. But a more recent attempt to make the meaning of religious statements depend upon moral statements has found some favour. In his oft quoted lecture 'An Empiricist's View of the Nature of Religious Belief'[5] R. B. Braithwaite argued that 'the primary use of religious assertions is to announce allegiance to a set of moral principles: without such allegiance there is no "true religion" '.[6] The trouble with reading the relationship of derivability in this way is that most theistic believers would reject it: religious belief is not merely a system of myths intended to commend certain ethical standards, and to represent it in such a way is an unhistorical travesty. Theistic belief is belief about the real existence of an intelligent agent which created and sustains the world, and to which individual human beings can relate. That such a belief may be false or meaningless is not a reason for interpreting it as an ethically influential myth – despite the fact that Braithwaite was writing in an era when logical positivism was still heaping semantic woe on religious language.

In the second section of this chapter I shall take it as established that there is (or are) valid secular moralities – usable moral concepts together with moral rules justified by reasons – which subsist independently of religion. I shall also take it that there are valid religious moralities which differ from secular moralities both in the authority which they claim and, to a greater or lesser extent, in the concepts which they employ and the moral commandments which they enjoin. I shall finally take it as admitted that most extant moralities are a hybrid of religious and secular influences in which conflicts must obviously arise when the religious or secular components pull in different ways over particular issues.

(ii) *Moral Gods and Godless Morals*

At the start I said that there were historical, logical and *motivational* relations between religion and morality. It is this last relationship which is most interesting in practical terms and which fuels Nietzsche's appalling dictum that if there is no God, anything would be permitted. It fuels this dictum because religious morality can be seen to provide very significant additional reasons (sometimes in the form of motives) for actually observing those important moral rules which are *de facto* common to both secular and religious moralities. If we follow J. L. Mackie [7] in saying that 'a ought to G' is roughly equivalent to 'There is a reason for a's G-ing' (together with 'there is something about the situation that sets up an expectation or presumption of a's G-ing'); then we can say that religious reasons or motives for doing G constitute what I shall call the *religious moral* obligation* for G-ing. But what are these distinctively religious motives or reasons which constitute an obligation for doing what is, *de facto*, anyway enjoined by secular morality for non-religious reasons?

There are, I believe, at least four elements in religious moral obligation. One is the belief that the existence of a righteous God will ensure ultimate moral justice. Innocent suffering *will* be rewarded in the end. The tabernacles of robbers *will* be cast down. It does not matter whether these ultimate vindications of morality are supposed to take place

---

* There are, of course, plenty of religious obligations which are not *moral* obligations, e.g., the orthodox Jew's obligation not to eat pork. What makes an obligation to do G, laid upon a believer as part of his religion, into a *moral* obligation to do G is that he would still encounter some sort of rule or obligation to do G apart from his religious belief. Thus, for example, 'you shall not bear false witness against your neighbour' is a religious *moral* obligation (perjury is also a serious secular offence); 'Pray to your Lord God and sacrifice to Him' is a religious *ritual* obligation (it has no validity or existence outside the religions in which the injunction occurs). In cases where it is unclear whether one has a ritual or moral obligation, e.g., 'abortion is forbidden', the status will have to be settled by a careful search of the *reasons* which are given for the alleged obligation: if some of them have a secular validity then we have a candidate for moral (rather than ritualistic) obligation.

eschatologically and in the next world or terrestrially and in this: in either case the influence on the believer will be towards doing good and avoiding evil in so far as he understands those concepts.

A second element is the belief that God, quite apart from any possible system of rewards and punishments, is some sort of ever-present loving person from whom nothing is hidden, to whom one is in fact responsible, and to whom one holds oneself responsible in such a way that to dishonour the responsibility is to suffer sin or separation.

A third belief implicit in much theistic religion is that the moral and other values which God embodies are rendered ultimate in the nature of things by that embodiment. Hence moral values are not a social or utilitarian convention subject to change and eventual extinction with mankind. They are an aspect of the creator. They are a permanent and ultimate part of things, even if our application and understanding of the values is subject to temporal change and revision.

Finally, what the theist accepts as moral rules, or rather *commandments*, have for him the special authority of God. They are not merely socially convenient recipes for living together. They have the authority of the Most High: whether directly, as in Exodus 19 and 20, or indirectly, as in Matthew 5 and 6.

It will be clear without laboured underlining that anyone holding beliefs of this sort will be subject to a powerful combination of reasons and motives for doing what he understands to be good and avoiding evil. He believes in ultimate moral retribution, in moral responsibility to an ever-present loved and loving person, in a final reality which in some way has moral values, and in a uniquely authoritative source for his moral principles.

From his awareness of this religious obligation, the theist's position tends to develop as follows: those who do not believe in God cannot have the obligational grounds which he has for acting morally. Therefore either the godless man has no grounds, or, at the very best, his grounds cannot be as strong as the theist's, since they can only be the grounds common to theist and non-theist *minus* the distinctively theistic grounds. It is from this position that careless and over-hasty persons rush into the dictum: 'if there is no God, then anything is permitted', meaning, roughly, that if *they* lost their belief in God *they* would feel cut adrift from a commitment to observe *their* morality; and that from *their* point of view the atheist is merely deceiving himself if he imagines he is really other than already cut off from the sources of moral obligation.

But the atheist is likely to reply that he too recognizes and experiences reasons for doing G which constitute moral obligation of a sort which is distinct from, and independent of, the religious obligation felt by the theist. Let us call this non-religious obligation to morality *secular moral obligation*. What elements enter into it? Apart from political and local distortions (akin, perhaps, to the violent distortions of religious morality caused by special cults and factions) the elements seem to have some relation to the abiding needs of the sort of social animal man is. David Hume in the *Enquiry concerning the Principles of Morals* (1752) distinguished five:

Benevolence is that aspect of human nature which Hume supposes – rightly I think – to manifest itself in an immediate desire for the good of others irrespective of consideration of one's own good. Not always, not with all people, but at least sometimes 'Some particle of the dove is kneaded into our frame together with the elements of the wolf and the serpent.'

Self-interest, in the restricted sense about to be given, is the element in social behaviour which makes us behave in ways acceptable to other people out of a recognition that there are occasions when my interest in seeing that other people observe a moral code towards me can only be served by my observing a similar code towards them. It is the 'do-as-you-would-be-done-by' element in morality, and it is not the same as selfishness. When we appeal to our children 'how would you like it if someone did *that* to *you*?' we are not inviting the child to be selfish but, on the contrary, to behave in a manner which will invite back the sort of behaviour the child itself would like.

The good regard of others comprehends all those family and social pressures which make us not wish to appear in a certain character to those who know us. To be thought of as a thief, a liar, or a cheat is to be estranged from society.

The good regard of oneself: as Hume puts it, 'Inward peace of mind, consciousness of integrity, a satisfactory review of our own conduct; these are circumstances, very requisite to happiness . . .' And again 'the immediate feeling of benevolence and friendship, humanity and kindness . . .' is in itself agreeable.[8]

But, if all these fail, there remains (as with the religious man) the *threat of civil punishment* to deter one from those activities which society finds peculiarly pernicious.

However the questions will still be asked: Does secular moral obli-

gation thus analysed provide, in practice, a completely satisfactory alternative to religious moral obligation? If it does not provide a completely
satisfactory alternative, how satisfactory an alternative does it provide? I
shall try to evolve an answer to these questions by considering some
objections to the secular moral obligation I have just analysed with
Hume's assistance.

First of all it may be said that 'secular moral obligation' is merely a
euphemism for selfishness. Among the five elements in secular moral
obligation only the first (benevolence) escapes the possibility of reduction
to concern for one's own comfort – physical, social or mental – and such
self-concern is not what is *properly* understood as 'moral obligation'.
But suppose I give up time in order to go and baby-sit for someone and
my account of why I do this refers to: (a) I just feel glad to be able to
help; (b) they may do the same for me one day (and (a) and (b) are
independent); (c) no one will think the worse of me for helping; (d) I
would be uneasy in myself if I did not help, knowing my help to be
needed and appreciated. Having given these as my reasons, it does not
appear to me that I have thereby diminished the moral quality of my
action, *nor* that my moral stature is diminished, *nor* – perhaps more
importantly – that the beneficiary of my action would feel uneasy or
offended or patronized by what I did in a way in which he or she would
not feel uneasy, offended or patronized were my action done from some
more 'proper' sense of obligation.

However one among the elements in my secular moral obligation – the
self-interest – may still be held unacceptable. Why is this? Partly, I think,
from the mistaken judgement that an action self-interested in the sense
given must always be morally inferior to some other possible action. But
more soundly, because if self-interest (i.e. action seeking its own return
as a reward) were the *only* aspect of secular moral obligation acting, then
we would rightly suspect that in a life lived entirely and exclusively
according to such a principle, morally acceptable actions would only
appear episodically and fortuitously as far as other people were concerned. But, *ex hypothesi*, self-interest, in the restricted sense given, is
not the only element in secular moral obligation; and in a life in which it
were we would be dealing with an immoral man, i.e., one in whom the
force of secular moral obligation did not properly operate. In much the
same way the religious man whose moral conduct was *only* activated by
hope of ultimate reward or fear of ultimate punishment would not be
one in whom the force of religious moral obligation properly operated

(nor, according to recent liberal theologies, would he stand much chance of the reward he sought).

But surely there could be a difference, in some instances, between the practical force of religious and secular morality? Suppose I am drawing money from a bank, and among the mound of used fivers I later find a £100 note (it is Scotland where such notes exist!) sticking to one of them, obviously there in error. No one else has noticed. My benevolence is not in question since no *person* loses by my retaining the £100. The do-as-you-would-be-done-by self-interest has no apparent relevance, and the same applies to the good regard of others. Could the good regard of myself come into play? Possibly, but only if I have a very unusually delicate moral disposition. Finally, no punishable offence appears to be committed. And thus the story ends – for the atheist; for the religious man not so. 'You shall not steal' – not ever, not even accidentally from impersonal institutions. Now the crux is not so much whether this additional element in the situation for the religious man actually makes a difference on a particular occasion. The crux is that for him an additional element exists. *He* is subject to reasons and motives which *for him* influence or add to the secular moral obligation which he shares with the atheist.

A further – and perhaps most forceful – objection to the adequacy of secular morality is that the components of religious moral obligation, unlike the components of secular moral obligation, recognize values which are absolute, which are always sacrosanct, quite apart from what may prove to be the transitory judgements of social convenience. Of course *some* theists (particularly Christians) are willing to allow for an evolution of ethical refinements; for example, few Christians would now wish to institutionalize slavery as is done in the Mosaic Law, or to ignore it in the manner of Jesus or St Paul. Nevertheless, a significant and enduring aspect of religious morality seems to be that what is encouraged and what forbidden, at least in terms of values if not also in the day-to-day recipes for expressing those values, is claimed to be known and absolute. God *is* love, truth, justice, etc. Thus a commandment embodying these values, e.g., 'love thy neighbour', holds always, even if at one time it may involve humanistic compassion for the non-believer, while at another it may mean burning the heretic alive for the good of his immortal soul. Now this means that when the theist claims that his moral values are not subject to variation under social or political pressure, his claim may be true, and yet those values are still able to be honestly expressed in apparently inconsistent actions. It is this possibility which, on the one hand, weakens the theist's claim that, for example, he would *never* have countenanced the attempt to exterminate European Jews, and, on the other hand, erodes the apparent strength of his objection that secular moral obligations can be socially conditioned in disagreeable ways. Perhaps they can. But *in effect* this is also possible when absolute religious values are interpreted for the purpose of particular acts.

At the end of the first section of this chapter I explicitly assumed that secular and religious moralities can and do subsist independently of each other even if, in most historical and contemporary situations, they influence each other in producing a hybrid of *more or less* agreed morality. I have now indicated what I believe to be some of the most important elements involved in religious and secular moral obligations, and I have argued that some of the more obvious objections to secular morality are not as strong as they might at first appear. But the point which emerges is that when religious and secular moralities agree *rather more than less* about which things are wrong and which right, the religious morality *augments* the secular moral obligation. A person may be activated by all four elements of religious moral obligation *and* by all five elements of secular moral obligation on the same occasion. So the removal of religious moral obligation will leave secular moral obligation intact. But it will also put more weight onto, make more important, secular moral obligation since that will be all the obligation that remains. Now while this gives an answer to the immature nonsense which believes that if there is no God we shall all run amuck, it also administers a rebuff to any claim that secular moral obligation is a perfect substitute for religious moral obligation when the two moralities enjoin the same things. Why? Because if religious belief disappears, the motives and reasons which lie behind our sense of moral obligation are *at least* diminished to the extent to which the motives and reasons which constituted religious moral obligation have disappeared.

The point is grudgingly admitted by Bernard Williams and it is only by the assertion of an unargued sceptical prejudice that he eludes its force: 'If God existed, there might well be special, and acceptable, reasons for subscribing to morality. The trouble is that the attempt to formulate those reasons in better than the crudest outline runs into the impossibility of thinking coherently about God.'⁹ Hume makes the same point more graciously in a passage of remarkable self-criticism:

You conclude, that religious doctrines and reasonings *can* have no influence on life, because they *ought* to have no influence; never considering, that men reason not in the same manner you do, but draw many consequences from the belief of a divine Existence, and suppose that the Deity will inflict punishments on vice, and bestow rewards on virtue, beyond what appears in the ordinary course of nature. Whether this reasoning of theirs be just or not, is no matter. Its influence on their life and conduct must still be the same. And, those, who attempt to disabuse them of such prejudices, may, for aught I know, be good reasoners, but I cannot allow them to be good citizens and politicians; since they free men from one restraint upon their passions, and make the infringement of the laws of society, in one respect, more easy and secure.[10]

Hume's point, and my conclusion, is that in societies in which what is enjoined by the secular morality is roughly the same as what is enjoined by the religious morality, the atheist is able to command a weaker sense of moral obligation for his secular morality than the theist is able to command for his morality. This is simply because the shared morality will for everyone be commended by the elements of secular obligation, but will be *additionally* commended to the theist by the elements of religious obligation. In such societies it is not *what is to be done* that is eroded by atheism, but rather *why you should do.*

But in this all we have is a practical inconvenience of atheism, not a serious philosophical objection to it. If atheism were recognized as the true account of the reality of the world, it could well transpire that the practical inconvenience for morality would be diminished because the elements in secular moral obligation would receive more attention and emphasis than hitherto.

A more vigorous defence of secular morality (and the one Hume indirectly adopts) is to say that it is *not* to be presumed that the injunctions of secular and religious morality are largely the same. Secular morality, derived perhaps from a recognition of the common human needs of individuals, is, according to this view, the fundamental source of what are distinctively *moral* concepts and rules. When religion creates obligations, derived perhaps from the supposed will of a god, it is at best setting up 'frivolous species of merit' and at worst perverting the name of morality with what are in reality merely theological or ritualistic obligations: the cruel and dogmatic observance of the Lord's Day by the old Presby-

terians for example, or the equally dogmatic and even more cruel insistence by the official Church of Rome that miserable poverty should be
made more miserable by observing the God-given duty to procreate children. Such religious 'moral' obligations are, according to this view, better
destroyed; 'better' in terms of the values of the secular morality, the
believer may retort, not 'better' in terms of the value of the religious life.
Perhaps so; nevertheless the first (secular) sense of 'better' is the one to
which the religious moralist himself appeals under pressure. When he
argues, for example, that his morality is 'better' than any secular alternative inasmuch as it will not be corrupted by fashionable political or
social creeds, he is arguing that in terms of some morality X, which can
also be accepted by the atheist, his, the religious morality, is more reliable
in its humanistic outcome than the merely secular morality. But X *is* a
secular morality: that is why it can be used to commend religious morality
to the atheist.

Now at this stage I want to conclude that although secular and religious moralities are independent of each other, nevertheless in the mixed
moral economy of the real world, the extensive overlap of precepts between the two moralities means that atheism (whether tacit or explicit)
is capable of removing *some* of the elements of obligation to do what is
morally right, usually without putting any new elements in their place.
(I exclude additional obligations which an atheistic pseudo-religion like
Marxism might stitch onto morality.) But the situation of atheism is in a
peculiar way worse than this. I refer in the first place to the question of
moral authority; and in the second place to what, for want of a better
phrase, I can only call the loss of metaphysical good and evil involved in
atheism. Let us take these in turn.

The first derives directly from the theistic acceptance of certain commandments and moral insights as having divine authority (typically the
Law delivered to Moses on Mount Sinai or the insights of the Sermon on
the Mount). Now in the atheist's morality, quite literally *nothing* corresponds to this superhuman authority. However much a Mill or a Russell
may urge and commend a moral principle, they can never give it the
unique authority of the omnipotent God whom they reject. But again
this only means that when atheist and theist are advocating *the same*
moral position, the theist can almost always do so with more power and
authority than the atheist, however much the latter may protest his
urgent concern with humanist, communist, socialist, social-democratic,
or whatever principles. (I once more emphasize *the same* because when

they are not the same the whole structure of claim and counter-claim is altered.) However, there is more to it. In the case of the loss of authority I would suggest that the atheist is so conscious of the potential damage he has done to the standing of the sort of morality to which he still (largely) wants to subscribe, that in the most hard-headed and influential cases he tends to substitute a new metaphysical authority in the place of God. Thus, for example, the Marxist talks not only about the dominance of the proletariat as a process with which we should co-operate, but as a commanding and inevitable process which will (like divine authority) dominate whether we co-operate or not. Similarly in many twentieth-century societies the dominance of the Party in a single-party state has been used not merely as a brute force to influence behaviour, but as a quasi-metaphysical existent to give *authority* to what is commanded. The point is simply that it is very difficult for the atheist to do entirely without something like the authority which he formally denies that moral commandments have through the existence and power of God.

The loss of what I have called metaphysical good and evil under atheism is more serious. One of the elements in religious moral obligations which I distinguished at the beginning of this section was the belief that moral values are in some way part of the ultimate nature of things, an aspect of the Creator not subject to eventual extinction with mankind. Now this belief may be shown to be irrational (because, for example, there are no good reasons for supposing that such a Creator exists) but it cannot be shown to be unimportant in the sense of *irrelevant* to human needs and aspirations. Why do I say that? For two reasons, one having to do with the impoverishment of moral categories, the other having to do with man's need to be aware of ultimate good and evil.

It is, I believe, one of the most glaring intellectual defects of the twentieth century that while on the one hand we have indulged and planned destruction and evil on an organized scale never before experienced or contemplated by man, on the other hand our concepts of good and evil have shrivelled to social minutiae and utilitarian niceties of a purely local and restricted character. We can thus go into paroxysms of moral anguish before the European Court of Human Rights about whether a bullying schoolboy would be improperly degraded by having his bottom smacked while *at the same time* we can virtually ignore the slaughter of thousands in a Cambodia or an El Salvador and can also equip ourselves for an Armageddon which contemplates burning away and poisoning most of the sources of life on earth.

I do not wish to turn what I hope has been a sober and thoughtful book on the philosophy of religion into an impassioned crusade against nuclear war or anything else. My point in the present context is only that the effect of atheism in secularizing morality has been and is to trivialize the language of morality by confining its concepts to social and humanistic needs which leave us bereft of the moral eternities of good and evil which alone seem able to measure the scale of the actual good and evil, creation and destruction, which we now contemplate as real possibilities.

What I am saying is that only when set against the powers of an eternal or divine good or of a Satanic evil can the things we are now capable of be adequately experienced in moral terms. The genetic mutilation of all living things, the poisoning of the earth, the burning of most of the cities of the northern hemisphere: these are moral enormities of vast significance, but all our secular atheistic moralities allow us to talk about are social rights, utilitarian needs, proletarian demands, and sophisticated interpersonal relationships. These things are assuredly important, but they have deprived us (and, for example, the C.N.D.) of the language of absolutes, of moral eternities, just when we (and perhaps it) most need the depths of such language to evaluate our own condition.

The need to feel, to have a lively awareness of, concepts of good (associated with creation) and of evil (associated with destruction) which go beyond considerations of social convenience and fair play, accounts in part, I would suggest, for the extraordinary worldwide success of such a book as Tolkien's *The Lord of the Rings*. Quite apart from its quality as writing, or its scholarly reconstruction of the language and mythology which might have made up an Anglo-Saxon epic, it contains a remarkably powerful representation of the forces of life and creation pitted against the forces of darkness and destruction (forces of evil *per se* which are very real and yet seem to elude entirely any ordinary analysis in terms of Humean or Marxist or Social-Democratic secular morality). The representation evokes again the sense of striving for a good dimly perceived against a destructive evil pressing ever closer. The greatest moral paradigms of literature are concerned with such strife: the Faust legend, *Pilgrim's Progress*, and, more recently (to mix small things with great), Louis MacNiece's radio play

The Dark Tower. It is almost as if man *needs* to measure himself against an eternal or metaphysical good and evil in order to get the measure of the best and worst he can experience or bring about in this world. And if such measure involves a divine association with the good (thought of as a force of creation, life and light) then an atheistic denial of that force, even if the denial were a correct representation of reality, would involve a serious impoverishment of man's moral consciousness.

My conclusions are that (i) since secular morality subsists independently of religious belief, the only relevant effect of atheism is to destroy the additional elements of religious obligation in cases where the injunctions of the secular and religious moralities are the same; (ii) nevertheless atheism restricts our moral concepts so that we can scarcely express the enormity of our own present potentiality for good and evil; (iii) atheism's denial of any alliance with eternal moral forces, thought of as forces of creation and life, is a serious impoverishment of man's spiritual* and moral endeavour.

But of course even if all this is true (and all of it is arguable) it would simply mean that atheism has practical, moral and spiritual disadvantages. It would not mean that atheism is false to the realities of the world, and *however much* we may deplore the disadvantageous effects of some state of affairs, that is not a reason for concluding that the state of affairs is other than it really is. It might, however, be a reason for ignoring or disguising the state of affairs if this were possible, and if the advantages to be gained therefrom were very great. When we couple this thought with the realization that the arguments do not decisively establish the falsity of theism or its incoherence, then some people may wish to conclude that our need for a moral God to augment godless morals is sufficient to justify belief in such a God. I shall return to this thought in the final chapter.

(iii) *A Meaningless Eternity*

In chapter three I drew attention to certain questions about the origin and nature of the universe and about man's place in it which I called *cosmic questions*. Typically these ask what the origin or reason for the universe is, why the stuff in it moves in orderly ways or settles into

---

* By 'spiritual' I do *not* refer to some non-physical world of life and activity which is the object of psychical research or quasi-religious belief. I use the word here simply as a convenient way of referring to human goals and activities which provide satisfactions which are not obviously physical.

stable patterns, and what purpose, if any, man has in the cosmic scheme of things. Two categorically opposed sets of answers were those provided by theism and those provided by the archetypal classical atheism of Democritus and the Epicureans. We saw how the cosmological arguments and the design arguments attempted to provide intellectually compelling reasons for accepting something like the theistic answers. We saw finally that these reasons were not compelling, although, if theism were shown to be a coherent possibility, the reasons in its favour provided by the two seminal arguments could be of some account.

I now return to the contrast between theism and atheism concerning the cosmic questions. I consider two issues. One is whether the 'positivistic naturalism' inherent in classical and much contemporary atheism is intellectually deficient. The other is whether atheism in all of its current forms is existentially and metaphysically unsatisfactory.

I have taken the phrase 'positivistic naturalism' from Patrick Masterson's *Atheism and Alienation*, where he remarks that the term 'may be said to connote the view according to which there is neither any basis nor any need to go beyond the world of experience and scientific explanation for an ultimate account of the meaning and value of reality in general and of human existence in particular'.[11] The calmest, most judicious, and most thorough embodiment of such a view (which in its historical contexts is often called Stratonian* atheism) is probably the philosophy of David Hume,[12] but in modern terms the view is vigorously and challengingly advocated by Antony Flew in *God and Philosophy*: 'the presumption, defeasible of course by adverse argument, must be that all qualities observed in things are qualities belonging by natural right to those things themselves; and hence that whatever characteristics we think ourselves able to discern in the universe as a whole are the underivative characteristics of the universe itself. This is, for us, atheism.'[13] In context Flew is specifically referring to the quality *order*, but his point is general and is that there is no intellectually compelling reason to go

---

* From the name of Strato of Lampsacus who died in 269 B.C., the third head of Aristotle's school of philosophy in Athens (the Lyceum). His revision of Aristotle's physics had the effect of removing purposes from nature. Stratonian atheism asks for positive reasons for *not* assuming that the universe contains within itself the ultimates of explanation. What I have called classical atheism (see p. 51) goes one step further than Stratonian atheism by providing an atomist account of the operations of the universe, i.e., a specific content to the Stratonian presumption.

beyond the world and its observable characteristics in explaining the world. Put in another way: no explanations *external* to the world are available to rational inquiry or necessary in explaining the world. All we can ever have are better and better explanations which come from *within* the world.

Now a great deal of argument (and for that matter my own philosophical upbringing) disposes me to accept positivistic naturalism as correct, but there are some questions which should be asked. In the first place *why* should one not go beyond the workings of the world in seeking explanations for the workings of the world, or reasons why things are as they are, or why anything exists at all, providing some genuine intellectual satisfaction is achieved thereby or some proper question faced up to, if not answered? It is surely the entire burden of the cosmological argument that there are intellectually compulsive reasons for seeking for an explanation beyond the sum of things as they are; and I would not wish to concede that the cosmological argument is totally and finally and in all respects unconvincing. At the very least it is arguable that two rational advantages are gained by going one step beyond the totality of the world in seeking explanations. One is that the number of explanatory principles may be reduced from two to one: from a world in which it is known that natural processes *and* intelligent agents (ourselves) bring about results, we may economically reduce explanation to a world in which ultimately everything is brought about by rational agents (ourselves and God or gods). What is more, such reduction is to a principle of explanation which is intrinsically more intelligible to us than the brute inexplicable facts of natural processes since *we are such rational agents*: in whatever way I am what I am, or know what I am in myself, I know myself as an agent differently from, and better than, I know the casual 'agency' of any natural processes. The second rational advantage to be gained by ignoring the limitations of positivistic naturalism is simply that such disregard *permits* (it does not oblige) those who wish it, to take *one more step* in the process of questioning and understanding reality: a step which some people feel is artificially denied them by the options of classical atheism. Let me put it in this way: if a sense of intellectual satisfaction is achieved, if what would otherwise be an ultimate enigma is in some way softened or resolved by a quest for explanations beyond the limits of the observable world, then surely the most rational presumption is that such a quest *is* permissible unless there are decisive reasons for concluding that its assumptions are incoherent.

In the second place, positivistic naturalism (and classical atheism) stifles and renders illegitimate any sense of purpose or hope evoked by contemplation of the universe or of our place in it. The universe is as it is; we are as we are: nothing to hope, nothing to seek for, no quest to be undertaken, no final purpose to be achieved. I agree that as a philosophical reason for rejecting atheism all this amounts to very little. But it does not amount to very little in terms of the values and purposes we put upon our lives. Of course if atheism were unarguably thrust upon us by *all* the available evidence and argument, and if *no* evidence and argument gave the slightest hint of coherence or probability to any theistic alternative, then we would have to lump it: dig our garden, procreate our children and die. But this is not the case. Theism is not *totally* devoid of rational respectability, and in that situation it may seem reasonable to take account of what one might call the existentialist or, if you prefer it, the utilitarian disadvantages of atheism.

I have so far spoken of atheism in the manifestation with which an English-speaking audience might be supposed to be most familiar – positivistic naturalism: the unenthusiastic restriction of our attention to this-worldly, social-centred, science-dominated considerations which in their popular acceptations do not so much explicitly deny as ignore theistic belief. But for much of the world two other sources of atheism are paramount: namely, some versions of existentialism, and, much more importantly, Marxism. I do not wish to discuss the former as a separate issue: partly because it has some of the aspects of a rather parochial literary movement rather than an argued philosophy; mainly because as a philosophy it can lurch between the extremes of fideistic individual commitment in, say, Kierkegaard (1813–55) and the indignant, at times almost adolescently violent atheism of, say, Sartre (1905–80). In short, existentialism can support atheism *or* religion. In as far as a consistent and orderly rejection of theism can be discerned in existentialism, the same comments apply as to naturalistic positivism: that the existentialist seems to deny God because he thinks God constitutes a premise inconsistent with individual freedom rather than because he soberly rejects the evidence for God's existence, makes no difference to the problem of ultimate unintelligibility posed by atheism. If the intelligibility of things is a problem for atheism, then it is a problem for atheism of any species: classical, positivist, existentialist or, for that matter, Marxist or Christian.

Marx himself (1813–83) seems to have thought very little about the philosophical worth of the evidence concerning the existence of God. He seems to have been an almost innate atheist, and his hostility to religion derives not so much from a conclusion that all of it is false, as from a conviction that it supplies an alien ideology which diverts man from his real task of creating himself by his own labour through the laws of economic and historical necessity. Marxism is full of hope and determination, and in this it is sharply distinct from classical atheism and positivistic naturalism. It poses a different quest: a quest for the realization of the full potential of man *now*, rather than the theistic quest for an eternity of truth and value and meaning in the whole nature of (created) things. Thus Marxism does not so much contradict theism, as affirm a whole ideological alternative, as it were a new religion, a system of secular salvation, which theoretically could have extinguished the questions and the hopes as well as the metaphysic upon which theism feeds. The cosmic questions do not get answered by the Marxist. They become irrelevant. Such is the promise; it is difficult to think of any other ideology in which the reality so consistently deviates from the promise: unless it be Christianity.

I said at the beginning of this chapter that the disadvantages of atheism also attach to the personalist reappraisals of theism which retain a religious vocabulary which has been deprived of any reference to the real existence of God as an external reality.[14] Without reiterating the points made in chapter one, it should now be clear why I say this. Let me take just one (currently fashionable) example of reinterpreted Christianity. In *Taking Leave of God* (London, 1980) Don Cupitt asserts that an objective metaphysical God is no longer intellectually secure as the basis for religion. But there is no need to worry about this. It is only a traditional mistake to regard the existence of a theistic God as something factual. God is the religious concern reified, and the religious concern is values which a person can autonomously accept. Possibly so, but the real loss here is just the same as if Cupitt were straightforwardly affirming atheism. Such a Godless husk of Christianity (however psychologically useful it might be) cannot commend itself by any reason to the person who autonomously rejects it. Theism can and does. Furthermore, Godless Christianity gives no more answer than classical atheism or positivistic naturalism to the great questions of our being: what is the origin of things, what is the purpose of life, what should I do, what may I hope?

In short, the limitations of atheism (fundamentally the limitations upon our ability, and perhaps our felt need, to explain the universe and understand our place and purpose in it) apply to any form of atheism, whether its origins be classical, positivist, existentialist, Marxist or Christian. The only difference is the degree to which each of these ideologies diverts our attention from the cosmic questions which lie at the roots of religion.

In the first two sections of this chapter I defended secular and social morality against the charge that it is invalid if theism is false or (which is for this purpose the same thing) believed to be false. The rules of secular morality can be and are perfectly easily evolved from the needs of man in society without reference to God, and the secular obligations or reasons why these rules should be observed by any individual stand whether or not they are augmented by religious reasons.

I then argued that although secular morality is independent of, and would therefore survive the destruction of, religious belief, nevertheless it would do so in a way which left profoundly unsatisfied both our aspirations to be allied with ultimate creative good against destructive evil, and our real and practical needs to find moral concepts which were full enough to express our own potentialities for good and evil.

In the final section I drew attention to the metaphysically and existentially stultifying effects of atheism. I shall now try to draw together some of the many paths trodden in this book.

8   DESTINATIONS

In the first chapter I tried to establish two things about the metaphysic of reality which is called theism. One was that it is the basic and common ground of Judaism, Christianity and Islam. The other was that because this common ground is so fundamental to all three religions, it cannot be abandoned without both depriving these religions of their characteristic claims to be true to the real nature of things, and so altering them that they cease to have any valid connection with their own original revelations or subsequent histories.

I then pointed out that since theism was the essential philosophical foundation of Christianity and Islam, it had always been supported by reasons, and could not be accepted on faith alone. Thus St Paul did not initiate a religious aberration when he wrote 'Ever since the creation of the world his invisible nature, namely, his external power and deity, has been clearly perceived in the things that have been made' (Romans 1:20). Instead he was linking Christianity in a perfectly natural way *both* to the traditions of Greek philosophical monotheism *and* to the perception that 'The heavens are telling the glory of God; and the firmament proclaims his handiwork' (Psalm 19): a linking which was carried out on behalf of Judaism by Philo and later by the Arab philosophers on behalf of Islam.

I further drew attention to the distinction between the causes of a belief and the reasons for it, and to the difference between saying a belief is reasonable and saying it is true. A true belief is one which happens to accord with the realities of the world, but a reasonable belief has two aspects. A belief is said to be reasonable, in the sense of being held by someone in a reasonable way, if the belief is sensitive to evidence – if it alters when new or better evidence is presented to the believer. But a belief may also be recognized as reasonable in itself when it is in fact supported by reasons or evidence of some sort, irrespective of how it is held by someone. Let us call these two aspects of reasonable belief: belief reasonably held, and belief reasonable in itself.

A belief is reasonable in itself if it is coherent (i.e. is internally consistent or possible or makes sense) and if it is also supported by reasons or evidence which give it some chance of being true (i.e. which give it some probability of being an accurate representation of the way the world is).

The questions I must now take further before drawing to a conclusion are: is theistic belief reasonable in itself, irrespective of whether I or you happen to accept it, and regardless of the way in which it is held by particular people? And finally, is theism more probably true than any comparable alternative?

(i) The Desert and the Garden

Suppose I am asked by a bemused victim of the Middle Earth industry: 'Is it reasonable to believe in the existence of Middle Earth and in the events of *The Lord of the Rings*?' The evidence – the narrative – is intricately coherent in every thinkable respect, and although not realistic in terms of all the physical realities of the world as it now is, the world could have been like that. What is more, the narrative is deeply realistic in much of its moral and personal experience. But is there any evidence which gives any probability to the real existence of Middle Earth? Well, perhaps. Consider the beautifully unified explanation it provides for all manner of trace superstitions and linguistic survivals scattered over northern Europe, not to mention the folk motif of the ring of power, etc. In the absence of other evidence, the case for the real existence of Middle Earth – like the case for the real existence of God – could be made quite powerful. But we *know* the inventor of Middle Earth. We *know* it is a new story, so the various bits of evidence which accord with its truth can be ruled out. Belief in the real existence of Middle Earth is unreasonable in itself; not because we lack favourable evidence, but because we *know* something which completely alters the value of the evidence. Now what should we say about belief in God?

The account of God which is taken for granted both in the historical events associated with theistic religions and in the day-to-day prayer, worship and devotion of those religions, makes God:

(a) creator and sustainer of all things;

(b) omnipotent, omniscient and eternal;

(c) an agent able to act everywhere without a body;

(d) morally concerned with mankind.

There may well be doubt amounting to flat disbelief that anything in fact exists which satisfies descriptions (a), (b) and (d), and anyway (b) needs qualifications and footnotes. But at least it seems possible to admit that there is nothing obviously or unambiguously incoherent in supposing that something could exist which satisfies these descriptions. Serious doubt about the coherence of the total description only appears when (c) is taken into the account. Unfortunately (c) is the crucial description upon which all the others depend. If it is incoherent, if it fails to describe any possible thing, then it makes no sense to talk of that thing being creator, or omniscient, or morally concerned. All these descriptions are descriptions of some sort of active agent or person, and that is what we have not got from item (c) or anywhere else. What is more if (c) were incoherent, it would make nonsense of all talk of God as an active agent or person – of Jehovah who *led* the Israelites out of Egypt, of God the Father who *raised* from the dead a previously existing human being, and of Allah who *instructed* his Prophet to record for him the teachings which mankind did not know.

Now we have seen above (pp. 110–13) that the supposition of a dispersed, bodiless, universal person or agent may or may not be coherent. The inferences are so intricate, and what is to count as relevant data is so elusive and complex, that no generally agreed way leads to any unified conclusion. Thoughtful people – Flew and Swinburne for example – legitimately fail to find common ground here. But what we can say is that there is *no agreed proof* that the supposition of a dispersed bodiless agent is *incoherent*. So can we instead decide the issue by reference to evidence that the belief is true?*

The problem is that – as we have seen throughout this book – the evidence for the truth of theistic belief is itself difficult to pin down. Even if we concede that it amounts to very little, the 'very little' may still form

---

* In the absence of any certainty that a belief is *incoherent*, any evidence that it is *true* will also be evidence that it is coherent, that it makes sense. Let me put this point more generally. Any belief, p, which is factually true, must be coherent. What is factually true is what is real, and what is real has to be coherent. It already *is*. Therefore any good evidence that p is true will also be evidence that p is coherent. On the other hand any belief p, which is *proved* to be incoherent, cannot be true. And *no* evidence can show that it is. (The whole point about an incoherent belief is that it cancels out its own possibility. It *cannot* be true because there isn't anything there that could be true.) Now since there is no agreed proof that theistic belief is incoherent, any evidence that it is true will also be evidence that it is coherent.

enough in the way of hints and possibilities for an intelligent person to put it together into a reasonable whole.

Let me first state the case for theistic belief as strongly as possible in a single paragraph, and then follow with a strong statement of the atheistic case. For reasons which will become apparent, I shall call the pro-theistic case 'The Garden' and the pro-atheistic case 'The Desert'.

The Garden. Belief in a vast intelligence (who is concerned with us) acting in and through all natural things (which he also created and sustains) provides some sort of answer to the quest for an origin and reason for the existence of the world, and some sort of answer to questions about the purpose of life. Similarly the order in natural processes, the predictable and regular changes in things, would be ultimately inexplicable if there were no intelligent orderer. What is more, although most direct awareness of this Being is overlaid by the particular images of particular historical religions, most religious experience can be described in terms of an awareness of *something* other-worldly in relation to which man finds his greatest joy and peace. This is most evident in experiences which are least specific in content – in numinous pantheist experiences, i.e. experiences which bring us closest to the creating and sustaining Being to which the cosmic questions already directed us. Furthermore, the selective revelation of that Being in religious experience is just what one would expect if he had chosen to keep the awareness of himself alive in each generation without compelling belief by some sort of M.G.M. spectacular. The same applies to the fine balance of evidence. This clearly leaves each individual free to decide *not* to believe in this Being: a freedom which we would antecedently expect to find if this Being were to be identified with the theistic God. Even human suffering can largely be shown to be consistent with the existence of a God who has allowed real human freedom, and human happiness would be less than explicable without such a God. (The point is succinctly made by Boethius (*c.* 480– 524): 'So it was not without reason that one of your disciples asked: "If there is a God, whence comes evil? But whence good, if there is not?"'[1]) There is powerful evidence that the earth is very special in the physical world. It is a paradise by comparison with all the rest of the universe known to us. It is a garden in the deserts of eternity. It is too beautiful to be there by chance. Finally there is the practical case for belief in a theistic God. Such a belief gives a significance to human life, and a hope without which we would all be embarked upon a journey from nowhere into nothing.

The Desert. The supposition that some intelligent being created and sustains the natural world, and gave it motion and order, serves no useful explanatory purpose. All genuine explanations come from within the world, and the existence of the world working in the way it does is the ultimate reality. At best religious experience is no more than a coloured version of the agnostic awe anyone may feel when acutely conscious of the fearful nothingness of ourselves in the sight of the vast emptiness of the universe. At worst such experience is totally explained by reference to cultural, psychological or environmental causes. The random and arbitrary evils suffered by individual living things, and sometimes by whole species, are decisive evidence against the existence of a caring God. The complex organisms on the earth are a stage in the physical evolution of things which might have occurred anywhere. They are not evidence of the providence of God. Even in practice the atheistic view is preferable to the theistic view: first, because in modern conditions man does not need the props of religion or feel their loss; secondly, because atheism does away with the unwholesome guilts and senses of sin engendered by religion; thirdly, because it releases our energies for the improvement of *this* world, and this is the only world there is, and this the only life we have.

Presented with these alternatives, I think that a reasonable person, honestly facing the arguments and evidence which support them, has a genuine rational choice. *Both* beliefs are reasonable in themselves. *Both* are supported by some evidence. It will, of course, be said that the wise man acting reasonably will incline to whichever is the more strongly supported by evidence. But the problem is that it is not completely agreed, even among 'wise men', which belief that is. So that despite my own judgement that one view is better evidenced as a truth about the reality of things than the other, I have to allow that the other view is reasonable in itself, and could be reasonably held. I do not have to insult my opponent's intelligence by looking for the causes of his belief, although causes will probably decide the issue if the evidence is very finely balanced.

Of course if it could be agreed that, for example, item (c) in the theistic description of God is incoherent, that would decide the issue. (It would have a similar effect on the evidence to discovering that Middle Earth was invented by Tolkien; the discovery would nullify as evidence all the unitary explanations and realism which had previously been used to show that the accounts of Middle Earth were probably true.) But such an agreement is not in sight, and in its absence one is thrown back upon other considerations in coming to a reasonable conclusion about the alternatives. For example – if we cannot decide that theism is probably true, would it nevertheless be reasonable to believe it because of its practical value to us?

So the quest moves on from an attempt to decide the issue between theism and atheism by reference to the way the ultimate reality of the world actually is, to an attempt to decide the issue by reference to the practical value of each belief. Is the Garden preferable to the Desert for human purposes (or *vice versa*)?

For example, it might be urged that when we take into account the fact that man does not live by bread alone, that ultimate purposes make a difference to the way we can view life, and that our moral strengths are feeble and in need of outside aid, it is *better* to believe in God; and this 'better' is a pragmatic reason for such belief. This way leads to the serene calm and confidence of the devout Christian or Muslim. The other way leads to an ultimately unsatisfying materialism and on to the rather pathetic heroics of the young Bertrand Russell,[2] the melancholy happiness of the Epicureans, or the emptiness of FitzGerald's *Rubaiyat*:

> One Moment in Annihilation's Waste,
> One Moment, of the Well of Life to taste –
>   The Stars are setting and the Caravan
> Starts for the Dawn of Nothing – Oh, make haste!

Surely, in this contrast, the reasonable man must choose theistic belief, and the life-enhancing power of one of the religions which depend upon it?

But this is a very dubious path to tread. We are saying that it does not matter whether the theistic metaphysic which underpins Christianity etc. is true or false, because the religious enterprise is anyway worth while *per se*. Isn't this exactly what Tillich, Robinson, Cupitt, and others whom I have criticized, are also saying? I think not. The critical difference is that a useful religious enterprise, underpinned by the theistic metaphysic, is underpinned by something which is in itself reasonable, even if its reasonableness is not strong enough to exclude its atheistic alternative. A useful religious enterprise which rests on nothing gives itself no way of commending itself except as useful. To the person who says 'I like the look of the religious enterprise, should I accept it?' someone like Cupitt can only reply with appeals to its intrinsic worth. The theist can do that *and* argue for the reasonableness of the metaphysic whose truth the religious enterprise actually presumes.

It is only in this chapter that I have referred to theism as a metaphysic of reality. It may now be clearer why I have adopted this phrase. Theism is not a religion in itself. It does not involve worship, prayer, devotion, serenity of mind, sin, forgiveness or any of the complex features of an actual religion. A religious practice or observation or devotion is not true or false, or even reasonable or unreasonable, except within its own confined terms of reference. But a metaphysic of reality *will* be coherent or incoherent, and *will* be reasonable or unreasonable according to whether the evidence shows it to be probably true or probably false. Moreover a theistic religion, Christianity for example, cannot be detached from its metaphysic without disaster. Why? Because the practice of the religion makes no sense without the truth of its underlying beliefs about what is real. The truth of the religion *depends upon* the coherence and truth of what it takes for granted; and if the Christian religion is not true, if there is no God, the question 'Does it work?' becomes, for many people, interesting at a much less serious level of commitment. That is why it is so important for Christianity that theism should be in some measure reasonable and probable, and most certainly not incoherent. If the theistic metaphysic is incoherent or false, Christianity is an agreeable picture of an unreal face.

If the theistic metaphysic is *a* reasonable belief, does the sort of evidence we have been looking at earlier indicate any *more* reasonable belief short of atheism? In my view it does. If you consider the difficulties created by God's supposed foreknowledge, his particular acts in the world, and above all by the fact of evil, you will observe that these difficulties all disappear if we abandon theistic description (d) – God's *concern* with us. The first three cosmic questions (p. 48) would be answered just as well by the supposition of a *deistic* god as by the supposition of a *theistic* God. A deistic god would be the designer, the reason why things are as they are, or why there is anything at all. He could be omnipotent, single and omniscient. He could know of us without finding us more interesting than we would find a colony of dust mites. The problem about the coherence of (c) would remain, but it would be no worse than for theism. But the snag here is that this belief, which is much *more* reasonable than theism, is valueless. Deism is like the Epicurean gods. It makes no difference to us whether such gods exist or not. Nothing comes of it. Deism takes away the intellectual pressure of the first three cosmic questions while leaving everything else – including the question concerning man's hopes and purposes – exactly where classical atheism leaves it. Such a god could provide *no* foundation for any belief in Judaism, Christianity or Islam, where the crucial message is always that God is with us, and we are in his care. As far as biblical religion is concerned, a deist god would take us to the end of verse 24 of the first chapter of Genesis and no further. (Curiously enough a pagan deity of the Greek pattern – a powerful god of the earth – could function for much of the Bible quite remarkably well, but would absolutely fail in the first 21 verses of Genesis, the beginning of St John's Gospel, and in other places where Jehovah is given cosmic properties.)

(ii) *Resting Places*

So I am concluding that theism may be coherent, but that the evidence that it is true is only enough to make it a weakly reasonable belief. The theistic God provides some sort of answer to all the cosmic questions, but there is far too much circumstantial argument of the sort 'things would be or could be thus if there were a God of the sort we believe in'; and this argument is in direct competition with the evidence of the problem of evil that they could *not* be thus. Nevertheless this possible coherence, and weak probability of truth, may be just enough to make it reasonable for a person to accept one of the religions which depend upon the theistic metaphysic. He may reasonably judge the religion to be of intrinsic value, and consciously acquiesce in the influences which cause him to accept it.

Deism carries the same doubts about its coherence as theism. It avoids all the contrary evidence of the problem of evil, but does so at the expense of becoming of no religious significance. A deist god would answer the first three cosmic questions in much the same way as a theistic God; the last it would leave blank. (I leave out of consideration various other religious metaphysics such as dualism since they involve more problems than either theism or deism.)

Atheism denies that the first three cosmic questions need answering, and supplies a variety of worldly purposes and values in answer to questions about man's values and aspirations. The prevalent forms of these include the brutally energetic social purposes of the Marxist, the welfare-conscious cosiness of the social democrat, and the worldly concerns of the consumer society. Given these as some of the social and personal consequences of atheism, and given them in contrast to the insight shared by almost all religions – that man does not live by bread alone – I am inclined to think that *for the generality of the world most of the surviving influences of theism are better than most of the present consequences of atheism.* But such a judgement is open to revision as the circumstances of society and man's understanding of himself change.

As I write this final paragraph, it seems to me that the decision for a thoughtful individual may, however, be at variance with what he judges to be best in social terms. There seem to be two possibilities. One is the mild and slightly sad Epicurean acceptance of such good things as the world can provide, coupled with the acknowledgement that things will go on and on in the ways in which we discover that they do go on and on, but to nowhere and from nothing that remotely concerns us, or could even be understood by us. The other alternative is the theistic hope which is supported by traces of real, if ambiguous, evidence that all things move from something which may be remotely like us towards something which has us as part of its creative purposes. But what those creative purposes are cannot be known. They can only be taken on the trust of Abraham, or Jesus, or Mahomet. As I write this last sentence, my mind inclines to the not altogether disagreeable Epicurean acceptance that the world is as it is, and is all there is; but the hope of other worlds somehow lingers.

AD FINEM NONDUM ADEPTUM

NOTES

1. The Way Forward

1. *The Coherence of Theism* (Oxford, 1977); *The Existence of God* (Oxford, 1979); *Faith and Reason* (Oxford, 1981).
2. From a review of J. L. Mackie's *The Miracle of Theism* in *The Times Higher Education Supplement*, 21 January 1983.
3. For example in *The Concept of Prayer* (London, 1965); *Death and Immortality* (London, 1970); *Religion without Explanation* (Blackwell, Oxford, 1976).
4. *The Honest to God Debate*, ed. J. Robinson and O. L. Edwards (London, 1963), p. 222.
5. *The Shaking of the Foundations* (Penguin Books, 1962), p. 63.
6. *The Honest to God Debate*, p. 220.
7. For example: Keith Ward, *Holding Fast to God* (London, 1982).
8. Richard Swinburne, *The Existence of God* (Oxford, 1979), p. 8.

2. Initial Obstructions

1. J. C. Flugel, *A Hundred Years of Psychology* (London, 1951), p. 340.
2. Freud, *Complete Works*, ed. J. Strachey (London, 1957), vol. XI, p. 123.
3. *Ibid.*, vol. XXI, p. 33.
4. *Ibid.*, p. 51.
5. Feuerbach, *The Essence of Christianity*, trans. George Elliot (London, 1854), pp. 12–14.

3. The Evidence for Belief in God: Public Arguments

1. For a collection of important papers on the ontological argument

see *The Many-Faced Argument*, ed. J. Hick and A. C. McGill (London, 1968). A useful but difficult monograph is Jonathan Barnes, *The Ontological Argument* (London, 1972). A. Plantinga's *The Nature of Necessity* (Oxford, 1974), ch. 10, is similarly useful but even more sophisticated.

2. Charles Hartshorne, *The Logic of Perfection* (Illinois, 1962). See also articles in *The Many-Faced Argument* (Note 1 above).

3. See *The Many-Faced Argument*, p. 120.

4. Hume, *Treatise of Human Nature*, I, ii, 6.

5. *Ibid.*, I, iii, 7; cf. Kant, *Critique of Pure Reason*, trans. N. Kemp Smith (London, 1933), p. 505.

6. Russell, *Why I Am Not a Christian* (London, 1957), pp. 144–68. Quotations are taken from pp. 147 and 149.

7. See, for example, Lucretius, *De Rerum Natura*, Book I, lines 215–20 and 265–70.

8. See Michael Durrant, 'St Thomas' Third Way', *Religious Studies*, 1969.

9. For a full and interesting account of this problem, see Bruce Vawter, *On Genesis: A New Reading* (London, 1977), pp. 37–41, or John Skinner, *A Critical and Exegetical Commentary on Genesis*, 2nd edn (Edinburgh, 1930), pp. 4–15.

10. Augustine, *City of God*, Book XI, ch. 6.

11. Joseph Silk, *The Big Bang* (San Francisco, 1980), p. 328.

12. Richard Swinburne, *The Existence of God* (Oxford, 1979), p. 48.

13. Kant, *Critique of Pure Reason*, Transcendental Dialectic, Book II, ch. III, section 3. The relevant passage reads: 'There are only three ways of proving the existence of a Deity on the grounds of speculative reason. All the paths leading to this end either begin with determinate experience and the special constitution of the world of sense-experience and rise, in accordance with the laws of causality, from it to the highest cause existing apart from the world; or they begin with a purely indeterminate experience, i.e. some empirical existent; or abstraction is made of all experience and the existence of a supreme cause is inferred from *a priori* concepts alone. The first is the *physico-theological* argument, the second is the *cosmological* argument and the third is the *ontological* argument.'

14. Swinburne, *op. cit.*, p. 118.

15. Antony Flew, *The Presumption of Atheism* (London, 1976), pp. 53–60.

16. Leibniz gives several such accounts apart from the one published in the *Theodicy*. Perhaps the best is in the paper 'On the Ultimate Origination of Things' for which see *Leibniz: Philosophical Writings*, ed. M. and C. R. Morris (London, 1934), pp. 32–41. Other statements of his argument can be found in 'The Principles of Nature and Grace, Founded on Reason' and in 'The Monadology', p. 26 and p. 9 respectively of the edition cited. All references to Leibniz in the text are to the pages of this readily available Everyman edition.

17. J. L. Mackie, *The Miracle of Theism* (Oxford, 1982), p. 81.

18. Extensive discussions of the cosmological argument can be found in A. Kenny, *The Five Ways* (London, 1969); W. L. Rowe, *The Cosmological Argument* (Princeton, 1975); W. L. Craig, *The Kalam Cosmological Argument* (London, 1979), a uniquely good exposition of the Islamic versions of this argument; and *idem, The Cosmological Argument from Plato to Leibniz* (London, 1980), a scholarly and useful contribution to this area of the history of ideas.

19. Leibniz, *op. cit.*, pp. 25 f.

20. *Ibid.*, p. 32.

21. See *The Stoics*, ed. J. M. Rist (California, 1978), p. 180.

22. Swinburne, *op. cit.*, pp. 124 f.

23. I find my wording in the first part of this paragraph inadvertently close to Swinburne's on p. 120 (*op. cit.*) There is no intention to follow him here, but since we are both expounding the same source (Leibniz) I suppose a similarity of exposition is almost unavoidable unless the original were hopelessly ambiguous – which it is not.

24. Leibniz, *op. cit.*, p. 33.

25. A useful and succinct summary of the discussion can be found in chapter 2 of H. A. Meynell's *The Intelligible Universe* (London, 1982).

26. In recent years the design argument has been badly served by books and only a little better by articles. Among books the following might be mentioned: A. Plantinga, *God and Other Minds* (Cornell, 1972), ch. 4, where, as John Hick remarked in a review, 'vast labours of logic' eventually extrude a rather minute conclusion; A. C. Ewing, *Value and Reality* (London, 1973), ch. 7; F. R. Tennant, *Philosophical Theology* (Cambridge, 1930), vol. II, ch. 4; J. C. A. Gaskin, *Hume's Philosophy of Religion* (London and New York, 1978), chs. 2 and 3. But the masterpiece on this subject is still, and is likely to remain, chapter XI of Hume's *Enquiry concerning Human Understanding* (1748) and almost the whole of his *Dialogues concerning Natural Religion* (1779).

27. *Life and Letters of Charles Darwin*, ed. F. Darwin (London, 1887), vol. I, p. 309.

28. *Ibid.*, p. 314.

29. Hume, *Dialogues concerning Natural Religion* (1779), Part XI.

30. Louis Dupré, 'The Argument of Design Today', in *Journal of Religion*, 1974.

31. Hume, *Dialogues*, towards the end of Part V.

32. Gaskin, *op. cit.* (Note 26), pp. 22–39.

33. Hume, *loc. cit.*

34. *Ibid.*, Part VII.

35. *Ibid.*, Part II.

36. *Ibid.*, Part XII. The words form part of a final paragraph probably appended to the unpublished manuscript in the year of Hume's death, 1776.

37. *Life and Letters of Charles Darwin*, *op. cit.* (Note 27), p. 316n.

4. The Evidence for Belief in God: Private Illuminations

1. J. L. Mackie, *The Miracle of Theism* (Oxford, 1982), p. 184.

2. Swinburne distinguishes between private and public perceptions in a similar way (see *The Existence of God*, Oxford, 1979, p. 248). We all owe him a debt in this matter, but in order to avoid lengthy and complicating additions to my argument in the main text I do not attempt to analyse our differences and agreements at this point.

3. Rudolf Otto, *The Idea of the Holy* (original German edition 1917; English translations Oxford, 1923, and Penguin Books, 1959). The first four chapters are critically important.

4. 'Numinous' is coined by Otto from the almost untranslatable Latin *numen*, meaning something like the will, power or sacred authority of a god.

5. H. D. Lewis, *Our Experience of God* (London, 1959), p. 102.

6. *Historical Selections in the Philosophy of Religion*, ed. Ninian Smart (London, 1962), pp. 306–39.

7. John Locke, *An Essay concerning Human Understanding* (1690), Book IV, ch. XIX 'Of Enthusiasm'.

8. *Royal Institute of Philosophy Lectures*, vol. 2 (London, 1969), p. 23.

9. Albert Einstein, *The World as I See It* (London, 1940), pp. 5 and 26.

10. Aelius Aristides, *The Sacred Teachings*. No published translation is known to me although a Loeb edition is in course of preparation. At

the date of writing only the first volume of a projected four has appeared, but even it indicates Aristides' veneration for Asclepius – not really surprising, since Aristides enjoyed ill health (and the leisure to write about it) from an early age. There were many others bearing the name 'Aristides' in antiquity. Our man might well be distinguished as Aristides the Unhealthy. It is probably mere chance that he also provides us with the first personal account of experience of pagan religion. This source was kindly drawn to my attention by Dr J. V. Luce.

11. William James, *The Varieties of Religious Experience* (Fontana edn, London, 1960), pp. 81–2.

12. See for example, W. T. Stace, *Time and Eternity* (Princeton, 1952), pp. 76 f.

13. R. A. Oakes, 'Religious Experience and Rational Certainty', *Religious Studies*, 1976.

14. Ronald Hepburn, *Christianity and Paradox* (London, 1958), pp. 24–60.

15. William James, *op. cit.*, p. 499.

16. I mean *not proven*: the past participle of the old Scots verb *preve* (not the current corruption of 'proved': the past participle of the English verb *prove*). With the negative the Scots verb carries the particular legal overtone – 'not *yet* proved, but the case may be reopened later'.

5. Arguments Against Belief in God: External Scepticism

1. Freud, *Complete Works*, ed. J. Strachey (London, 1961), vol. XXI, p. 31. In view of Freud's present rather diminished reputation as a scientist it may seem odd to cite him in connection with the scientific attitude. But, as I say in the text, Freud *intended* to adopt the methods and attitudes of positivistic science. That we can now see that he failed to adopt them rigorously in his own work does not alter his positivistic sympathies.

2. A. J. Ayer, *Language, Truth and Logic*, 2nd edn (London, 1946), pp. 116 and 118.

3. Antony Flew's essay in the symposium 'Theology and Falsification' has been reprinted about sixteen times. It is most readily accessible (in company with the responses by R. M. Hare and Basil Mitchell) in *New Essays in Philosophical Theology*, ed. Antony Flew and Alasdair MacIntyre (London, 1955), or in *The Philosophy of Religion*, ed. Basil Mitchell (Oxford, 1971). For Flew's second thoughts as well as the original

essay see his *The Presumption of Atheism* (London, 1976), pp. 71–80.

4. See, for example, John Hick's 'Theology and Verification' in *The Philosophy of Religion, op. cit.*

5. J. L. Mackie, *The Miracle of Theism* (Oxford, 1982), pp. 215–29.

6. Useful summaries can be found in E. R. MacCormac, *Metaphor and Myth in Science and Religion* (Carolina, 1976), ch. 2; J. H. Gill, *Ian Ramsey* (London, 1976), chs. 1 and 2.

7. Mackie, *op. cit.*, p. 3.

8. Anthony Flew, *God and Philosophy* (London, 1966), p. 37.

9. For a concise and important discussion of these problems see Terence Penelhum, *Survival and Disembodied Existence* (London, 1970).

10. John Locke, *An Essay concerning Human Understanding* (1690), first chapter, section 4.

11. For a discussion of Hume's theory of knowledge in its relation to religion see my *Hume's Philosophy of Religion* (London and New York, 1978), ch. 5. For a more general assessment of his meaning–empiricism see Jonathan Bennett, *Locke Berkeley Hume* (Oxford, 1971), pp. 222–34.

6. *Arguments Against Belief in God: Internal Dilemmas*

1. See *Dialogues concerning Natural Religion* (1779), Part X. No such questions occur in any extant work of Epicurus. Possible sources for Hume are Bayle's *Dictionary*, the article on Paulicians, note E, or (for both of them) *On the Anger of God*, ch. 13, by Lactantius (260–340), for which see *The Works of Lactantius*, trans. W. Fletcher (Edinburgh, 1871, or London, 1951). A somewhat similar form of words occurs in Sextus Empiricus (second century A.D.), but there is no attribution to Epicurus. See *Outlines of Pyrrhonism*, III, iii.

2. My very sharp rejection of this solution would have been less convincing in the Middle Ages. See, for example, Chaucer's 'The Clarke's Tale' in which the Marquis selects the peasant girl Griselde to be his bride, and then subjects her to all manner of barbarous treatment in order to try her patience and love for him. The story is told to illustrate the virtue of patience and submission (to God?); but told *now* it merely sounds absurd or draws attention to the Marquis as a criminal lunatic.

3. For this intriguing discussion see J. L. Mackie, 'Evil and Omnipotence', in *Mind*, 1955; Antony Flew, 'Divine Omnipotence and Human Freedom', in *New Essays in Philosophical Theology*, ed. A. Flew and

A. MacIntyre (London, 1955); Alvin Plantinga, 'The Free Will Defence', in *The Philosophy of Religion*, ed. B. Mitchell (Oxford, 1971); Flew, 'Compatibilism, Free Will and God', in *Philosophy*, 1973; Mackie, *The Miracle of Theism* (Oxford, 1982), pp. 162–76; *et al.*

4. *The Brothers Karamazov*, Book 4, ch. 4, is perhaps the most fervent outcry in all literature against a God permitting men the freedom to inflict the suffering they do inflict.

5. *Dialogues*, part XI.

6. John Hick, *Evil and the God of Love* (London, 1966), p. 371.

7. See for example S. C. Hackett, *The Resurrection of Theism* (Chicago, 1957), pp. 286–7.

8. Note particularly Plotinus (*c.* 205–70), *The Enneads*, I. 5 (7), and the whole of II, 7. By the time Augustine (354–430) is writing the Neoplatonist philosophy of eternity has thoroughly entered Christian theology as a means of accounting for God's immutability and for saying that the 'world was not created in time but with time'. See *Confessions*, XI, 13 and *City of God*, XI, 6. A century later Boethius (*c.* 480–524), at the very end of classical philosophical writing, bequeathed an influential account of time and eternity similarly influenced by Neoplatonism to medieval scholasticism. See *Of the Trinity IV* and the conclusion to *The Consolation of Philosophy*.

9. The expression and the thought here are inadvertently close to that of Parmenides of Elea (*c.* 510 B.C.) whose metaphysical system 'Eleatic Monism' taught that time, plurality and motion are merely what *seems*. The world of intelligible reality is an unchanging unity.

10. Typical are such exponents of Process Theology as Charles Hartshorne and John Cobb. From what has already been said in the text (see p. 121) it will be seen that the systematic reasonableness of Swinburne's arguments about omniscience makes him a notable representative of the social democratic view.

11. See, for example, the Articles of Religion of 1571, particularly Articles 10–12 and 17, where the text struggles to commend good works while allowing that they cannot *really* help since God already knows whom he has chosen.

12. James Hogg, *The Private Memoirs and Confessions of a Justified Sinner* (Oxford, 1969), p. 123. The *Confessions* were first published in 1824.

13. *Ibid.*, p. 135.

14. For an example in brief compass of an attempt to argue (other than from timelessness) that free actions are possible given that God knows

them in advance, see Brian Davies, *An Introduction to the Philosophy of Religion* (Oxford, 1982), pp. 88–90.

15. Hume, *Enquiry concerning Human Understanding* (1748), Section X, Part i, in a footnote.

16. H. G. Wells could scarcely have written a better story than *The Man Who Could Work Miracles*, but a more philosophically careful title would have been *The Man Who Could Work Prodigies*.

17. R. Swinburne, *The Concept of Miracle* (London, 1970), p. 26.

18. *Ibid.*, p. 32.

19. See my *Hume's Philosophy of Religion* (London and New York, 1978), ch. 7.

20. *American Philosophical Quarterly*, 1965, p. 43.

21. Alasdair MacIntyre, *Difficulties in Christian Belief* (London, 1959), p. 50. See also Ninian Smart, *Philosophers and Religious Truth* (London, 1964), p. 38; *et al.*

7. The Limitations of Atheism

1. In the context of a book on classical civilization this generalization would need too much explanation and discussion to be of value. There were important moral philosophies in antiquity which were not related to religion, and there must have been, as in all societies, person-to-person moral acts which took place without reference to religion or religious superstition. But for present purposes the undoubtedly close relation in classical antiquity between religious duties and public duties, and between national and local customs and religious observances, is, I trust, sufficient to permit the generalization in the text.

2. Shelley, *Prometheus Unbound*, line 305.

3. Kant, *Critique of Practical Reason*, Book II, chs. 2–5. My very compressed paragraph cannot begin to do justice to Kant's arguments but space forbids a fuller account.

4. C. D. Broad, *Five Types of Ethical Theory* (London, 1930), pp. 141 f.

5. Originally the ninth Arthur Stanley Eddington Memorial Lecture (Cambridge, 1955), but see *The Philosophy of Religion*, ed. Basil Mitchell (Oxford, 1971), pp. 72–91.

6. *Ibid.*, p. 82.

7. J. L. Mackie, *Ethics: Inventing Right and Wrong* (Penguin Books, 1977), p. 74.

8. David Hume, *Enquiry concerning the Principles of Morals*, ed. L. A. Selby-Bigge (Oxford, 1902), pp. 282f.

9. Bernard Williams, *Morality: An Introduction to Ethics* (Penguin Books, 1973), p. 86.

10. David Hume, *Enquiry concerning Human Understanding*, ed. L. A. Selby-Bigge (Oxford, 1902), p. 147.

11. Patrick Masterson, *Atheism and Alienation* (Penguin Books, 1973), p. 103.

12. See my *Hume's Philosophy of Religion* (London and New York, 1978).

13. Antony Flew, *God and Philosophy* (London, 1966), p. 69.

14. For an exceptionally hard-headed exposé of such reappraisals see the article 'God and the Theologians' by Alasdair MacIntyre in *The Honest to God Debate*, ed. D. L. Edwards (London, 1963). The specific matter is now going out of date but every subsequent decade has produced its versions of the dottiness to which MacIntyre is drawing attention.

8. Destinations

1. *The Consolation of Philosophy*, 1:4.

2. Bertrand Russell, *Mysticism and Logic* (Penguin Books, 1953), pp. 58–60. The item referred to was originally written in 1903.

GLOSSARY

AGNOSTICISM: the view that there is not enough, or not good enough, evidence to decide whether God exists or not. Such a view admits the possibility that evidence may be forthcoming and hence that the existence of God or gods is a coherent possibility. (cf. Atheism and Scepticism.)

ANTHROPOMORPHISM: with reference to religion means ascribing to the deity human characteristics, frequently (and apparently acceptably) thoughts, intentions, and commands; less frequently (and usually unacceptably) human appearance or passions.

ATHEISM: originally the denial of the existence of God or gods generally believed in within a given society (thus to the Romans the early Christians were atheists); now, usually, the denial of the existence of anything corresponding to any of the concepts of god held by any extant religion.

COMPARATIVE RELIGION: the description and comparison of the beliefs, concepts and worships occurring in different religions.

COSMOLOGICAL ARGUMENT: the argument that God must exist because his existence is required to explain why anything exists. But there is a serious terminological confusion here which often results in argument to a first cause or a prime mover being called cosmological argument. See chapter three, section iii.

DEISM: (a) belief in a single god not otherwise known by revelation who set the universe in motion or caused it to exist and be what it is and thereafter left it entirely alone, or (b), as an historical term, the name for the views expressed by those eighteenth-century English and French thinkers who argued that natural theology (q.v.) is sufficient without revealed religion (q.v.).

DESIGN ARGUMENT: the argument that God exists because his creative intelligence can be observed in the order and/or purposiveness to be found in the natural world. See chapter three, section iv.

DUALISM: when used with reference to religion means belief in two conflicting deities, one good (or creative), the other evil (or destructive).

FIDEISM: belief that the teachings of Christianity or Islam or whatever are justified because all knowledge rests upon premises accepted on faith.

GOD: there are many concepts of god and everyone is an atheist with respect to some of the concepts. No concise account of the meaning of this word can be given. I try to fix and justify the sense in which it will be used in this book in chapter one.

MONOTHEISM: belief in *one* god (not necessarily the Christian).

MORAL EVIL: suffering which occurs as a result of the free actions of sentient moral agents.

MYSTICISM: the aspect of religion (of whatever type) which emphasizes 'the possibility of union with the divine nature by means of ecstatic contemplation' (*Shorter O.E.D.*).

NATURAL EVIL: suffering caused by the workings of the natural world independently of any human agent's free actions.

NATURAL RELIGION or NATURAL THEOLOGY: the body of knowledge about God or the gods which may be attained by human reason alone without the aid of revelation. (Whether there is such a body of knowledge and how large it is are subjects of debate.) See chapter three.

ONTOLOGICAL ARGUMENT: the argument that God exists because a full understanding of what is meant by the word 'God' involves his necessary existence. See chapter three, section i.

PAGANISM: (a) in general, belief in gods other than the one acknowledged in the 'true' religion – usually taken to be the Christian; (b) in particular, the polytheistic religions of Greece and Rome which were overcome by Christianity in the second to fifth centuries of our era. In this book the word will be used only in the particular sense.

PANTHEISM: belief that god is identical with nature as a whole.

PERSONALISM: the view that Christianity can be sustained if its traditional language is retained while the concept of God is redefined to accord with one's own loss of faith or the incredulity of one's contemporaries. (I hope usefulness will excuse the novelty. See chapter one.)

PHILOSOPHY OF RELIGION: the disinterested, rational discussion of the truth of religious claims, the meaningfulness of religious language, and the coherence of religious concepts.

POLYTHEISM: belief in a multiplicity of gods.

REVEALED RELIGION or REVEALED THEOLOGY: knowledge about God (or the gods) which could only be got from a particular revelation of his nature or purposes such as is contained in the Bible or Koran.

SCEPTICISM: when used with reference to religion generally means the view that in such matters nothing could ever count as evidence one way or the other because, for example, the human understanding cannot cope with such 'remote and obscure' subjects, or because the central concept 'God' is incoherent.

TELEOLOGICAL ARGUMENT: the particular version of the Design Argument (q.v.) which refers to the purposiveness (or adaptation of means to ends) which seems to occur in nature.

THEISM: as the word is most commonly used, it means belief in a single and eternal God who created all things and continues to sustain and work within his creation. In this sense the Judaic, Islamic and Christian religions are all theistic religions (rather than, for example, deistic religions).

AFTERTHOUGHT

To view as a whole so great an extent of subject matter, to harmonize and bring together so many diverse varieties of discourse, to connect smoothly what follows with what goes before, ... was by no means an easy undertaking. But such as it is, it is at least written with a concern for the truth. Its other qualities I leave to the judgement of my readers.

Isocrates' Apology
c. 354 B.C.

INDEX

Footnotes in the main text are indexed thus: 69n, 121n, etc.
End notes are not indexed with regard to persons. Subjects are indexed thus: 185n3, 182n18, etc.
The glossary is not indexed.

MORE ABOUT PENGUINS, PELICANS
AND PUFFINS

For further information about books available from Penguins please write to Dept EP, Penguin Books Ltd, Harmondsworth, Middlesex UB7 0DA.

In the U.S.A.: For a complete list of books available from Penguins in the United States write to Dept DG, Penguin Books, 299 Murray Hill Parkway, East Rutherford, New Jersey 07073.

In Canada: For a complete list of books available from Penguins in Canada write to Penguin Books Canada Ltd, 2801 John Street, Markham, Ontario L3R 1B4.

In Australia: For a complete list of books available from Penguins in Australia write to the Marketing Department, Penguin Books Australia Ltd, P.O. Box 257, Ringwood, Victoria 3134.

In New Zealand: For a complete list of books available from Penguins in New Zealand write to the Marketing Department, Penguin Books (N.Z.) Ltd, P.O. Box 4019, Auckland 10.

In India: For a complete list of books available from Penguins in India write to Penguin Overseas Ltd, 706 Eros Apartments, 56 Nehru Place, New Delhi 110019.

Penguin Reference Books

The Penguin Dictionary of Religions

Edited by John R. Hinnells

A guide to all the major religions from ancient times to the modern day.

This fascinating and informative dictionary encompasses religions past and present, throughout the world. Written by an international team of authorities, it discusses the rites, rituals and beliefs of each religion, as well as their gods and holy figures, their sacred books and iconography.

Illustrated with charts, maps and line drawings, complete with a full bibliography and index, *The Penguin Dictionary of Religions* will be interesting and invaluable for both academic and general readers.

Published in Pelicans

God and the Gods

Walter Beltz

Creating a unique picture of the 'perfect man', the myths of the Bible are a deeply influential part of our cultural heritage.

Here Walter Beltz takes the Judaeo-Christian myths independently of their immediate religious connotations, and gives us a fascinating study in the tradition of Robert Graves's *Greek Myths*. Sketching the Old and New Testament stories, he explores and explains their origins: relating them to earlier religions and myths, to political events, to writings and tales outside the canon; drawing on his knowledge of Hebrew, Greek and Latin, as well as on a vast body of learning and scholarship.

Published in Pelicans

God and the New Physics

Paul Davies

How did the world begin – and how will it end?
What is life?
What is matter?
What is mind?

These questions are not new; what is new, argues Paul Davies, is that we may be on the verge of answering them. Here he explains, in clear, jargon-free language, how far the recent explosive discoveries of the new physics are revolutionizing our view of the world and, in particular, throwing light on many of the questions formerly posed by religion.

Science has come of age, Professor Davies believes, and can now offer a surer path to God than religion. In this important, exciting and highly readable book, he explains why.

'There is a wealth of interesting ideas here' – *The Times Literary Supplement*

'The author is an excellent writer. He not only explains with fluent simplicity some of the profoundest questions of cosmology, but he is also well read in theology' – *Daily Telegraph*

Published by Penguins

The Dead Sea Scrolls

John Allegro

This is a revised edition of the best popular account of the Dead Sea Scrolls.

John Allegro has long been connected with this exciting field of research, both as an expert linguist and as trustee and secretary of the Dead Sea Scrolls Fund. In this new edition he has reappraised the discoveries, with their particular importance for New Testament studies, in the light of the very latest trends, and has discussed the possibility of future finds. Hitherto unpublished texts concerning the Essenes have been added to the book, which now includes a completely new set of plates.

The Dead Sea Scrolls in English

G. Vermes

Many books have been written about the Dead Sea Scrolls since their discovery in 1947, but until now the ordinary reader has had little opportunity to get to know the texts themselves, and so to make any personal judgement of their value or relevance. In this volume a clear, faithful translation of the non-biblical scrolls from the Qumran caves is accompanied by brief introductory comment on each, and by a general description of the beliefs, customs, organization, and history of the Community they derive from.

Published by Penguins

Islam

Alfred Guillaume

The cultural background of the Arab peoples has been formed as much by Muhammadanism as has that of Europe and America by Christianity. The great awakening of the Muslim world which is now in progress, the emergence of new Muslim states such as Pakistan, Libya, Jordan and Saudi Arabia, and the ever closer contact between the West and the Middle East make an understanding of the spirit of Islam essential to the informed Westerner. Professor Guillaume provides the elements of such an understanding in this book. He deals in turn with Muhammad, the founder of Islam; the Qurān, its holy book; the evolution of Muhammadanism as a system of faith, law, religion and philosophy; and the varying schools of thought and the intense devotional life that have grown up within it. He also discusses the changes that are now taking place in the Islamic viewpoint as the Muslim peoples prepare to take their full part in the modern world.

The Way of the Sufi

Idries Shah

'A short time in the presence of the Friends (the Sufis) is better than a hundred years' sincere, obedient dedication.'

Idries Shah here reveals the secrets of the Sufi and explains some of their more startling achievements. Drawing from a wide selection of their teachings and classical writings, he offers a unique and readable introduction to a body of thought vitally relevant to the contemporary world.

'A key book' – Doris Lessing in the *Observer*

'More wisdom than I have found in any other book this year' – Pat Williams on 'The Critics' (BBC Radio)

'His work is as exciting as a good novel' – *The Times Literary Supplement*

Published by Penguins

Mysticism

F. C. Harpold

In this clear, simple and illuminating book, the author combines a study of mysticism – as experience, as spiritual knowledge and as a way of life – with an illustrative anthology of mystical writings. Drawing material from all over the world, the anthology includes not only selections from the Christian mystics, but also from the *Upanishads* and the *Bhagavad Gita*, from Plato and Plotinius, from the Sufi mystics of Islam, from Dante and even from the 'nature' mystic, Richard Jefferies.

Complementing each other, Dr Harpold's study and anthology knit together to form a brilliant and original introduction to mysticism.

Buddhism

Christmas Humphreys

The religion-philosophy known to the West as Buddhism is in number of adherents and range of teaching one of the largest in the world. Born in India in the sixth century B.C., it became the religion of Ceylon, Siam, Burma and Cambodia, which adhere to the older or Southern School, while the developed Mahayana School is found in various forms in Tibet, Mongolia, China, Korea and Japan. Its range of thought is equally vast. It includes the most exalted philosophy yet achieved by man, a psychology from which the West is slowly beginning to learn, a religion which has satisfied untold millions for 2,500 years, a Middle Way of self-development to self-enlightenment and a range and depth of spiritual science, mysticism and religious art which cannot be found elsewhere.

To compress such a wealth of human thought into a single volume is difficult, but here is not only the history and development of Buddhism and the teaching of the various Schools, but also its condition in the world today.

Published by Penguins

Judaism

Isidore Epstein

The comprehensive account of Judaism as a religious and distinctive way of life, presented against a background of 4,000 years of Jewish history.

From the westward migration of Abraham, the progenitor of the Jewish people, to the establishment of the modern state of Israel, *Judaism* traces the rise, growth and development of the beliefs, teachings and practices of Judaism, as well as its aspirations and ideals.

It also discusses the spiritual movements and influences which have helped to shape the Jewish religion in its varied manifestations; and describes the contributions made in turn by a succession of prophets, legislators, priests, psalmists, sages, rabbis, philosophers and mystics, by which Judaism has come to be the living religious force it is today. In the treatment of its themes the book strives to maintain a balance between the factual and the interpretative, and aims throughout at clarity and simplicity in presentation and exposition.

A History of Christianity

Paul Johnson

'Masterly ... It combines great wealth of scholarship, including many fascinating byways as well as the main highways, with a vigorous, confident style, a kind of innate intensity which carries the narrative along so that it rarely falters and is never dull ... It is a huge and crowded canvas – a tremendous theme running through twenty centuries of history; a cosmic soap opera involving kings and beggars, philosophers and crackpots, scholars and illiterate *exaltés*, popes and pilgrims and wild anchorites in the wilderness, with a story-line at once of infinite variety and inexorable necessity ... Johnson works out his own presentation of it all with verve, imaginative insight and the lofty self-confidence of a practised editorialist' – Malcolm Muggeridge in the *New Statesman*

Published in Pelicans

Philosophy Through Its Past

Edited and Introduced by Ted Honderich

The central concerns of the great philosophers – from Plato to Wittgenstein – explored and interpreted by the greatest philosophers of our day.

From Gregory Vlastos on 'Plato: The Individual as an Object of Love', to Arthur Danto on 'Sartre: Shame, or, The Problem of Other Minds', this book explores the central concerns of the past masters of philosophy. It extends across a whole spectrum of approaches: some essays lean towards the historical, seeking truth as much as possible in the thought of the great master, while others are more inclined to suppose that philosophy advances, so that attention to the past must be selective, and certainly judgemental. All of them however, illuminate the vital past of philosophy, for the issues discussed are not only perplexing and challenging, but very much alive.

This anthology of distinguished essays forms a companion volume to *Philosophy As It Is*.